December 1984

Dear Laurence —
    for calm times together
dear friend —
            I do g love from
        Caroline X x

EDWARD CARPENTER
SELECTED WRITINGS

Sex still goes first, and hands eyes mouth brain
follow; from the midst of belly and thighs radiate
the knowledge of self, religion, and immortality.

(Towards Democracy)

EDWARD CARPENTER

SELECTED WRITINGS
VOLUME 1: SEX

WITH AN INTRODUCTION
BY NOËL GREIG

Volume One: Sex in this Gay Modern Classics edition
of Edward Carpenter's *Selected Writings* was first
published in September 1984 by GMP Publishers Ltd,
P O Box 247, London N15 6RW. The *Selected Writings*
are edited by David Fernbach and Noël Greig.

British Library Cataloguing in Publication Data

Carpenter , Edward[l],*1844–1929*
  Selected Writings.
  V. 1 : Sex
  1. Socialism
  I. Title
  335   HX73

  ISBN 0-907040-44-6
  ISBN 0-907040-43-8 Pbk

The cover portrait is from a monochrome photograph of
Edward Carpenter aged 42, hand tinted by Sally Slight.
This book was set in Trump Medieval by M C Typeset
of Chatham, Kent, and printed and bound by
Billing & Sons Ltd of Worcester.

The editors would like to dedicate this book to Anton Everts, who helped it on its way, but did not live to see it finished. 'He shall not grow old, as we that are left grow old.'

Note on the edition

This edition of Edward Carpenter's *Selected Writings* was one of the first projects planned by Gay Men's Press after its foundation in 1979. After several years in the pipeline, it is now appearing in our Gay Modern Classics series.

Preparation of the *Selected Writings* has been the joint work of Noël Greig, and David Fernbach of GMP. The format we chose was to have three volumes grouped broadly by subject: on *Sex*, *Society*, and *Spirit*. Though selection involves by nature both re-ordering and omission, our aim all along has been to allow Edward Carpenter to speak to the contemporary reader for himself, and this aim has governed the selection made.

Carpenter published a far larger number of books than can be accommodated in our three volumes, yet the manner in which they were generally constructed has made it possible to minimise the violence done by the selection process. His books are in most cases collections of essays grouped around a common theme; these had often been previously published separately as articles or pamphlets, and new material was frequently added when a new edition was prepared. We have therefore been able to avoid, on the whole, arbitrarily chosen extracts, and the great bulk of these three volumes is made up of texts that were in each case written as a unity.

Considerations of size, and timescale, have led to three separate books rather than one giant volume. But the *Selected Writings* is designed as an integral whole. Volume One contains an essay on Edward Carpenter by Noël Greig which serves as introduction to the whole edition; Volume Two likewise contains a section of photographs and Volume Three a bibliography.

Where the texts selected are published in more than one variant, our policy has been to follow the latest edition prepared by Carpenter himself. The only changes made are a certain standardising and modernising of spelling, punctuation, and style of footnote references. All footnotes are relegated here to the back of the book. Carpenter's own notes have been given a numerical ordering, and editorial notes a printer's mark to clearly distinguish them.

Introduction

Not Easy to Sum Up

In 1931, a book entitled *Edward Carpenter: In Appreciation* was published. Carpenter had died in 1929 and the book was a collection of essays by those who had known him. One of the contributors was the novelist E. M. Forster. He wrote:

> If I am as deep as a pond and you as a lake, Edward Carpenter was the sea.[1]

In 1944, Forster reminisced on Carpenter once more, this time in a short radio address. The occasion was the hundredth anniversary of Carpenter's birth. He opened with the question:

> Do you know the name Edward Carpenter?[2]

but he needed no answer, for he knew that the man who had been written of in *In Appreciation* was fast being forgotten. In that address, Forster described someone who had been:

> a poet, prose writer, a prophet, a socialist, a mystic, a manual labourer, an anti-vivisectionist, an art-critic, etcetera.[3]

He told how, despite the gathering obscurity surrounding the name, Edward Carpenter had contributed much to a developing vision of the world, and the world had much to thank him for.

What was that vision? What was the contribution? Why is Edward Carpenter, in Forster's words, 'not easy to sum up'? Let us take a look at his literary output for some clues. I'd like you to imagine that we have stumbled on a complete shelf of his works. It would be a reasonably long shelf, and the volumes would span a period from the 1870s to the 1920s – a crucial passage of years in the history of these islands: the mid-Victorian heyday of certainties and industrial muscle, leading the English towards Empire; the renewal of radical criticism of capitalism, with native and international revolutionary groupings emerging; imperialist dogfights between the European powers, leading into a 'war to end all wars' (followed by the silhouette of an even more ghastly conflict); an explosion of socialist hope, with the Russian Revolution; the triumph of the democratic state, with the incorporation of Labour politics into the parliamentary process; great movements of art and literature reflecting all these things.

So, we take a look along the shelf, and see that our author has responded to his times more than fully. There are books and pamphlets on science, industry, art, religion, economics, sex, marriage, women, the Empire, war, police, prisons, nature, vivisection, nudism, anthropology, Walt Whitman, Beethoven, Wagner, anarchism, socialism, market gardening, pollution, the East, mysticism, transcendentalism. There are articles on current events, the meaning of pain, pacifism, the minimum wage, the right to work. There is poetic verse, there are plays, songs and short stories. Let's imagine them all lined up, in chronological order. We would look along the shelf, and hear the echo of E. M. Forster – 'Not easy to sum up'. A harsher verdict would be 'eclectic', for this display of seemingly unrelated subjects, themes and preoccupations seems to indicate a mind that could not settle. Nor does the world seem to have cherished this output, for almost all of this work has long been out of print. If his name is known at all, it is perhaps for a long poem he wrote – *Towards Democracy* – which is possibly more acknowledged than read. Yet here perhaps there may be some clue for us, since Carpenter himself said of it:

> the other books are only supports and buttresses and steps of access to that.[4]

Here, then, may be the starting-point for the academic sleuth – no need to track down the course of the work from the early 'try-outs' to the later works of genius, for Carpenter has given the game away himself – *Towards*

Democracy was his most important work, his greatest achievement. He said it (and we shall see how his contemporaries said it), so the task in hand would seem to be to examine the rest of the work and see where each piece held its place on the ladder of achievement. Then we should have our writer charted, dated, fully analysed and plainly explained. A neat graph pinning down the man, his vision and his contribution to history.

Edward Carpenter does not work that way. In the first place, he began *Towards Democracy* in 1881, long before he embarked upon the bulk of his work. What can that mean? If the other books were 'supports and buttresses and steps of access to that', did everything else get worse? Did he and his admirers get it wrong, allowing the book a status it never deserved? (You'd find evidence for that case too, for Havelock Ellis did let slip he at first considered the work to be merely 'Whitman and water').[5] If so, then the hunt would be on for the *truly* great and as yet totally unacknowledged work – the greatest prize for the literary gumshoe. If this were to be the attempt we should still be disappointed. Edward Carpenter does not work that way.

Alright, you say, let's try a different approach. Along comes a tidy archivist, to regroup everything under appropriate headings: Anarchism, Beauty, Civilization, Drama, etcetera, so sacrificing chronological order to academic efficiency. That would be helpful in getting at Edward Carpenter from certain angles, but it would miss the key to the man. For Edward Carpenter made an attempt to live his life as a whole. He wished to link all aspects of himself – the inner and the outer, the intellectual and the spiritual, the physical and the emotional – with all aspects of the world. So then, his work is a reflection of his preoccupations, desires, actions, dreams and experiences, and as such it bears all the marks of life's to's and fro's. If we look into his life, we can see beyond a seemingly disconnected series of writings to patterns of thought running through all, emerging at times in one form, at times another, sometimes forcefully and sometimes falteringly. The shelf of books is not a ladder of achievement, it is Edward's diary to the world.

Here perhaps we have one reason for the silence of these

past decades. Take out a selection of his work under a particular heading, and there will be things that are fresh and interesting, yet not enough to justify his place as a key figure in the development of our culture. Dismantle his work into its sections and sub-sections and you dismantle his life, dismantle the meaning of his life. *Towards Democracy* may be the essence of all the other work, but not because it was the finally accomplished and crowning achievement. It was the nearest he got to distilling his soul, and is thus the centre of a circle, as opposed to the pinnacle of a ladder. To rediscover him fully, we must regard him not simply as a 'political' writer, but also as a deeply personal one, indeed a poet. We must allow him to catch at our hearts as well as our minds.

If, then, you will trust my belief that the personal, emotional response is as important as the literary, academic one, perhaps the voices of his friends and loved ones have much to tell us. Read *In Appreciation* and you will be in no doubt that it was not just E. M. Forster who regarded Carpenter as a force to be reckoned with. In that volume, you will find a very broad range indeed of individuals of differing age, class, nationality, all of whom acknowledge the powerful influence he exerted over their lives. Reference to *Towards Democracy* features in many of these accounts, as with Havelock Ellis, who eventually discovered:

> an original voice and one that made a direct appeal to me. I introduced the book to friends, and before long some of them, going beyond me, were cherishing *Towards Democracy* as a kind of Bible.[6]

Katharine Bruce Glasier echoes this:

> It is no exaggeration for many of us inside and outside the political Socialist movement to say that Walt Whitman's *Leaves of Grass* and Edward Carpenter's *Towards Democracy* have become as a kind of Twentieth-Century Old and New Testament. . .[7]

He touched the intelligentsia certainly – the world of Ellis, Edith Lees, Shaw, Forster, Olive Schreiner, Laurence Housman, D. H. Lawrence – yet *In Appreciation* brings us to another world, one which draws us closer to Edward. The world of the workers. He came from an educated back-ground (more of that later) but he drew loyalty from such as C. T. Cramp, then Industrial General Secretary of the NUR. To this man, Carpenter was 'one of the greatest and most clear-sighted teachers that society has ever known':[8]

> his house was a rendezvous for all sorts and conditions of men, particularly at week-ends. The Sheffield cutler, engineer, miner or railwayman met poet, musician or dramatist beneath his roof and all were made to feel one of a great family.[9]

There was W. J. Godfrey who 'having been an active socialist since 1905', remembers:

> clearly what must have been his last public appearance . . . when he spoke slowly and haltingly for a few minutes to a working-class audience. Although poss-ibly few of them appreciated or knew of his works, it was clear they realised that here was one who under-stood them, believed in them, and belonged to them.[10]

The picture fleshes itself out. A man from the stuffy, mid-Victorian bourgeoisie who stepped out from his own class to receive love from the workers, to give them love. It goes further, beyond the boundaries of nation. Illit Gröndhal from Norway tells us that:

> To become a friend of Edward Carpenter's was to be enlisted in a band of friends reaching through all nations.[11]

Charles Sixsmith records how, on a visit to Italy, Carpenter was cashing a note in a bank, when:

> the bank manager, seeing the signature, said 'Are you *the* Edward Carpenter?' and the identity being estab-lished, we were invited to his home, where Edward's books were in evidence, and thus began a lasting friendship . . .[12]

Throughout *In Appreciation*, all give voice to the belief that Carpenter spoke not to them alone, but to the future. Forster remarks:

he may have a message for the future, for the generations unborn;[13]

and C. T. Cramp says:

I cannot imagine that his works will ever grow stale or out of date in a world which must always admire sanity, courage, and a life of beauty. He has gone, but his spirit will never die and his memory will always be green.[14]

Here then are voices from the past, crying passionate belief in the gifts he gave to them and to the world. Yet look for him on the library shelves and you will look long. Seek him out in the reading-lists of Labour history and the search will be tedious. You may come across a book, by Godfrey Elton, called *England Arise*. It was published in 1931, that is, the same year as *In Appreciation*. The title of the book, as we are told in the foreword, is taken from one of Carpenter's song lyrics:

The world-famous 'Red Flag' was written to express the aspirations of revolutionary movements the world over. 'England Arise', which now rivals 'The Red Flag' in popularity in the British Labour movement, was composed to celebrate the first victories of the new native British Socialism.[15]

The book is subtitled 'A Study in the Pioneering Days of the Labour Movement', and so the reader might well expect to discover within it, just how and why Carpenter had been vital to that movement. Not so. He is given four pages, in which *Towards Democracy* is once more given its due, and then he is gone again, with the more familiar names of Hyndman, Keir Hardie and William Morris taking centre stage. It is like searching for a Will-o'-the-Wisp, and again comes Forster's helpless little sigh over the radio in 1944:

He was a very good man, certainly an unusual one, possibly a great one, and he is not easy to sum up.[16]

We seem to step even further from a sensible and helpful discussion of his place in history with comments such as this, from Edith Lees:

When one is with Carpenter one feels that what we call
the miraculous is no violation but only an enlargement
of nature's laws.[17]

And when Guido Ferrando speaks, the theme approaches
the tone more appropriately reserved for saints and other
myths:

I shall always remember, as long as I live, the sense of
elation, of blissful peace which enwrapt my soul when
I stood for the first time in front of Edward Carpenter,
my hand in his warm grasp, his vivid piercing eyes
looking deep into mine, his noble delicate features
radiant with a luminous smile.[18]

Now perhaps you will snap shut this book, and tell me
that I have failed to bring you that sense of the man which I
believe is central to understanding his work. Yet it is
undeniable that he struck chords in the hearts and imaginations of all he touched. I do believe that he spoke to his
generation in ways which enabled it to make connections
between its desires and dreams, and the fragmented sort of
existence the present state of society offered. I believe he
can do that for us today when, perhaps even more so, the
parts of our existence are crushed into categories and the
sense of wholeness with ourselves, with each other, with
history, with nature, recedes even further. He certainly had
this effect on me, and so I must add to this attempt to 'get at'
the man through his effects on others, by mentioning how
someone who was born exactly one hundred years before
me, added to my own store of understanding of the world
and myself.

I first stumbled upon Edward Carpenter in 1977 – as a
footnote. I was researching for a play which dealt, in part,
with Victorian attitudes towards homosexuality. There was
a reference to a man who turned his back upon a well-
heeled, Brighton-born and Cambridge-educated background,
to settle in the North of England amongst the workers.
Eventually, so the story went, he played a major role in the
national drive towards a party of Labour (having been a key
figure in the socialist revival of the 1880s). Eventually, too,

he declared his homosexuality, discussed the issue in his writings, and celebrated it by setting up home with his lover, a working-class chap from Sheffield called George Merrill.

Here was a revelation. To date, my knowledge of homosexuality in 19th century England had been confined to scandals and trials amid the setting of West End socialites, penniless male prostitutes and tortured MPs. The reckless courage of Oscar Wilde, the self-loathing of Bosie, the double life of Casement, the bordellos of Cleveland Street all spoke of the wealthy once again holding the power of cash over the poor. The history of homosexuality seemed the usual tedious list of 'famous names' and the anonymous exploited. I'd read Wilde's *The Soul of Man under Socialism* and been stirred by it – it was clear that his radical political views were as threatening to the Establishment as his sexual desires (indeed it was the act of treason of taking working-class boys to upper-class clubs which sealed his fate). Yet nowhere was there evidence that within the working class – within its organisations and its common life – were there openly homosexual persons whose relationships were not bound by cash-barter. So here was this man Carpenter 'coming out' in the Labour movement of the late 19th century, not as a wealthy renter of boys, but as an equal partner with a working-class man, and as a literary advocate of homosexuality.

I later came to realise that the picture was less simple and rosy. Carpenter was limited by his class, his temperament and the times he lived in. It was to be another century before homosexuals were to engage more fully – or at least more effectively, on a mass basis – in the socialist debate. All the same, that first brief description of Carpenter and Merrill fired my imagination. Here was proof that a movement in which I held faith – the impulse towards a radical shift in the structures of society – held within its early stages an open advocation of something even closer to me – my own sexuality. Some sense of isolation dissolved – the feeling of having no personal part in the movements of history. In the early 1970s, the starting-point for many of us in the Gay Liberation Movement was the phrase 'the personal is political'. For myself, Edward Carpenter gave this a historical dimension.

Now I am writing in a very personal way, but then again, nothing we are able to speak of ourselves is personal in the sense of ultimately 'private'. You may care little about homosexuality in 19th century England, or the Gay Liberation Movement of the 20th century, or my reactions to either. Yet if I am able to tell you how Carpenter spoke to me, what 'personal' feelings of my own connected with his politics, his life, his writings, that is because of a movement of history to which he contributed – a movement which demands a world where all have equal access not simply to the material comforts, but to the desires of our bodies and the joys of our souls:

> I conceive a millennium on earth – a millennium not of riches, nor of mechanical facilities, nor of intellectual facilities, nor absolutely of immunity from disease, nor absolutely of immunity from pain; but a time when men and women all over the earth shall ascend and enter into relation with their bodies – shall attain freedom and joy . . .[19]

My response to Carpenter is not unique. Over the past few years there has been a steady trickle of revived interest in Carpenter. Gay and feminist work has offered some serious studies, including a couple of plays; there has been one major biography. All have acknowledged his sexuality and most have given it the value he gave it – that is, a central focus in his life and work. Through these works, a widening circle of people have come to appreciate Carpenter's contribution to the socialist debate. Yet still the circle is limited, and I think that may be for the same reasons why Carpenter was, in his own lifetime, shunted into the sidings. The same reasons why E. M. Forster found him hard to 'sum up'. The same reasons why to approach his writings from a rigidly academic, literary or conventionally political angle, from an 'objective' standpoint, is to be blind to what he was truly concerned with – the questions of the heart and the soul. Such questions do not travel easily alongside the bread-and-butter matters of organised politics and material progress, agendas and schedules. We hear brave battling words from those who speak up in public against the

injustices of the world (Carpenter would have applauded
them, would have been up on the platform speaking too), yet
his most intense wish was to bring within that public arena
those things which unite us all, but for which we are denied
a common language, which are relegated to the 'private' and
are muffled in platitude and confusion. He is not easy to
sum up, for how can we distil into a neat paragraph those
things we grope to understand? The questions of the heart
and soul.

Questions of the Heart and Soul

Of that which exists in the Soul, political freedom
and institutions of equality, and so forth, are but the
shadows (necessarily thrown); and Democracy in
States or Constitutions but the shadow of that which
first expresses itself in the glance of the eye or the
appearance of the skin.

Without that first the others are of no account, and
need not be further mentioned.[20]

Sex still goes first, and hands eyes mouth brain
follow; from the midst of belly and thighs radiate the
knowledge of self, religion, and immortality.[21]

How are the makers of agendas and schedules to deal with
a man who sought to discover the intimate relationship
between a political development and a personal sensuality?
Such things may prove too deep for those who are concerned
(often necessarily) with the pressing tasks of seeing immediate justice done, and certainly when Carpenter wrote those
words, history was driving in another direction. The path of
progress was taking the material route – and in the face of
the hideous deformities which the 19th century had imposed on the lives of the masses, who could *not* fight for
better housing, clean air, decent work conditions? Carpenter
certainly did, he became a supporter of Labour and a fighter
for the working class. Not just as a literary commentator,
but as a foot-slogger, speaker, demonstrator, pamphleteer.
Yet it was the byways of his own dreams he sought in the
end, and the hard-nosed, bread-and-butter politicians had no

time to stop for such things. Nor do they now, nor did they when E. M. Forster wrote:

> I do not think that he has any message for us, the citizens of 1930; we seem condemned to mechanisation, and our problem is to mechanise in the right direction and not the wrong one . . .[22]

I believe Carpenter spoke for a generation of socialists who conceived of a politics where the inner life of the individual was reflected in the organisation of society. The influence of anarchist thought was evident in this, as it was in the radical movements of the 1880s. But, as Forster said:

> The Labour movement took another course, and advanced by committee meetings and statistics towards a State-owned factory attached to State-supervised recreation-grounds. Edward's heart beat no warmer at such joys. He felt no enthusiasm over municipal baths and municipally provided bathing-drawers. What he wanted was News from Nowhere and the place that is still nowhere, wildness, the rapture of unpolluted streams, sunrise and sunset over the moors, and in the midst of these the working people whom he loved, passionately in touch with one another and with the natural glories around them.[23]

What was it that drew his gaze from the physical mutilations imposed by a dog-eat-dog society, towards the inner poverty of life? The answer lies with his own class background, from his reflections on the ways in which his own young soul had been bound and stifled, the ways in which his sisters were suffocated. The cry lifted up in *Towards Democracy* was as much directed to his own past as to a hoped-for future world, and once again, here is the key to understanding his writing – his life.

He was born in Brighton, on August 29th, 1844, at 45 Brunswick Square – a haughty curve of Georgiana facing onto the sea – and in early childhood had begun to feel the trap sprung for his soul:

> The social life which encircled us at Brighton was artificial enough . . . I hated the life, was miserable in it

– the heartless conventionalities, silly proprieties – but
I never imagined, it never occurred to me, that there
was any other life.[24]

He had witnessed how that world had poisoned the well of
his sisters' lives:

> the life, and with it the character, of the ordinary
> 'young lady' of that period ... was tragic in its
> emptiness ... In a place like Brighton there were
> hundreds, perhaps, of households, in which girls were
> growing up with but one idea in life, that of taking
> their 'proper place in society'. A few meagre accom-
> plishments – plentiful balls and dinner-parties,
> theatres and concerts – and to loaf up and down the
> parade, criticising each other, were the means to bring
> about this desirable result! There was absolutely
> nothing else to do or live for.[25]

So then, when he wrote in *Towards Democracy* of:

> strong healthy boys who positively believe they will
> starve unless they enter the hated professions held out
> to them;[26]

and of:

> avenues of young girls and women, with sideway
> flopping heads, debarred from Work, debarred from
> natural Sexuality, weary to death with nothing to
> do . . .[27]

he was railing against the iron-maiden of 'respectability' he
had grown up within. A world which polluted and confused
the young mind, full of:

> children who have been taught to mix the nonsense
> manners and diarrhoea of drawing-rooms with their
> ideals of right and wrong; to despise manual labour and
> to reverence ridicule; to eat and drink and dress and
> sleep in unbelief and against all their natural instincts;
> and in all things to mingle the disgust of repletion with
> the very thought of pleasure – till their young judg-
> ments are confused and their instincts actually cease
> to be a guide to them.[28]

Yet, trapped though he felt himself to be, Edward did believe in personal change, and he did manage to wrench himself away from that suffocating world. His writings reflect that journey, tracing it now this way, now that, following the dictates of his longings, recording what he felt and saw along the way, and what he was seeking.

The changes he made were certainly against the grain of that age, when upward mobility and the shoring-up of the material securities were the order of the day. For this, he was little understood by his own class. His great-niece Ida G. Hyett related how:

> Once . . . I ventured to ask my Aunt Sophy whether she did not think her brother Edward a wonderful man, and she answered: 'Well, my dear, I feel that he might have done *so much more* with his life. His talents were so great that it seems a pity he has made so little use of them.'[29]

Today the phrase 'dropping out' would be employed against him – and as with many of his actions, the accompanying motives do have resonances with our own recent times. When, in the 1960s, a large section of young people (often higher-educated) did 'drop out', the rejection of a system of life (career structure, status, guaranteed income, etc.) also went hand in hand with dreams of a world that did not exist. Dreams that were often interlarded with wedges of pie-in-the-sky, but which, like Carpenter's dreams, connected those longings with an understanding that to achieve such a better place, personal change was part of the process – that without personal development and the desire for it, political change would be a hollow victory. The outcrop of exotic behaviour, mysticism, communes, etc. of our own times was a resurfacing of a tradition of thought and action to which Carpenter belongs. It comes back to us on the great ebb and flow of history from time to time, in various guises – sometimes in group adventures, such as the Cathars of the 12th century, the Seekers, Ranters and Diggers of our English Revolution, or as individual commentators such as Rousseau, George / Sand, Whitman, Shelley, Blake. It will continue to come back, until the world is no longer dragged along by the scruff of its neck by those who place our lives at the mercy of their power. Until then, these anarchistic, communitarian, free spirits will rise time and again despite repression or (in the more sophisticated world) ridicule. Edward Carpenter was part of that tradition. To him, the past, present and future were indivisible, as were the parts of each individual human existence, as were the parts of the whole of nature. He knew in his fibre that change, development, progress and history had to include the unknowns of the human heart. He knew this because he had listened to his own heart and, in the face of a set of laws, morals, manners and customs that boomed out 'Impossible!', he had formed the strength to change. It was not easy, yet once achieved, it seemed the simplest thing in the world:

> Wonderful! The doors that were closed stand open. Yet how slight a thing it is.
> The upturning of a palm? the curve of a lip, an eyelid? Nothing.
> Nothing that can be seen with the mortal eye or heard by the ear, nothing that can be definitely thought, spoken, or written in a book —
> Yet the doors that were treble-bolted and barred, and the doors weed-overgrown and with rusty old hinges,
> Fly open themselves.[30]

Just as the Gay Liberation Movement was the response of countless individuals struggling to declare their own sexuality, so too did Edward Carpenter's struggle give warnings, in the mid-Victorian night, of what was to come:

> there was that other need ... that of my affectional nature, that hunger which had indeed hunted me down since I was a child. I can hardly bear even now to think of my early life ... the denial and systematic ignoring of the obvious facts of the heart and of sex ...[31]

The door did eventually open though, and:

> I soon discovered that others of like temperament to myself were abundant in all directions, and to be found in every class of society; and I need not say that from that time forward life was changed for me. I found

sympathy, understanding, love, in a hundred unexpected forms, and my world of the heart became as rich in that which it needed as before it had seemed fruitless and barren.[32]

Here, in his sense of a personal unity, are the seeds of his socialism. He saw the movements of history – the possibility of great shifts – through the movements of his own life. For him, change was laid up in the hearts of women and men:

as these sufferings of women, of one kind and another, have been the great inspiring cause and impetus of the Women's Movement . . . so I do not practically doubt that the similar sufferings of the Uranian class of men are destined in their turn to lead to another wide-reaching social organisation and forward movement . . .[33]

These are – to me at any rate – thrilling words. Yet they are the product of something much more complex and difficult: a lived life. Who knows what mysterious chemistry of biology and circumstance brews up our individual characters? Yet it must be that Edward's notions of change took root in the long and painful evolution of his own life. He knew that change was a process, not an event. It can be exhilarating, can produce fine expressions of hope, but it can also be exhausting and debilitating. His temperament and constitution were shaped by that battle to repossess his heart, and at times there is a cautious tone to his writings, a wariness, which reflects the difficulties of it all. As Laurence Housman says:

in his public utterances on behalf of certain under-dogs – especially on behalf of homosexuals – his manner of speaking often struck me as too indirect and evasive for his pleading to get really home . . .[34]

The dogged attempt to 'go gradual' makes me wonder what strains were felt by the nervous system and what cast of character it produced. He was, after all, loving men and attempting to open out some discussion of homosexuality at a very dangerous time. I suspect his self-imposed caution accounted for a nervous system which did at times erupt in irritability and delicate health. His friend Henry Salt tells us:

> constitutionally delicate, he only kept his weaknesses in check by a carefully cultivated will-power akin to that of the yogi . . . This internal strain and conflict in Carpenter left its mark very strongly on his personal appearance.[35]

So then, he was certainly not the rash, defiant martyr – could never have been an Oscar Wilde – although he did steer a dangerous course at times. In the end, it was the 'gradual' qualities that Housman valued him for. Not because of their immediate effect, but for their future influence:

> though his method of approach and argument had a gradualness that sometimes seemed almost diffident, I have no doubt at all . . . that the outspokenness of the present age on things that were 'unmentionable' a generation ago is very largely due to his life and influence, and to the moral courage which the beauty of his own life and character inspired in others.[36]

Here again, we learn that to fully appreciate the writings, we should attempt to feel the life through which they wove. A life which began in the respectable Brighton cage, but from which he flew (his sisters, not having even the deformed advantages of being male, left behind to loaf on their sofas). He entered a university career at Cambridge, studying maths and taking clerical orders, finally achieving a fellowship. In short, he 'did well' and seemed all set for a comfortable and ordered life. Under the surface though, other forces were at work:

> after a time it began to pall upon me and bore me. There was a vein of what might be called painful earnestness in my character. These talking machines were, many of them, very obnoxious to me. And then of what avail was the brain, when the heart demanded so much, and demanding was still unsatisfied?[37]

The Church was no answer, either, and he was to

renounce that path. All this debilitated him – 'by the end of '72 I was obviously ill and incapacitated' – but a long Italian holiday worked some changes. That country helped to unite in his mind the beauty of southern art and nature with another particular influence – the writings of Walt Whitman. He had received copies of Whitman's writings some years previously and:

> From that time forward a profound change set in within me . . . What made me cling to the little blue book from the beginning was largely the poems which celebrate comradeship. That thought, so near and personal to me, I had never before seen or heard fairly expressed . . .[38]

Italy was a sensual reminder of another age, which found a voice in Whitman's poems and a resonance in Edward's heart:

> the Greek ideal of the free and gracious life of man at one with nature and the cosmos – so remote from the current ideals of commercialism and Christianity![39]

It was in Italy, experiencing a healing and a calming, where the ground was smoothed for an inspirational thought:

> It had come on me with great force that I would go and throw in my lot with the mass-people and the manual workers.[40]

Something had happened which was sudden, dramatic, and unsought. The straitjacket of his previous existence and the sensuality of southern culture did not remain as two styles of existence which were both foreign to him (one by temperament, the other by culture), but produced out of their opposition a lightning-flash. A new course presented itself – not retreat to the tomb of bourgeois respectability, nor an attempt to live out the fantasy of a mythical Greek utopia, but a decision to realise his desires amongst those in his own land who had not yet been stifled by bourgeois culture and 'respectability'. Where did this inspirational thought come from? Not from a progress chart he had worked out carefully at his desk. Not from a logical process of thought. There was nothing in his previous existence which had suggested such a solution. With hindsight it was (as we shall see) the absolutely right one for him, but the process which brought it about was mysterious – it was the deep spiritual needs which are so hard to chart and which are the motor of change in history, whether of individuals or of the masses. Carpenter spent much of his life attempting to understand these changes within himself, and in so doing, wondered upon the greater changes of the species, of personal relations and the relations of society. The mystery of personal evolution led him to the mysteries of political evolution. These thoughts came to centre on one word: Exfoliation.

Exfoliation: The Desire for Change

> If the question is: What is the cause of Variation among animals? some approximation towards an answer ought to be got by each person asking himself, 'Why do I vary?' Why – he might say – am I a different person from what I was ten years ago, or when I was a boy?[41]

At a time when the effect of external forces and of environment were establishing themselves as crucial factors in the development of personality, Carpenter was beginning to seek out the other side of the matter – the *desire* for evolution coming from within. The facts of his own life – of his own half-realised desires acting upon him and seeking for the light – taught him to reject mechanical Darwinism (and later encouraged him to regard a strictly Marxist approach as a useful, yet limited tool). He refused to see himself or others merely as objects worked upon; rather as creatures with the will to change, and therefore with the power of self-transformation. The escape from a world of money and manners to a shared existence with the Sheffield workers, then later to the small farm-holding in Derbyshire with George Merrill, did not happen quickly or with ease. He was already in his late forties when he met Merrill, and in his fifties when they set up home together. This left its mark upon his health and his moods, but he had come near to being the creature he wished to be:

Who shall say that the lark, by the mere love of soaring and singing in the face of the sun, has not altered the shape of its wings . . . ?[42]

Just as the lark seeks its desires, so he, in the inky pitch of 19th century morality, came towards his desire to love other men, openly. It was a rocky track, as we shall see. Over the years he must have meditated upon that sudden resolution to 'throw in my lot with the mass-people' and this was surely in his mind when he wrote:

The order seems to be: first, a feeling – a dim want or desire; then the feeling becomes conscious of itself, takes shape in thought; the thought becomes more defined and issues in a distinct plan . . . The process appears as a movement from within outwards . . .[43]

By his later years, he had incorporated this individual experience into a philosophy embracing us all:

It may be that as to individuals the revelation of a new vision often comes quite suddenly, and *generally* perhaps after a period of great suffering, so to society at large a similar revelation will arrive – 'like the lightning which cometh out of the East and shineth even unto the West' – with unexpected swiftness.[44]

He wrote *Pagan and Christian Creeds* in 1919. In it, he was attempting to grasp the unity of the psychological evolution of the species, to see how it had led to a pit of individual loneliness and mass destruction, and to divine the process which he believed *would* lead to a better world. Strong as his faith in our regeneration was, however, he was not unrealistic. His remark that 'still more and more terrible struggles *may* be necessary' for the liberation of the creature within, is chilling indeed for those of us who live at a time when nuclear missiles grow thick as wheatfields from the soil.

This philosophy of evolution is far from a 'survival of the fittest' attitude, where severe competition for material sustenance is the keynote. Of course, that is one part of the reality of existence, and much blood has been spilt because of it – although it is interesting to note (as did he) that only a system which elevates competition totally could see in the animal life of distant archipelagos a 'natural' justification for a boom-and-bankruptcy economy! Well, Darwin had a theory and Marx had an analysis, and the material drive for food has caused death, and the mercenary drive for minerals, oil, land and profits has caused mass death, but what of the other side, which Carpenter draws us to? Many a lark may have died in the attempt to reach the sun, but it was not an attempt to grasp the sun for herself alone. Today we fear nature – it is a thing to be subdued, to be hidden from, to be raided and hacked about. We are taught that the products of nature and of our own labours have to be policed, or we should all be at each other's throats in an instant. It is difficult to prove otherwise, for we are given little opportunity to organise ourselves in more sensible ways. Within organised politics there is an assumption that we must be *led* to communality, organised into it. In a sense, this may be true, given the ways in which the modern State has robbed its citizens of the sense of self. Yet without an understanding that the desire for unity and wholeness with the self and with others is present (sleeping though it may be), such leadership or organisation will only trample further on the human soul.

That desire for communality can be glimpsed though, even in the most ghastly situations. At a time of war it appears, in a perverted, uncalled-for way, but nevertheless there:

> I think I now begin to understand why to thousands, and one may say millions, this War (even with all its horrors) has been a relief and an escape, why it has brought alertness of mind and brightness of eyes with it. And the answer is: Because – dreadful and wicked though it be – it has meant to so many a life in the open-air; it has meant health, good food, a common cause, comradeship with others, and a dozen positive things, instead of the inhuman monotonies and negations of a life of slave labour under the heel of commercialism. I understand that wicked as the War is, it is in its essence the outcome and result of something more wicked; and I pray that when after-

wards the millions return to their homes they will see
to it that never again shall the soulless régime of the
past be reinstated, but that industrial life shall go
forward into a new land – the land of freedom and of
joy.[45]

The war (it was the First World War of which he spoke)
did not produce a conflict between the old dead hand and the
soul's longings sufficient to lead to the new evolution of
society. He must have felt despair at this, and at the failure
of the socialist agenda to inspire the masses to change the
basic social relations. But by then the 'questions of the heart
and soul' were definitely not part of the agenda, and he knew
that only a political philosophy which addressed itself to
those questions on an equal footing with the bread-and-
butter issues, could produce the regeneration he longed for.
He wished for a politics which recognised the inner longing
and the outer necessity as having equal validity in the story
of our evolution as individuals and as social beings, a
politics which recognised:

> this inner force producing modification in man and
> animals – to try and find out of what nature it is, what
> is the law, and what are the limits of its action . . .[46]

In short, he wanted a political philosophy (and therefore
programme) which reflected his own evolution: not one
which demanded he adapt himself to it, but adapted itself
(continuously and creatively) to his personal needs and to
the needs of every single individual. The core of the theory
of exfoliation is that, if function precedes organisation,
desire precedes function. The urge to give life and form to
his homosexuality had no basis in any possible material
benefit or gain. Quite the reverse, he was contemplating
something that had meant suicide and social ruin for
countless men. The laws of his own self-modification went
beyond bread-and-butter, and his instincts told him that he
was not alone in this. He saw that 'communality' could only
be based upon the recognition that:

> Every human being, like every animal or plant or tree,
> has a law of growth of its own . . .[47]

and he believed in a form of social organisation which did not reduce our individual variety in its search for material equality:

> One tree bears oranges, another bears roses. The joy that any such healthy tree has in its work is evident. But only on condition that it is *free*, to produce according to its nature. To try to compel a rose-tree to bear oranges would be madness – a madness similar to that which prevails at present in the whole of our industrial world.[48]

Where the theory of exfoliation (which Carpenter took from Lamarck and expanded upon according to his own experience) differs from the theories of Darwin and Marx, is that 'imagination' (for which read 'desire', 'inspiration', 'joy', or what you like) is not regarded as the final achievement of evolution, but as the original motor:

> it fixes the attention on that which appears last in the order of Time, as the most important in order of causation, rather than on that which appears first . . . Thus in the growth of a plant we find leaf after leaf appearing, petal within petal – a continual exfoliation of husks, sepals, petals stamens and what-not; but the object of all this movement, and that which in a sense sets it all in motion, namely the seed, is the very last thing of all to be manifested.[49]

This is a great challenge to the scientific approach of Marxism, which tells us that only by a social application of the 'laws' of historical materialism can we create the space for our humanity to flower. In one sense that is true, for the imagination is crippled by lack of bread (decent housing, clothes, etc.), but the presentation of this theory as *the* solution, as fixed and immutable, misses the possibility that the theory may be one manoeuvre in the story of our evolution – an intellectually conscious attempt to re-shape the social environment which has been produced by deeper, less easily identified desires. This is dangerous thought, for we have seen how words such as 'joy', 'desire', 'will' have been used by regimes of death and destruction, how appeals to the 'unconscious', the 'non-rational' have ended up with death-camps and genocide. Yet we cannot avoid the fact that those appeals have worked, have struck some chord with the masses, fed some hunger which is there. In the end, the masses have been cheated by those words, led to another war, another total destruction, but is the answer to ignore the appeal which those words made? A scientific theory of the evolution of the species may serve to discredit a myth that Original Sin subjugates us all to God; a scientific analysis of economic forces may serve to produce an understanding that poverty is not 'natural' or necessary. Until both can see that *they* have not produced or allowed the imagination to flower, but that imagination has created them in order to find itself, they can only be fresh prisons for the imagination:

> All our modern science, for instance, is founded on the acceptation of mechanical cause and effect as a basic fact of consciousness; but when that base gives way the entire structure will cave in, and a new edifice will have to be reared . . .
>
> Thus, although the experimental investigatory coral-reef accretion method of modern science is very valuable within its range, it must not be forgotten that the human mind does not progress more than temporarily by this method – that its progression is a matter of growth from within, and involves a continual *breaking away of the bases* of all thought-structures; so that while this latter – i.e., the progression of the systemic consciousness of man – is necessary and continuous, the rise and fall of his thought-systems is accidental, so to speak, and discontinuous.[50]

It was not simply in his own life that he saw desire as the motor of change. When he went to live amongst the workers in Sheffield, he saw the same process at work. In the smallest, everyday things he found hope that people could reject the mechanisation of their lives:

> So great is the pleasure of free creative work that thousands and hundreds of thousands of folk – as is well known – after their day of leaden and slave-like labour in the factories, do actually on their return

> home plunge into some sort of hobby of their own —
> whether gardening, or cabinet-work, leatherwork,
> copper-embossing, painting, or what not. Tired as they
> are they still are drawn onwards by the desire to
> express themselves, to create something of their
> own . . .[51]

He believed that in such activities, insignificant as they
seemed, could be heard — in the face of the great hammer of
industry — the 'No' of the people. To him, one person
conceiving one self-made object of craft and beauty was an
echo of the desire for a different world. Here was the form of
the new society within the husk of the old, and he trusted in
this individual experience far more than any grand plan or
scheme. He asks us, over and over, to look inside ourselves
to see through a society where we are asked to endure a
'natural' race with each other for jobs, housing, career,
status, sexual gratification; endure, too, the complex structures of bureaucracies and institutions which mark out the
tracks. For this looking within is just what the society of the
consumer-individual does *not* wish us to do. To do so might
bring forth a tidal wave of voices, declaring the blight
imposed upon the human spirit by such a system. A people
who cannot express their feelings, have no access to them,
cannot say 'No' to that which is doled out:

> The very extensive and wealthy classes who today
> control production and derive their riches from the
> enslavement of labour, dread above all things the
> *freeing* of the worker and the prospect of the latter
> becoming self-determining and master of his fate.
> Though it is notorious that the present dispensation
> produces a rather futile, mean, and miserable master-
> class, together with a dismal, weary, and sad-eyed
> worker class, yet the whole political and social engine
> is concentrated on the effort to maintain it as it is, and
> to disguise or conceal its evil character. The lifting of
> this coffin-lid would be the signal of a Resurrection
> such as the world has hardly yet dreamed of.[52]

The evolution of the species to a true communality was,
to Carpenter, as much about the sharing of the wealth of our

emotional lives as about the sharing of the material wealth of the world. Such ideas were a direct threat to the old, dead culture within which he lived. Why was the Free Love movement so reviled? (the phrase is still a slur today on the lips of many) – because it talked of a free exchange of feelings, whereas in the present circumstances love, like anything else, had to be paid for. The unpredictable, whimsical, unprogrammable desires for love and creativity have no place in a system where all must go to the market-place to achieve humanity. When Carpenter, Annie Besant, Olive Schreiner and other socialists demanded that love be freed, it was not a cry for a 'permissive' oasis in an otherwise unchanged society, but for a total change in our relations to each other. Imagine, if you can, a Labour politician of today who could say:

> Not till our whole commercial system, with its barter and sale of human labour and human love for gain, is done away with, and not till a whole new code of ideals and customs of life has come in, will women really be free . . . their cause is also the cause of the oppressed labourer over the whole earth, and the labourer has to remember that his cause is theirs.[53]

In the milling slums of Sheffield, where survival meant mutual support, he must have seen an active, day-to-day caring which underlined his belief that love was the true spark of revolution:

> For after all it is not in the main on account of ourselves that we cherish a grudge against the 'common enemy' and dispute his authority, but for the sake of those we love. For ourselves we may be indifferent or acquiescent; but somehow for those others, for those divine ones who have taken our hearts into their keeping, we resent the idea that *they* can perish.[54]

A struggle for change which springs from such sentiments must carry within it the seeds of a world where a serious, intelligent attempt to understand our emotions is not mocked and trivialised, or seen as fit pastime only for the leisured and the educated. Here was a trust that, once we unlock the cages of our hearts to each other, we will not need systems of government to enact laws for us, police forces to control us, theologians to define our morality, industrial entrepreneurs to suggest our material wants. He himself had struggled out of a kind of coffin, and amongst the workers he found reassurance that within the mass of the people there was the same desire for self-liberation:

> The truth is that the germ of the Beauty-sense is slumbering in the hearts of all peoples . . . But it is very commonly starved out on the one hand by sheer poverty or paralysed on the other by mere superfluity of wealth.[55]

So he looked to the lives of the many for signals of the new social relations, of the new form of society evolving within the old. Once again, he did not expect instant results:

> the New Morality – to look *within*, to feel and refer to the needs of others almost as instinctively as to one's own, to refuse to regard any *thing* as in itself good or bad, and to look upon all beings, oneself included, as ends in themselves and not as a means of personal self-advancement and glorification – while it is the more natural, it is also the more difficult in a sense, as providing no set pattern or rule. But surely the time has arrived for its adoption. It is the morality which must underlie the freer, more varied forms of the society of the future; and it is the only escape from the corruption of the old order.[56]

These 'freer and more varied forms' striving for the light, he saw in the lives of those around him. The anecdotes which pepper his writings are not given as picturesque 'colour', but as sound proof that human evolution has further to go:

> I know a boy who slaves in a dirty workshop for ten hours or so a day. When he gets home – and a very poor home at that – he actually, after he has had his tea, descends into the *cellar* and by the dim light of a tallow candle and with poor tools begins work again, making little cabinets or corner-cupboards, or a model of an aeroplane. Such people are true artists; and *all* work of course ought to be of a similar nature – that is, of the nature of an Art.[57]

In that future world, the boy creeping home from mind-numbing drudgery to make models in his cellar would no longer be a symbol of the soul's resistance. His joy of creating freely would beat at the very heart of society, for behind the small creative act, undertaken freely, he sensed the greater desires of the spirit:

> now for the first time in History both the masses and the thinkers of all the advanced nations of the world are consciously feeling their way towards the establishment of a socialistic and communal life on a vast scale. The present competitive society is more and more rapidly becoming a mere dead formula and husk within which the outlines of the new and *human* society are already discernible.[58]

As I have said, he knew that insights and visions could never produce overnight changes. For him, the inspirational thought could light a path to the future:

> I dream that these are the fibres and nerves of a body that lies within the outer body of society,
> A network, an innumerable vast interlocked ramification, slowly being built up – all dear lovers and friends, all families, groups, all peoples, nations, all times, all worlds perhaps –
> Of which the outer similitudes and shells, like the minute cells of an organism, are shed and die in endless multitudes with continual decay and corruption . . .[59]

It was his inspiration of setting his life down with the masses which enabled him to shed the husk of his own dead class, and to eventually apply that experience to his meditations upon nature and society. It would be worth our while to take a look at the journey he made, in the light of those ideas centring on exfoliation.

Only Connect: The Politics of Friendship

The phrase 'Only connect' was used by E. M. Forster in his novel *Howard's End*, and he believed it to be the most important he had ever written. It was in fact George Merrill who had helped Forster connect his inner feelings with his whole life and the lives of others. Merrill had touched Forster in a friendly, sensual way, and the writer felt a physical shock of recognition concerning his own sexuality, one which was to influence the rest of his life.

This sense of connecting his own inner feelings with those around him was an important part of Carpenter's development, and it is interesting to see how, in his early life, this came through a certain identification with women. From the Brighton days he had seen how circumstances had pulled his sisters down to a genteel monotony, and it is no surprise that he was drawn to those women who fought back. Such a woman was Jane Olivia Daubeny, with whom he made that visit to Italy. Her story can be found in his book *Sketches from Life*, where she appears under the guise of 'Francesca':

> There are some natures so keen, so intense, that they seem as if they were never made for this patchwork world of broken resolves, lukewarm alliances, half-avowed principles and half-disavowed creeds. They can never accommodate themselves to it; they are at war with it all the time. They neither quite understand others, nor are quite understood. They suffer, and at times they inflict suffering. Tragic almost always is their fate. The hungry sea beating for ever unsatisfied against a sullen shore is as near to its goal as they; the lightning-flash at mid-noon casts upon our ordinary work-a-day world no stranger illumination.[60]

Certainly here was a temperament with which he could identify parts of himself, and it was Jane's mind which:

> served to liberate my mind, corrected in many respects the native vagueness of my thought, and certainly helped me greatly on the road to choose my own way in life.[61]

Thus Jane urged Carpenter, at his time of great doubt at Cambridge and in the Church, to seek the change:

> It is terrible to me to know how you suffer. Your letter last night made me cold to the finger-ends. One thing

is clear anyhow, your present life is intolerable, *change it you must . . .*[62]

Not sexually drawn to women, he was moved and influenced by the treatment doled out to them – although I should also mention that not all his friends believed he was in total sympathy with them. Henry Salt remarks:

> Women he was supposed to understand, but that he did *not* understand them was the opinion of Olive Schreiner, Isabella Ford, and those of his female friends who knew him best.[63]

When it came to working-class women, there is certainly evidence of a distance. The reasons for this are not too hard to guess at – jealousy, or something of that nature, for by the time he was in contact with such women, he was in the thick of developing close relationships with men. That is, very often with the husbands of those women. At that point, theory and aspiration collided with the reality of the moment – the desire for generosity in love coming face-to-face with the miserly greed for possession. He attempted to come to grips with this, and he wrote of it. The exchange of letters with his friends should be read alongside the theoretical writings, for they are good evidence of the desire for the new battling with the ways of the old.

All that was to come. After Italy he began the long attempt, going cautiously, first as a University Extension Lecturer in the North, then closer and closer to his ideal. It was uncharted territory and he was in for some shocks. In those days before mass media, communities separated only by a hundred miles or so could seem as foreign to each other as the tribes of Asia:

> When living in Brighton as a boy . . . I used to hear of the miners in the North whose coal . . . we were in the habit of burning. And I used to think what grand fellows those miners must be . . . what strong and well-grown men, and honoured by the nation, as of course they ought to be. Fate or destiny have led me, in these later years, to live within three or four miles of the coal pits of North-East Derbyshire; and now I know the miners of that locality well . . . I shall never forget

the moment when first I watched the arrival of this train. Instead of the fine hearty fellows my boyish imagination had pictured, there descended from the overcrowded carriages ... a shambling ragged crew, whose thin legs and worn features spoke only too clearly of want and overwork ... Rickety limbs, contracted chests, hacking coughs and hollow cheeks, abounded ... these men who do some of society's most needed work are left, through ignorance, neglect, and oppression, to become its bitter enemies. And one can only ask, Where are the splendours and the joys of life which should be their portion?[64]

In a society which attempts to reduce all life to a mechanised standard of human existence, it is useful to look towards the outcasts of that society. From their treatment we can learn something of the morality of the system. From their struggles and desires we can glean signals for the future. Carpenter knew this had to be his course (did he not know in his heart that, despite social advantage, he was an outcast? There were threads between his sisters, himself, such as Jane, and those miners):

> If I am not level with the lowest I am nothing; and if I did not know for a certainty that the craziest sot in the village is my equal, and were not proud to have him walk with me as my friend, I would not write another word – for in this is my strength.[65]

He knew that he was:

> profoundly ignorant of commercial life. The manners, customs, ideas, ideals, the types of people ... all formed a strange contrast to Cambridge and Brighton.[66]

How easy it would have been to have found relief for his renegade sexuality in the niches of the dinner-party, opera-going world, or the self-satisfied networks of the clerical and academic cloisters. He did not seek it there. A century before homosexuals stepped out of the closets en masse, to add our voices to the demands for great changes amongst the masses, Edward Carpenter took that route as an individual.

It had to be an individual step in the dark then, but the action was taken with the consciousness that it could only be complete through a sympathy with and a development amongst the greater masses – the outcasts. In the process of making these connections, he came to develop a notion of politics where 'friendship' and 'personal relations' were as vital as 'economy' and 'money flow'.

Today, perhaps even more than then, we live at a time where 'friendship' tends to fall into the same category of things which includes 'leisure time', 'weekends', 'hobbies' – that is, institutionalised refuges from the world of work. Our personal relations are regarded as that area of life which is 'private', where we go to refresh ourselves for the 'public' daily struggle which will resume tomorrow. It is in this privatised context that our struggles with love, desire, jealousy and loneliness take place. We return home exhausted from work (or, these days, more likely from hunting for work), shut the door on the world and enter this 'private' life of the emotions.

Knowing already that unity was a major theme in Carpenter's journey, it is clear that such a situation would not satisfy him. The keynote is in a letter to Charles Oates, of December 1887:

> We are going to form by degrees a body of friends who will be tied together by the strongest general bond, and also by personal attachments.[67]

That strong general bond was a common cause – the movement for socialism, and it is true to say that for a short period towards the end of the 19th century, many socialists encouraged an approach to politics that encompassed the personal and the individual. In this, they were not alone in history. In the early 19th century a generation of utopian socialists, drawing inspiration from the Lanark mill-owner turned radical, Robert Owen – and many of them women – envisaged a process of change where the questions of sexuality and the relations between the sexes were not to be postponed till 'after the revolution', but were seen as motors of true revolution. Carpenter, Olive Schreiner, Besant *et al* were inheritors of that movement, and Carpenter arrived in the thick of the radicalism of the 1880s with the already formed desire to find his common humanity through a sharing of his emotional life with his political comrades. It was excellent timing on the part of history, for by adding his voice to the larger trend, he broadened and amplified the discussion in such a way that those ideas were to be secured for future generations.

The phrase 'the personal is political' was never used by Carpenter, yet this basic principle of today's gay and feminist movements was at the heart of his beliefs. He saw, from his own life, how we struggle with our complicated emotions behind locked doors, never encouraged to share our fears and dreams with others, never taught how to, and therefore restrained from acting upon them. This threatens the keepers of power not one jot. The belief in the 'natural-ness' of certain feelings (jealousy, competitiveness, posses-siveness), the lip-service given to any public discussion of them (the thin talk of 'love' from the Church, the odd 'honest' tv play) is to the advantage of every politician who seeks power over our lives.

Carpenter's 'band of friends' was not to be some inward-looking coterie of aesthetes, but an attempt to engage the whole self with the world and so change the world. How strange to think, now, that there was a movement of labour which held within it the seeds of challenge to a static view of our natures. It did not regard progress simply as the accumulation of goods and services, but as an advance to a form of society where our inner desires could gain full expression. In practice, of course, the attempts of Carpenter and his circle to pull together the 'inner' life with the 'outer' exhibited all the messiness and frustrations of day-to-day existence. He was helped greatly, though, by the workers he came to know. Perhaps, unconsciously, he knew that here was a class of people who, because of the circumstances they found themselves in – thrust together willy-nilly, in overcrowded, grim conditions – could not help but reveal things which in the world of 'manners' and private bed-rooms, remained veiled. Read the letters from the three Georges – Merrill, Hukin and Adams – and you'll find a frankness which would sit uneasily in the armchairs of polite society. Myths begin to crumble (as they must have for Carpenter). A class which, we are told, was steadfastly intolerant towards homosexuality could not have produced the conditions where George Merrill was able to express his emotions for men with a quite reasonable degree of openness – as with this letter to Carpenter, written in 1886:

> Dear Ted . . . I shall be glad to see thy dear face again as I have such longings to kiss those sweet lips of thine. I will wait till I hear from you, first. So I must close dear heart as I am feeling a little low and lonesome. I'm always with thee every night in spirit, fondest love from your dear Boy G XXX.[68]

In Carpenter's own written study on Merrill, we find a young man who had grown up in dire poverty, yet had an access to emotions which were so firmly suppressed in the society of starched linen and six-course meals from which Carpenter came. If anyone represented Carpenter's belief that a true socialism existed in the hearts of the many, then it was Merrill:

> I'm so sorry for [. . .] the impediment in my speech. I think I should be able to do a little good for the social cause if I could converse better, but never mind it may wear away when I get to you and read for you. I do feel it very much at times. I thought about you all last night dear . . . love from your affectionate Sonny X.[69]

Merrill was to arrive in the nineties. Before that, in the 1880s, when Carpenter had begun to put down roots in Sheffield, there were other relationships forming. Merrill, in his frankness, might be seen as an exception to the picture we are often given of working-class inarticulacy, but the letters from other friends give the lie to that. George Hukin, a razor-grinder by trade, met Carpenter through the Sheffield Socialist Society, and their relationship did not simply include the energetic comradeship of political organising round the town. It was deeply emotional and for a time sexual:

> Dear Edward . . . it is so good of you to love me so. I dont think I ever felt so happy in my life as I have felt lately. And I'm sure I love you more than any other friend I have in the world.[70]

And again, the same access to emotions seen in Merrill:

> yes, Ted, it did help me a great deal that talk we had in
> bed that Monday morning – oh how often I wanted to
> tell you about it – ever since that first night I slept with
> you at Millthorpe. You dont know how miserable I
> have felt all day long just because I wanted to tell you,
> and yet somehow I was afraid to. But I shall not be
> afraid to tell you anything in future if only you will let
> me, Ted.[71]

Then there is George Adams, born in utter poverty in the
Sheffield slums, who worked at a variety of dismal jobs till
he eventually – with wife Lucy and their children – moved
to Millthorpe with Carpenter. Here again, the same ease in
expressing affection:

> I am pleased to hear from you, and hope you will not be
> able to do without me, I miss you very much, when
> you come back be strong, dont overwork yourself and
> dont get cross.[72]

Remember that this was no Bloomsbury Set of sophisti-
cates, with the leisure to transform their emotional lives
into literature. They are the expressions of a group living
near to the bread-line. It may be that Edward's personal
influence sparked such men as these to express their
affections in these ways – but even so, it is entirely within
Carpenter's philosophy that the *desire* for expression was
already there. Yet the passionate articulacy in the letters of
these men when writing of broader events shows that their
class position was no bar to fine, poetic expressions of ideas
and feelings. In 1887, after a brutal police attack on an
unemployed demonstration in Trafalgar Square (the first-
named 'Bloody Sunday') which Carpenter had attended and
where he had been injured by a baton, Adams wrote:

> the victory they steal from us today does not prove
> they will win tomorrow, and if it should not come
> while we live, we can get pleasure in dying fighting for
> it.[73]

As mentioned, jealousy probably played some part in his
distance with working-class women. In 1887 he wrote to a

friend about George and Fannie Hukin:

> tho' they are *both* very affectionate, it causes me horrible spasms of jealousy to see them. . .[74]

and it is clear from Hukin's letters to Carpenter that he had a tough time of it himself:

> Surely Ted, if you knew how we both love you, you would not be so unhappy, and cause us to be so miserable . . . if we didn't both of us love you so much I dont think we should love each other as much as we do.[75]

Carpenter was apparently not past causing a rumpus when the mood was on him. Henry Salt gives us an account (*In Appreciation*, pp. 185–6) of his moods, all of which had been given names by his friends – 'Cambridge' was 'just a little stiff and distant'; 'hall porter' was 'indicative of a certain external lassitude' and 'On the pounce' sent everyone running for cover!

Through the letters we can glimpse a socialist movement which was attempting an openness on matters that were rarely seen as vital to political debates. Those connections with the emotional lives of others, often painful, must have provided the material for his essays on personal relations. The essays gain depth when read alongside the letters, for all are aspects of a movement which strove to seek the links between personal desires and political change. From this vantage point, Carpenter was able to develop a radical critique of the emotions, linking what we experience as 'private' (that is, not of the world) with the material process of history. The essay 'On Jealousy' goes far in reversing the notion that our emotions live outside of historical time:

> with the growth of individualism in life and love, with the rise of the sense of property under civilisation and the accentuation of every personal feeling . . . the passion becomes one of fearful and convulsive power and fury. . .[76]

Today we have national newsrags which applaud these grossly exaggerated emotions – a film actress publicly announces in banner headlines that she would kill if her husband 'cheated' on her. This is the token of her great love, to which our hearts are meant to warm and which we are meant to see as a 'natural' aspect of a loving relationship. Well, jealousy does exist and we cannot wish it away, but perhaps we should attempt, as Carpenter did, to seek its different causes and so perhaps understand that it is not inevitable. He suggested that there were two major 'types' of jealousy – the first that which:

> arises perhaps from the real uniqueness of the relationship between two persons . . . and the endeavour to stamp this uniqueness on the whole relationship, sexual and moral.[77]

This may die away, quite naturally, 'without damaging the intimacy and uniqueness of the alliance'. Then there is the other kind of jealousy which:

> rests on the sense of property . . . This kind of jealousy is more especially the product of immediate social conditions, and is in that sense artificial. Though probably not quite so heart-rending as the other, it is often passionate enough, and lasts on indefinitely, like a chronic disease.[78]

What he sought was a politics which desired a world in which we should be free of such inner chains. A world where:

> as the sense of property declines, and as Love rises more and more out of mere blind confusion with the sex-act, we may fairly hope that the artificial jealousy will disappear altogether, and that the other form of the passion will subside again into a comparatively reasonable human emotion.[79]

Where is that world?

As capitalism presents itself more and more forcefully not as *a* form of society, but as *the* form, it needs to induce in us the feeling that we have arrived at our humanity, that history has stopped, that its institutions reflect our needs. So dies the sense of journey, the belief that the story continues, that human needs will find new forms of social organisation to express themselves. A people who see emotions as 'fixed' will cease to quest for other forms of living. If jealousy is seen as 'natural', then this 'personal' and 'private' emotion will continue to erupt publicly, with rich film stars boasting of it and husbands let off lightly for killing their wives because of it. The freeing of love would not only bring joy to our lives, it would save lives and for that reason alone it should be at the centre of any political programme. It might also be that, in a type of society which has at its heart the notion of personal relations constantly *developing*, the great fear of death itself would lessen. If our personal relations (and thus our lives) appear fixed or 'stuck', and if we are so trapped in a caul of ignorance that we regard this situation as inevitable, 'natural' and desirable, how can we accept the final stage of our earthly evolution:

> Daily we pass, like shadows in a dreamland,
>   And careless answer in the old curt tone,
> Till Death breaks suddenly between us, and
>   With a great cry we know we have not known.[80]

It is terrible, and true, that in a world where emotions become the object of embarrassment, sniggers and nudges, it takes a death to shock us into recognition of the wealth we have let slip through our fingers. Yet to Edward, this was not inevitable. For him, the new seed within the dead husk of the old, dead society was the vision of radically altered personal relations. The means to break the husk lay in the heart of every individual. He called this old world 'civilisation'. He saw the power it held, with its systems of power and wealth held up by ignorance and fear, but for him it was a stage in history, not the end of it.

The Husk of the Old

England! for good or evil it is useless to attempt to conceal yourself – I know you too well.

Do you think your smooth-faced Respectability will save you? or that Cowardice carries a master-key of the universe in its pocket – scrambling miserably out of the ditch on the heads of those beneath it?

Do you think that it is a fine thing to grind cheap goods out of the hard labour of ill-paid boys? and do you imagine that all your Commerce Shows and Manufactures are anything at all compared with the bodies and souls of these?

Do you suppose I have not heard your talk about Morality and Religion and set it face to face in my soul to the instinct of one clean naked unashamed Man?[81]

The disunity – imbalance – which he had felt in himself he saw in the world around him. The industrial, Empire-building world named this imbalance 'civilisation', pronounced it good and presented it as a full-stop to history. Carpenter saw it as a disease. His criticisms of modern science flowed from this observation:

Science has failed because she has attempted to carry out the investigation of nature from the intellectual side alone – neglecting the other constituents necessarily involved in the problem. She has failed because she has attempted an impossible task; for the discovery of a permanently valid and purely *intellectual* representation of the universe is simply impossible. Such a thing does not exist.

The various theories and views of nature which we hold are merely the fugitive envelopes of the successive stages of human growth – each set of theories and views belonging organically to the moral and emotional stage which has been reached, and being in some sort the expression of it; so that the attempt at any given time to set up an explanation of phenomena which shall be valid in itself and without reference to the mental condition of those who set it up, necessarily ends in failure . . .[82]

Such words peeved many, at that time of the labelling of the universe. Life was being separated out and the parts of existence pinned down for examination like so many dead butterflies. While much good did come from this – and he did not deny it – the process of division and specialisation took us further and further from a sense of wholeness, in ourselves or with each other.

It was in Sheffield in the 1880s that he began to see how, with others, he could work for a change:

> early in '86 quite an important local event occurred . . . One or two of us beat round the town and got together a few Socialists and advanced Radicals; we persuaded William Morris to come down . . . and the result of that was the formation of the Society.[83]

What Carpenter and the Sheffield Socialist Society shared with Morris (who had recently, with Hyndman, formed the Social Democratic Federation) was the vision of a new society growing up within the framework of the old. It was Whitman's picture of 'Creation's incessant unrest, exfoliation' reflected in the process of social regeneration. It was the transformation which Carpenter had experienced in himself – 'one skin cast leaves another behind, and that another, and that yet another' – writ large. Yet he knew that the disease called 'civilisation' would not blow away in an afternoon:

> The chief difficulty, then, which arises in people's minds at the thought of a free non-governmental society does not concern its desirability – they are agreed as a rule that it would be desirable – but concerns its practicability. And much of this difficulty is derived from the society of the present. People see, in fact, that an internecine competition for subsistence is the ruling force of life today, and the chief incentive to production, and they infer that without government society would dissolve into a mere chaos of plunder on the one hand, and of laziness on the other. It is this difficulty which has first to be removed.[84]

The task of removal would be enormous, since the fear of poverty characterising the life of the wage-slave, and the fear of losing the commercial race that drives the entrepreneur, had a strong grip on the souls of all:

> We are like shipwrecked folk clambering up a cliff. The waves are raging below. Each one clings by handhold or foothold where he may, and in the panic if he push his neighbour from a point of vantage, it is to be regretted certainly, but it cannot be helped.[85]

He did not know how the leap would be made. He did know that, once all were assured of 'not only an old-age pension, but a decent provision for all our days of the actual necessaries of life', society would not sink into a trance of inactivity or a welter of barbarism.

In our time, as the states of the world, with no attempt at apology, spend their billions on weapons of destruction whilst millions starve, it seems such a small thing to assure 'provision for all our days of the actual necessaries of life'. Such a simple thing, yet so dangerous to those systems of government whose power rests upon a morality which declares we are all 'naturally' greedy, competitive and anti-social. This is how we exist under the present system, and if it were by some magic stroke done away with, our response would be conditioned by our present circumstances:

> Perhaps, as many would maintain, nine-tenths of the population would say 'I'm blessed if I'll ever do another stroke of work' . . . and rightly enough too. . .[86]

To many, such a state of affairs would be the end of everything. To Capenter it would be the beginning:

> let us suppose, since a bare living has been assured to us, and we are in no danger of actual starvation, that we all take a good long holiday, and abstain religiously from doing anything. Suppose that we simply twirl our thumbs in idleness for two, three, four, or six months. Still, is it not obvious that at the end of that time nine-tenths of the population would find sheer idleness appallingly dreary, and that they would *set themselves* to work at some thing or other – to produce comforts or conveniences rising above the level of sheer necessity – objects of use or beauty, either for themselves, or for their families or neighbours, or even conceivably for society at large; that, in fact, a spontaneous and free production of goods would spring up, followed of course by a spontaneous free exchange – a self-supporting society, based not on individual dread and anxiety, but on the common fulness of life and energy?[87]

Further:

> the work done would be useful ... If a man were a
> cabinet-maker and made a chest of drawers, either for
> himself or a neighbour, he would make it so that the
> drawers would open and shut: but nine-tenths of the
> chests made on commercial principles are such that
> the drawers will neither open nor shut. They are not
> meant to be useful; they are meant to have the
> semblance of being useful; but they are really made to
> *sell*. To sell, and by selling yield a profit.[88]

So, in Sheffield, he was drawn to the socialist movement
'not ... so much in its actual constructive programme'
(though he agreed with that, and helped shape it), but rather
because it 'enshrined a most glowing and vital enthusiasm
towards the realisation of a new society'[89] – one where
beauty and creativity could emerge from the cellars and take
possession of the world. For him, the programme was not
the goal but the vehicle, and he believed that:

> this general programme is the one along which western
> society will work in the near future; that is, till such
> time as the State, qua State, and all efficient Govern-
> ment, are superseded by the voluntary and instinctive
> consent and mutual helpfulness of the people – when
> of course the more especially Anarchist ideal would be
> realised.[90]

In 1887 the Sheffield Socialists opened a café meeting-
place. Carpenter lived on the premises and 'occupied a large
attic at the top of the house, *almost* high enough to escape
the smells of the street below.' Around this time he
produced *England's Ideal* – 'descended from the transcen-
dental generative thought of "Towards Democracy" on the
one hand, and my new-found acquaintance with practical
life on the other'.[91] The influence of Marxist economic
thought is evident in the book, for despite his dreaming
visions, he was not uninterested in the intellectual analysis
of capitalism. Hyndman's *England for All* – a work which
established Marx's theory of surplus-value amongst the
radicals of the 1870s and '80s – was part of his education:

My ideas had been taking a socialistic shape for many years; but they were lacking in definite outline – that definition which is so necessary for all action. That outline as regards the industrial situation was given me by reading Hyndman's *England for All.* However open to criticism the Marxian theory of surplus-value must be (and *every* theory must ultimately succumb to criticism) it certainly fulfilled a want for the time by giving a definite text for the social argument . . .

From that time forward I worked definitely along the Socialist line: with a drift, as was natural, towards Anarchism.[92]

In 1889 *Civilisation, Its Cause and Cure* was published (there were to be 16 editions, through to the completed set of essays in 1921). In the preface to the final edition he recollects how the original lecture on 'Civilisation' – given to the Fabian Society in 1888 – and the subsequent book of essays, were both furiously attacked:

The whole trend of thought of the time was against its conclusions; and it is perhaps worth while to recall these facts in order to measure how far we have travelled in these thirty years. For today (I think we may say) these conclusions are generally admitted as correct; and the views which seemed so hazarded and precarious at the earlier date are now fairly established and accepted.[93]

In 1889 however his criticisms of modern science were thrown back in his face and he was accused of 'desiring to return to the state of primitive man'.[94] That was not his drift, for as in all things, he saw the positive aspects of modern scientific achievements. He wanted an improbable, sandal-wearing dreamland no more than he desired an intolerable machine-dominated wasteland. What he desired was to sift from history the helpful and progressive elements in our evolution and our social relations, and to use those as lamps for the future.

The outlines of the new world were, for Carpenter, to be seen in the individual lives of those around him. If, under the most tedious and deathlike form of common existence, people could still give signs of their love of beauty and free creativity, what worlds awaited when communal life was freely chosen and ordered?

> In these days of thoroughly 'business-like' commercial practicality, it is pleasant to think that a character combining in one the political idealism of the Communist and the roving emotional temperament of the Minstrel should even be possible. Such however was the character of my old friend, Joseph Blount; . . . one of the people – of native feeling, dignity, gentleness, in the very poorest walks, and of that desire for and belief in a better social life, which runs through the thoughts of the real workers in all lands . . .[95]

It was the 'organic, vital, almost physiological morality of the common life'[96] which would produce the new morality, and here he must be referring to those expressions of caring which he witnessed in the grimmest of surroundings. He believed that it was as much in the ways people formed their own commonsensical social relations, as in political agenda, that the key to the 'societies of the future' could be found. 'Common sense' is in fact a phrase which pops up regularly in his writings, spelling out his trust that people do have a sense of what is best for them. Policies and programmes of reconstruction, with their tendency to atrophy into mirror-images of the systems they are intended to replace, he did not so much trust. He could see the future waiting live and ready in the activities of those around him:

> Mrs Usher, large-bosomed and large-hearted, would move on the outskirts of our open-air meetings, armed with a bundle of literature. She was an excellent saleswoman and few could resist her hearty appeal 'Buy this pamphlet, love, it will do you good!'[97]

Of course, such self-education and activity was not the beginning of any sudden revolution. Indeed there had been, throughout the century, an aspect of working-class self-help which had been encouraged by the ruling class – so much better for the poor to take care of themselves. Parliament naturally kept a watchful eye and a controlling hand on such activities, and gradually the friendly societies and co-

operative organisations were absorbed into the legal structure of the land, came to benefit from the economic system,
and any radical notions that had accompanied those spontaneous working-class associations melted away. Much
material relief came to the poor through these compromises
with the state, and lives were made less unbearable, but
Carpenter was not interested in municipally supplied
bathing-drawers, nor the corporation-approved hobby-
centre.

In those last decades of the 19th century, it did seem that
a radical challenge was emerging, and one which would not
be absorbed. The Socialist League (split off from the SDF)
came under the influence of the anarchists; militant
unionism tested its strength in a series of strikes; intense
local activity – as in Sheffield – was widespread. Popular
agitation and intellectual debate seemed to be linking arms
and marching on the State, an understanding of personal life
seemed to water the movement, a new order was glimpsed.
It was not to be. In 1887 a resolution was passed to form a
party of labour in the House of Commons. Seen as desirable
by many, the shadow of a new respectability was cast – the
respectability of Labour leaders, aping their masters in suits
and bowlers, out for votes. That was to be some way off yet,
but it was to come – and many of the ideas which Carpenter
and his circle believed in were soon cast aside as irrelevant,
'crankish' and 'cultish', with anarchist philosophies purged
from the political debate. The matters of the heart, of love,
of sex, and an order of society where such things would have
the same value at least as annual production figures, were
reduced to scoffs about naturists and sandal-wearers. The
husk of the old was not yet broken.

The Independent Labour Party was founded at Leeds in
1892 – the same year in which the police, through the good
services of their agents, began to depict anarchists (through
the 'Walsall bomb affair') as cloaked figures with lit fuses in
their hands. The decade closed with the Boer War and a tidal
wave of jingoism engulfing the nation (it was a practice run
for the First World War); a soldier-loving, militaristic mood
was not conducive to any discussion of sexuality and
socially conditioned gender roles. The Wilde trials certainly
took place in an atmosphere where the ruling elite wanted

to state clearly and publicly that it would not tolerate within its ranks any 'questionable' practices. Carpenter was to retreat somewhat from the industrial struggle – not simply out of necessity, due to the mounting reaction, but for his own inner reasons. He continued as a supporter of labour and of its party, though he knew that party-organisation, however necessary at a particular moment in history, would ossify into another tradition, another net for the human soul:

> That neither Hyndman in his time, nor Morris in his, nor the Fabian Society in theirs, nor Keir Hardie, nor Kropotkin, nor Blatchford, nor any other individual or body, succeeded in capturing the social movement during these years and moulding it to his or their hearts' desire, must always be matter for congratulation. For once pocketed by any clique it would have pined and swindled into an insignificant thing; but, as I have just tried to show, the real movement of this period has been far too great for such a destiny. It is like a great river, fed by currents and streams flowing into it from the most various directions and gathering a force which no man can now control and a volume too great to be confined.[98]

The coincidence of external forces and inner desires which produced Carpenter's retreat was symbolised by his move from Sheffield to a rural existence in Derbyshire. It was less a negative response 'to what was happening on the political front, more an advance towards his own personal socialism. He was not a worker, and his temperament, health and class background dictated he would not live out his days in the Sheffield slums. It would be easy to dismiss him as a 'sight-seer', yet his actions were far removed from those members of the middle classes who descended to the workers to perform 'good deeds'. It is clear that his friends and allies amongst the workers did not see him in that light, and so we should trust their feelings. Yet he must have been aware that his contribution was not to be part of the masses as he had dreamt in Italy. 'Civilisation' was to continue for some time more – its damaging effects somewhat ameliorated perhaps by the establishment of a party representing the masses (and thereby ensuring a longer life for the underlying disease). His attempt at a 'simplification of life' at Millthorpe was his own personal comment on the deficiencies of a left-wing politics, now established in the institution of the State, which had a design for the future that included sound housing with no damp, access to all the material riches of the earth, but was set fair to reducing each living soul to the status of the machines which serviced their bodies:

> it may at first sound extravagant to use the word disease in connection with Civilisation at all, but a little thought should show that the association is not ill-grounded. To take the matter on its physical side first, I find that . . . the number of accredited doctors and surgeons in the United Kingdom is put at over 23,000. It the extent of the national sickness is such that we require 23,000 medical men to attend us, it must surely be rather serious! And *they* do not cure us. Wherever we look today, in mansion or in slum, we see the features and hear the complaints of ill-health; the difficulty is really to find a healthy person.[99]

What he desired for the world was the unity he sought for himself. He did not find its outline in the organised politics which grew from the radical movements of the late 19th century. In his writings and at Millthorpe he continued the attempt at combining the intellectual approach to that world with the day-to-day application of it.

Millthorpe: A Personal Socialism and a Philosophy of the Personal

Having been introduced to Marx by Hyndman, he was typically not content to leave these new insights separate from his own material existence. In 1883 he produced a pamphlet on *Modern Moneylending and the Meaning of Dividends*. In this he examined his own material circumstances (rather good at the time, his father's inheritance of £6,000 having just come to him). He asked himself what was the best means of putting his own surplus to social use. Millthorpe was to be the answer.

The farm at Millthorpe was an experiment in communality, co-operative production and the simplification of life. It became the material realisation of his ideas and ideals, in particular the desire to draw closer to nature. For in the end, it was Walt Whitman and Thoreau who sparked him more than Marx or Hyndman. As E. M. Forster said in 1944:

> he was not really interested in industrialisation, though he tried to be and he loved the industrial workers individually.[100]

In the 'singularly beautiful Derbyshire valley with plentiful woods, streams and moors'[101] he farmed his seven acres. From 1883 to '98 with the help of two families – first the Fearnehough's, then the Adams'. Then an event occurred which was (with the inspirational 'flash' in Italy) one of the most significant of his life. George and Lucy Adams had left, and:

> the next day – trundling with the help of two boys all his worldly goods in a handcart over the hills, and through a disheartening blizzard of snow – George Merrill arrived.[102]

Now Carpenter was to establish, in a practical sort of way, the comrade-love of which he had sung in his poems, had yearned for all his life. Here was the person to whom he could say:

> Indeed, thou art so deep within my heart,
> I fear not Death. And though I die, and fail,
> Falling through stupors, senselessness, oblivion,
> Down to the roots of being; still, thou art there.
> I shall but sleep as I have slept before,
> So oft, in dreamless peace, close-linked with thee.[103]

It may not seem so very earth-shattering today for two men to live together openly, but remember that four years previously, the Wilde trials had heralded suicide, ruin and emigration for hundreds of homosexual men. In 1898 Havelock Ellis had been prosecuted for his own writings on sexuality, Scotland Yard having determined to strike a blow

at a cause connected closely in their minds with anarchism.
There was a growing climate of opinion which saw all forms
of non-marital, non-procreative sexuality as a danger, and
Carpenter was risking more than his reputation in setting
up house with Merrill:

> If the Fates pointed favourably I need hardly say that
> my friends (with a few exceptions) pointed the other
> way![104]

and we can be sure that their worries were not confined to
the fact of who should do the housework with no woman
present (although those doubts *were* expressed). Certainly
his isolation in the North gave him some protection, as did
his position as a respected political speaker, but there must
have been some moments of real fear. Worse to come,
though, was rejection by colleagues in the Labour movement – they were on the highroad to respectability and he
was on the path to isolation from the main stream of
political development.

Millthorpe became the secure base – rooted in Nature –
where he could develop his notion of a daily-lived communality. It was a hard life (there is much talk of colds and
coughs and draughts in all the letters!), with slog-work in
the fields and a long haul with a cart each week to sell the
produce at the Sheffield market. As age encroached he
eventually left much of the work to Merrill, but there is
little sense of Marie-Antoinette 'toy farm' escapism:

> I worked for hours and for whole days together out in
> the open field, or garden, or digging drains with pick
> and shovel, or carting along the roads . . .
>   It was a considerable strain. With my somewhat
> vague aspiring mind, to be imprisoned in the rude
> details of a most material life was often irksome. Yet a
> consuming passion drove me on – a desire to know, to
> do something real, an evil conscience perhaps of the
> past unreality of my existence. I was compelled to eat
> it all out.[105]

Millthorpe provided not only the base for a material, and
eventually a sexual realisation of his quest, but also
provided the security for another journey – to India –

towards an understanding of what may loosely be described as the spiritual aspect of life. In 1890 he set sail for the sub-continent, where he was to meet a wise man (a Gñani):

> here in this man it was of absorbing interest to feel one came in contact with the root-thought of all existence – the intense *consciousness* (not conviction merely) of the oneness of all life . . . After seeing Whitman, the amazing representative of the same spirit in all its voluminous modern unfoldment – seven years before – this visit to the Eastern sage was like going back to the pure lucid intensely transparent source of some mighty and turbulent stream.[106]

Despite all this, he did not off-load his conviction that the other route to wisdom and understanding was in the day-to-day of people's lives. In a letter to George Hukin he writes:

> Bombay was very interesting – I managed to pick up acquaintance with sundry native post office and railway clerks and tramway men, and they gave me regular entertainment at the house of one of their number in a back street in the city; I also went to a native theatre and an opium den and a cotton mill.[107]

Hukin, in reply to one of Carpenter's letters, comments on the Gñani and cosmic wisdom that it '*is* a relief to hear that you are not likely to get merged in it all'.[108] Carpenter was not likely to. As with everything else which came along, he was not about to go all overboard on one aspect as '*the* solution':

> The Eastern teaching has or has had a tendency to err on one side, the Western on the other. The Indian methods and attitude cause an ingathering and quiescence of the mind, accompanied often by great illumination; but if carried to excess they result in over-quiescence, and even torpor. The Western habits tend towards an over-activity and external distraction of the mind, which may result in disintegration. The true line (as in other cases) is not in mediocrity, but in a bold and sane acceptance of both sides . . . Growth is

the method and the solution. The soul goes out and
returns, goes out and returns; and this is its daily,
almost hourly, action – just as it is an epitome of the
æonian life-history of every individual.[109]

Carpenter's soul took him to India, then returned him to
England and Millthorpe. He met George Merrill shortly after
his return. As I have mentioned, his developing role as
reclusive commentator – as opposed to foot-slogging activist
– coincided with all this. He was still to sally forth on
lecture tours, to give support for particular causes (he stood
witness at the trial of the Walsall anarchists), to speak
against the Boer War. It was, however, his developing
personal life with George Merrill and the little hut at the
bottom of the garden where he would sit and write that was
the main focus from now. It was inevitable that within this
context his writings should begin to reflect his meditations
on the nature of personal relations and sexuality – and a
great deal of trouble they caused him, too.

In 1894 he wrote three pamphlets – *Sex Love, Women* and
Marriage – all published by the Manchester Labour Press. In
June 1895, Fisher Unwin signed a contract to publish them
as a book, entitled *Love's Coming-of-Age*. In the January of
that year, the Labour Press printed – for private circulation –
a fourth pamphlet, *Homogenic Love*. Although this was not
sold but was 'sent round pretty freely to those who I thought
would be interested in the subject or able to contribute
views or information upon it',[110] the nature of the contents
created quite a to-do:

> Even in this quiet way the pamphlet created some
> alarm – and in the dove-cotes of Fleet Street (as I heard)
> caused no little fluttering and agitation. . .[111]

Still, all might have passed off smoothly enough, had not
Oscar Wilde been arrested that year and 'from that moment
a sheer panic prevailed over *all* questions of sex, and
especially of course questions of the Intermediate Sex'. The
upshot was that Fisher Unwin reneged upon the agreement
to publish *Love's Coming-of-Age* (even though *Homogenic
Love* was not to be included) and went so far as to refuse to
sell any further copies of *Towards Democracy*. Carpenter
approached other publishers:

– but they all shook their heads. The Wilde trial had done its work; and silence must henceforth reign on sex-subjects.[112]

'The Wilde trial had done its work' – a telling phrase. For indeed, the function of that business was less concerned with ruining one man (though it certainly did that) than with battening down the hatches on any public recognition of sexual radicalism. A society which was preparing to put guns into the hands of its young men, to defend an Empire, was not out to have the basic assumptions of 'natural' manly, aggressive virility criticised, mocked or discussed.

Reading those pamphlets now, Laurence Housman's remarks concerning Carpenter's sometimes tentative approach to sexuality come to mind. Earlier I suggested that his own cautious temperament had much to do with this, yet here we see another factor – historical circumstance – hedging him around. In his autobiography he remarks upon this:

> In '96 no 'respectable' publisher would touch the volume, and yet today [1915] the tide of such literature has flowed so full and fast that my book has already become quite a little old-fashioned and demure! But the severe resistance and rigidity of public opinion at the time made the volume very difficult to write. The readiness, the absolute determination of people to *misunderstand* if they possibly could, rendered it very difficult to guard against misunderstandings, and as a matter of fact nearly every chapter in the book was written four or five times over before I was satisfied with it.[113]

In this attempt to proceed with caution, the writings do at times appear not only over-timid, but even to retreat on his own perceptions of the world in order to make a case. There are paragraphs which seem irritatingly vague – even to the point of contradicting his own understanding of the difference between individual temperament and social conditioning:

> Man, the ordinary human male, is a curious animal. While mastering the world with his pluck, skill,

enterprise, he is in matters of Love for the most part a
child . . . In this he differs from the other sex; and the
difference can be seen in earliest years. When the boy is
on his rocking horse, the girl is caressing her doll.[114]

There are passages which bear out Olive Schreiner's remark
that he did not truly understand women, and he admits that
'*Love's Coming-of-Age* ought of course (like some parts of
England's Ideal) to have been written by a woman . . .'[115]

That aside, there is still much that we can gain from his
writings upon sex and sexuality, and when we turn to *The
Intermediate Sex* we find the reflection of his lived attempt
to place his homosexuality *in* the world. It is in these
writings that he earns his place in that movement of history
which is not restricted to gays alone, but ultimately
involves all people who desire to 'ascend and enter into
relation with their bodies'.[116]

The Intermediate Sex

Starting with the privately printed pamphlet on *Homogenic
Love*, Carpenter published a series of essays on homosexuality that were collected into a book in 1908, *The Intermediate Sex*. This was regularly reprinted every three or four
years, and remained for several decades the most positive
text available in English from which gay people could draw
support and hope.

Carpenter's views on the nature of homosexuality share
the qualities which mark his writings in general. Insightful
yet non-dogmatic. Given that he did not believe a purely
objective explanation was possible for anything, even in the
case of the physical world, he certainly did not approach the
question of homosexuality as an objective theoretician
looking at the phenomenon from outside. In writing on
homosexuality Carpenter was seeking first of all to express
his own nature, and only secondly enlisting the fragmentary
facts and theories that science might provide.

In *Towards Democracy* he had already celebrated in
poetic form his love for other men. This book, which for so
many in the early socialist movement was 'a kind of bible',

is unequivocal enough in its hymn to a comrade-love
founded frankly on sex:

> The love of men for each other — so tender, heroic,
> constant;
> That has come all down the ages, in every clime, in
> every nation.
> Always so true, so well assured of itself, overleaping
> barriers of age, of rank of distance,
> Flag of the camp of Freedom. . .

Only after hymning in similar vein the love of women for
each other — 'so rapt, intense, so confiding-close, so
burning-passionate' — does Carpenter come on to add: 'And
(not less) the love of men for women, and of women for
men', and it is rather the future than the past of heterosex-
uality that is commended: 'on a newer greater scale than it
has hitherto been conceived'.[117]

More concretely, there is his poem to George Hukin:

> A man who understands and accepts all human life
> and character,
> Keen and swift of brain, heart tender and true, and
> low voice ringing so clear,
> And my dear comrade.[118]

And even:

> I enter the young prostitute's chamber, where he is
> arranging the photographs of fashionable beauties and
> favourite companions, and stay with him; we are at
> ease and understand each other.[119]

It was, however, a further step forward to move from the
literary celebration of homogenic love to an openly political
defence of homosexuality. True to his nature, Carpenter
approached this cautiously, and again in the context of
sex-love in general. But the early 1890s were a propitious
time to begin this propaganda. As well as the aesthetic
movement around Oscar Wilde (whom Carpenter in fact
never met), John Addington Symonds, living an invalid in
Switzerland, produced in 1891 his privately printed booklet
A Problem in Modern Ethics, which broke new ground in

arguing the positive contribution of love between men. But though Symonds was, like Carpenter, influenced by Whitman, he was far from sharing Carpenter's socialism or his support for women's liberation. In 1892 Symonds began a collaboration with Havelock Ellis on their book *Sexual Inversion*, and also met Carpenter when he visited England. Early in 1893, however, Symonds died, and the mantle of public champion of homosexuality fell naturally on Carpenter.

In this 1894 pamphlet and the essays that followed, Carpenter draws both on the work of Symonds and Ellis, and that of the Germans K. H. Ulrichs, Albert Moll and Magnus Hirschfeld. But while striving for the respectability of science, he was equally concerned to fit his defence of homosexuality into his general philosophy in which sex-love held such a central part. In these writings, Carpenter still does not write quite openly as a gay person; he only came out to that full extent in *My Days and Dreams*, published in 1916.[120] Yet no one can have read *The Intermediate Sex* without being quite aware of the author's personal identification with his subject. Thus Carpenter writes of:

> The instinctive artistic nature of the male of this class, his sensitive spirit, his wavelike emotional temperament, combined with hardihood of intellect and body; and the frank, free nature of the female, her masculine independence and strength wedded to thoroughly feminine grace of form and manner.[121]

Again:

> The normal type of Uranian man . . . while possessing thoroughly masculine powers of mind and body, combines with them the tenderer and more emotional soul-nature of the woman . . . like women they read characters at a glance, and know, without knowing how, what is passing in the minds of others.[122]

And so on.

The themes of *The Intermediate Sex* include the standard ones of homosexual apologetics. The tradition of heroic Greece; the great artists; the relation of teacher and pupil.

Much of this can also be found, and as well expressed, in Symonds, who wrote a few years earlier. Where Carpenter stands out, and most strikingly, is his linking of homosexual liberation with the struggle of women and the attenuation of the gender division, in a way that prefigures the themes of radical sexual politics three-quarters of a century later.

Whitman had already championed 'loving comradeship' as the 'counterpart, without which [American Democracy] will be incomplete, in vain, and incapable of perpetuating itself' – prophetic words.[123] Carpenter developed this theme in alignment with a socialist and feminist movement that set itself more far-reaching social goals than the Republican party in the United States. He still held to the Whitmanesque image of a political 'comrade-love'. Heroic bonding is needed to deal with the 'hydra-headed monsters at least as numerous as the tyrants of old',[124] yet he notes how among women, too:

> such comrade-alliances are becoming increasingly common, and especially perhaps among the more cultured classes of women, who are working out the great cause of their sex's liberation.[125]

And although Whitman also championed independent womanhood, Carpenter's vision of a rapprochement of the sexes has a different and more feminine emphasis. Both the homogenic woman and man, 'through their double nature, command of life in all its phases, and a certain freemasonry of the secrets of the two sexes ... may well fulfil their function as reconcilers and interpreters',[126] and 'above all [their temperament] has fitted them, and fits them, for distinction and service in affairs of the heart':

> It is hard to imagine human beings more skilled in these matters than are the Intermediates. For indeed no one else can possibly respond to and understand, as they do, all the fluctuations and interactions of the masculine and feminine in human life.[127]

For Carpenter, as we have seen, 'affairs of the heart' did not refer to a private sphere outside of social life. On the contrary. And so:

> If the day is coming . . . when Love is at last to take its rightful place as the binding and directing force of society (instead of the Cash-nexus), and society is to be transmuted in consequence to a higher form, then undoubtedly the superior types of Uranians . . . will have an important part to play in the transformation.[128]

This leads on to what is always a crucial question for defenders of homosexuality. Is homogenic love the fixed attribute of a closely defined minority, or a potential contained in every human being? On this question, Carpenter is somewhat torn. It was always his conviction, as it spontaneously seems to many gay people even today, that 'in my case the temperament . . . has been absolutely inborn, and not induced by any outside example or teaching'.[129] The insights of psychoanalysis have since superseded this alternative, yet making a public defence of homosexuality when Victoria was still queen, it was far more necessary than today to cling to the idea that we were 'born that way' as a defence of gay people's right to a place in society. Thus Carpenter writes of the homogenic or 'Uranian' temperament as 'instinctive and congenital, mentally and physically, and therefore twined in the very roots of individual life and practically ineradicable'. This was particularly to stress that Urnings were not to be confused with 'that class of persons . . . who out of mere carnal curiosity or extravagance of desire, or from the dearth of opportunities for a more normal satisfaction . . . adopt some homosexual practices'.[130] But even if today we see our 'temperament' as acquired early in life, rather than congenital, it still holds true that it is 'twined in the very roots'.

The term 'Uranian' (from *uranos*, Greek for heaven; 'Urning' is the German form) was coined by Ulrichs in the 1860s, and Ulrichs championed very forcefully both the congenital theory of homosexuality and the idea of the 'feminine soul in a male body' (and vice versa). This theme, which also persists down to our own day, Carpenter again echoes more than a little. And though noting that 'we are not obliged to accept [Ulrich's] theory about the crosswise connection between "soul" and "body", since at best these words are somewhat vague and indefinite',[131] he adopts the 'Uranian' conception even in the fourth (1902) part of *Towards Democracy*, writing (in 'O Child of Uranus'): 'Thy Woman-soul within a Man's form dwelling'.[132]

The psychological vocabulary available to Carpenter was the limited one of pre-Freudian times. It was not the dogmas of Ulrichs that were important to Carpenter, but the conviction that gayness was 'twined in the very roots of individual life' and involved a psychical shift towards the feminine in men, and towards the masculine in women. Yet the relative vagueness of Carpenter's psychology, by modern standards, and his Lamarckian concept of exfoliation as an evolution inspired from within, enabled him to combine the assertion that gayness was 'congenital' with the apparently contradictory asertion (from today's standpoint) that 'the capacity of their [the Uranians'] kind of attachment also exists – though in a germinal and undeveloped state – in the breast of mankind at large'.[133]

Viewed historically, this seeming contradiction expresses Carpenter's position midway between the rigid and defensive view of Ulrichs that gays were a small minority defined firmly by biology, and the view of gay liberation, a century later, that 'gay shows the way' to a future for humanity free from the tyranny of gender and the horrors it involves (the male specialisation in warfare above all else). And in Carpenter's boldest statements on 'the place of the Uranian in society', he prefigures in truly remarkable terms the radical sexual politics of the 1970s:

> it is possible that the Uranian spirit may lead to something like a general enthusiasm of Humanity, and that the Uranian people may be destined to form the advance guard of that great movement which will one day transform the common life by substituting the bond of personal affection and compassion for the monetary, legal and other external ties which now control and confine society.[134]

If the Uranian spirit is to produce such a 'general enthusiasm', it must clearly spread, as Carpenter acknowledged, far more widely than the present gay minority. It is interesting to note that even Magnus Hirschfeld, in Carpenter's day, could estimate the proportion of the population who were essentially gay as no more than 1½ to 2 per cent. Fifty years later Kinsey's estimate of around 5 per cent became generally accepted, yet today this again seems a wide underestimate. Carpenter may have been wrong in viewing gayness as congenital and seeing its spread as a biological process, but what matters above all in historical perspective is his splendid intuition that gay people were not fated to remain a 'deviant' minority, and that homogenic love had an essential part to play in social regeneration.

The New Morality

Nowadays it is a commonplace amongst those who have taken up (or made an attempt at) radical sexual politics, to question those attitudes which reduce another human being to sex-object status. Carpenter attempts to extend this consciousness towards a general discussion of morality:

> in comparing, as we did a page or two back, the sex-needs and the hunger-needs of the human race we left out of account one great difference, namely that while food (the object of hunger) has no moral rights of its own [though this of course is not true of *animal* food; E. C.'s footnote], and can be appropriated without misgiving on that score, the object of sex is a person, and cannot be used for private advantage without the most dire infringement of the law of equality. The moment Man rises into any sort of consciousness of the equal rights of others with himself his love-needs open up this terrible problem. His needs are no less – perhaps they are greater – than they were before, but they are stricken with a deadly swound at the thought that there is something even greater than them . . .
>
> It is not perhaps till the great current of sexual love is checked and brought into conflict with the other parts of his being that the whole nature of the man, sexual and moral, under the tremendous stress rises into consciousness and reveals in fire its god-like quality.[135]

So, he wished a morality which sprang from within each

individual, not imposed by the 'Thou Shalt Not' in the face of desire:

> It is clear, I think, that if sex is to be treated rationally, that is, neither superstitiously on the one hand, nor licentiously on the other, we must be willing to admit that both the satisfaction of the passion and the non-satisfaction of it are desirable and beautiful.[136]

This sort of theme is worlds away from the stony-faced, authoritarian 'self-control' we are taught, or the dead-eyed, casual 'permissiveness' we are more recently allowed. For as long as sex is seen as something outside of ourselves, it will always be either a monster to control (and there will always be legions of meddlers pestering us to do as such), or the gilded apple to devour (and there will always be crowds of entrepreneurs selling it to us):

> Until these subjects are openly put before children and young people with some degree of intelligent and sympathetic handling, it can scarcely be expected that anything but the utmost confusion, in mind and in morals, should reign in the matters of Sex. That we should leave our children to pick up their information about the most sacred, the most profound and vital, of all human functions, from the mere gutter, and to learn to know it first from the lips of ignorance and vice, seems almost incredible, and certainly indicates the deep-rooted unbelief and uncleanness of our own thoughts.[137]

Only when sexual pleasure is no longer thought of as something to be either fought off or bought, can we begin to regain a sense of unity with our individual selves and with each other:

> Sex-pleasures afford a kind of type of all pleasure. The dissatisfaction which at times follows on them is the same as follows on all pleasure which is *sought*, and which does not come unsought. The dissatisfaction is not in the nature of pleasure itself but in the nature of *seeking*. In going off in pursuit of things external, the 'I' (since it really has everything and needs nothing) deceives itself, goes out from its true home, tears itself

asunder, and admits a gap or rent in its own being. This, it must be supposed, is what is meant by *sin* – the separation or sundering of one's being – and all the pain that goes therewith. It all consists in *seeking* those external things and pleasures; not (a thousand times be it said) in the external things or pleasures themselves . . . for us to go out of ourselves to run after *them*, to allow ourselves to be divided and rent in twain by *their* attraction, that is an inversion of the order of heaven.[138]

What he wished for was to make public that which we are taught is utterly private. Not in the prurient, sniggering way in which sex is slyly hawked in the High Streets, on the screens and in the press these days (like indulged children we are 'permitted' those perverted glimpses of our own desires by a society which is a wasteland of sexual frustration), but in a sensible, open-handed way. Yet now, as then:

Our public opinion, our literature, our customs, our laws, are saturated with the notion of the uncleanness of Sex, and are so making the conditions of its cleanness more and more difficult . . .
Till this dirty and dismal sentiment with regard to the human body is removed there can be little hope of anything like a free and gracious public life.[139]

Certainly this denial of sex had ensured that at least half the population – women – would have no part in public life whatsoever. They were 'ladies' or 'drudges' and in both cases serfs, their 'nervous and sexual systems' ruined, their biology seen as fit mark for legal and economic dependency. Now that economic recession is (as then) re-establishing the call for women to take their 'natural' place in the home, his observations ring depressingly true:

Few men again realise, or trouble themselves to realise, what a life this of the working housewife is. They are accustomed to look upon their own employment, whatever it may be, as 'work' (perhaps because it brings with it 'wages'); the woman's they regard as a kind of pastime. They forget . . . that the woman has no eight hours day, that her work is always staring her in the face, and waiting for her, even on into the night; that the body is wearied, and the mind narrowed down,'scratched to death by mice and rats' in a perpetual round of petty cares.[140]

Today (perhaps) women have a margin of freedom which their 19th century sisters had not – yet still they live under conditions which forbid 'natural and spontaneous gesture as unbecoming and suspicious – and indeed in any public place as liable to the attention of the policeman'.[141] Just as he wanted freedom of expression of his own nature, he wished the same for women. For him, there was no political solution 'which will not include the redemption of the terms "free woman" and "free love" to their *true* and rightful significance'.[142] Once this were achieved, and mutually consenting relationships between individuals were possible (that is, *moral* relationships), 'marriage' would find its true place in the order of society:

> The modern Monogamic Marriage however, certified and sanctioned by Church and State, though apparently directed to this ideal, has for the most part fallen short of it. For in constituting – as in a vast number of cases – a union resting on *nothing* but the outside pressure of Church or State, it constituted a thing obviously and by its nature bad and degrading; while in its more successful instances by a too great exclusiveness it has condemned itself to a fatal narrowness and stuffiness.[143]

His belief in the sense of unity (first with oneself, then with others and nature) as the basis of morality, enabled him to see clearly through a system where love is choked with 'egoism, lust and meanness':

> surely it is not very difficult . . . to imagine so sincere and natural a trust between man and wife that neither would be greatly alarmed at the other's friendship with a third person, nor conclude at once that it meant mere infidelity – or difficult even to imagine that such a friendship might be hailed as a gain by both parties.[144]

Here now he is aware of the yelps of horror which such imaginings would produce, in those who could not 'see in such intimacies anything but a confusion of all sex-relations and a chaos of mere animal desire'.[145] He could only know, from his own nature, that this would not be so – for although he experienced various passions and jealousies, made several experiments with relationships, tended towards one central relationship (though maintaining others, right through the years with Merrill), it was not so much the difficulties accompanying sexuality that nearly ruined him, but the early denial of it.

It is not easy to sum up his essays on sex and love; I can tell you that, as well as the wider speculations he made, these were accompanied by practical suggestions for aiding the emergence of a new morality in relationships. It would be a morality not based upon the Right and the Wrong of theological or legal authority, but one which comes from each individual experiencing her or his actions as taking place in the context of wider, universal principles. In the concluding passages to *Pagan and Christian Creeds* his desire to discover those principles – and to use them as a barometer for present social organisation – is made clear:

> As a kind of rude general philosophy we may say that there are only two main factors in life, namely, *Love* and *Ignorance*. And of these we may also say that the two are not in the same plane: one is positive and substantial, the other is negative and merely illusory. It may be thought at first that Fear and Hatred and Cruelty, and the like, are very positive things, but in the end we see that they are due merely to *absence* of perception, to dulness of understanding. Or we may put the statement in a rather less crude form, and say that there are only two factors in life: (1) the sense of Unity with others (and with Nature) – which covers Love, Faith, Courage, Truth, and so forth, and (2) Non-perception of the same – which covers Enmity, Fear, Hatred, Self-pity, Cruelty, Jealousy, Meanness and an endless similar list. The present world which we see around us, with its idiotic wars, its senseless jealousies of nations and classes, its fears and greeds

and vanities and its futile endeavours – as of people struggling in a swamp – to find one's own salvation by treading others underfoot, is a negative phenomenon. Ignorance, *non*-perception, are at the root of it.[146]

So then it is that each person, struggling with sexual desires which in themselves take no account of the rights and desires of other individuals, is experiencing the great universal tug-of-war between Ignorance and Love. Beyond the necessities of fundamental economic and political changes, there is Love:

and it needs man's highest ingenuity and capacity to become skilled in it – but in the public mind it is an art utterly neglected and despised, and it is only by a very few (and those not always the most 'respectable') that it is really cultivated . . .
    And so too the whole modern period of commercial civilisation and Christianity has been fatal to love . . . They have bred the self-regarding consciousness in the highest degree; and so – though they may have had their uses and their parts to play in the history of mankind, they have been fatal to the communal spirit in society, and they have been fatal to the glad expression of the soul in private life.[147]

The 'modern nation' which England was becoming was not to direct its attention to such things. Nor was the party of Labour which was growing within its institutions. A combination of class-advantage, temperament, and dogged determination had led Carpenter to establish for himself a rough approximation of the type of existence he wished, but it was not to be the model for a world of the immediate future. The mass-world was lurching along the path where the individual perception had no place in the mass-experience; mass-entertainment, mass-ideology, mass-murder were to be the order of the day. Yet how can we join together, in a creative and radical way, if we do not recognise that at the very core:

we only know what we see ourselves.
    This is the complete answer to the idea of an exact

Realism. There is no such thing. It is as impossible in
Art as it is in Science. Every object, every scene is
inexhaustible; the person who contemplates it can
only *pick out* for representation what appeals to him.
Neither Art nor Science can catalogue the leaves of a
tree.[148]

Nor can the varieties of our individual human perceptions
be catalogued, and it is his vision of a mass-society
organised around the principle of freeing the individual at
last which is perhaps of most interest to us today. Not the
sort of mass-society where all are numbed by laws and
bureaucracy to take our place as mere numbers in a
computer's memory; nor the sort of individuality which can
only express itself in accumulation, competition and status.
He saw in neither of those the release in imagination which
he regarded as the spring of personal evolution and the key
to social evolution:

In a well-painted picture there isn't a grain of paint
which is mere material. All is expression. And yet life
is a greater art than painting pictures. Modern civilised
folk are like people sitting helplessly in the midst of
heaps of paint-cans and brushes – and ever accumulat-
ing more; but when they are going to produce anything
lovely or worth looking at in their own lives, Heaven
only knows.[149]

His especial care for the artist – be it the boy in his cellar
constructing models, Beethoven creating his sonatas, or a
washer-woman (drudge that she is) rescuing something of
her own soul in the grimmest of conditions by taking a care
in her work – is as a reflection of that future world, where
art and life would link arms. At the moment (then as now),
the artist is generally disconnected from the mass-life,
weighted down as it is by custom and tradition. When an
artist expresses new feeling, 'an Angel has come down from
heaven':

yet no one says a word about it! The human multitude
stares and sees nothing, like a herd of cows chewing
the cud . . . Tradition and Custom of course are against
him. They have been framed to express what has been

felt before, but what have they to do with anything
new? . . .

Thus there is an everlasting feud between the
Individual and the Tradition. For each new feeling
must come to light through the Individual first. Nay
more, there is something original, authentic, in *every*
individual . . . Only go far enough, deep enough, into
your own nature and you are sure to haul up something
which will get you into trouble with the world![150]

At the present time, it is the duty of the artist to give form to
new ideas, but 'this feud between the Individual and
Tradition covers the ground not only of Art but of social
affairs', for:

the ideas which are going to dominate the life of
an epoch . . . appear in Art simultaneously or beforehand . . .

These outgrowths, these correspondences of Art and
Life are at any period 'in the air', and affecting whole
masses of people at the same time. But though they are
so, they have to manifest themselves through individuals first.[151]

Yet beyond 'all this variety, this individuality of flavour in
the great artists of the world' he discerned an underlying
unity:

Read Kalidása, and you might be reading Shakespeare.
The sixteen centuries between the two poets, and all
the distance of East from West, are in vain to disguise
their fraternity. In whatever race or nation or language
a great work may appear, lo! it is but another petal of
the same red rose, a leaf of the old World-tree.[152]

This unity of variety is a shadow of the unity he predicted
for the future of the world.

As the years passed it must have saddened him to see the
parliamentary process debilitate the broad socialist movement within which public debate along these lines was
possible. Still, he pursued his theme of a true communality
of life emerging from the freeing of the individual. For him
this was 'the great main problem which lies before this age
for solution' and:

one of the greatest services a man can do is – by psychologic study and manifold experience, by poetical expression, especially in lyrical form, and by philosophic thought and investigation – to make clear to himself and the world what he means by the letter 'I', what he means by his 'self'.[153]

It is only by this means that we can come to understand how, beneath the varieties of our perceptions, there is a unity, that 'Self' *is* interdependent – but in ways far different from those of custom, tradition, laws, etc. At this, the individualism of the age we live in would baulk:

The little self-conscious mind (of the civilised man) no doubt protests against all this. It desires to think of itself as a separate and definite identity, distinct from (and perhaps superior to) all others . . .[154]

And yet:

The personal self can only 'survive' by ever fading and changing towards the universal . . . Continual *expansion* is a normal condition of consciousness. Time is an integral element of it. Consciousness must continually grow. Through memory it preserves the past, through the present it adds to its stores.[155]

It was this embracing of the idea of universality by each and every self-conscious individual which would shape the 'Religion of the future', which:

must come from the bosom itself of the modern peoples; it must be recognition by Humanity as a whole of the Common Life which has really underlain all the various religions of the past; it must be the certainty of the organic unity of mankind, of the brotherhood of all sentient creatures, freeing itself from all local doctrine and prejudice, and expressing itself in any and every available form.[156]

That recognition of our common humanity would at last break the power of custom and tradition – the power which on the one hand blights our personal relations with jealousy, greed and ambition, and on the other enables the states of

the world to terrorise us with prisons, armies, threats of
mass destruction. It might seem a hopeless dream, this
yearning of his for that time of unity – and a pitifully small
thing to place faith in, faced with the horrors which the
politicians plant in the soil nowadays. Yet, most other
methods having failed, perhaps it is the one thing which
might save us. In 1981, some fifteen women from Wales
walked to a small village in England. It is called Greenham
Common. There, the government planned to locate atomic
missiles. The women set up camp, to protest at the
escalation of plans to wage a war which would rob them and
their children of life, rob perhaps the whole beautiful planet
of life. A year later, some 30,000 women ringed the camp,
holding hands and singing for peace. When they left, they
attached personal items to the wire-mesh surrounding the
camp – photographs of their children, their lovers and loved
ones, nappies, toys, scraps, poems. Again, what are 30,000
women and that circle against the hardware of death
sprouting up across the globe? And yet that force of Love
might just win us life, defeat the negotiations of Ignorance
that are taking place behind locked doors. Perhaps it is the
most tangible thing after all:

> Our union with Nature and humanity is a *fact*, which
> – whether we recognise it or not – is at the base of our
> lives; slumbering, yet ready to wake in our conscious-
> ness when the due time arrives.[157]

The awakening will not be easy. In his own individual life
Carpenter had experienced a terrible struggle. He had
witnessed it in others, seen lives wrecked in the pursuit of
ideals, had participated in the tremendous efforts to force
even the smallest practical changes in the lives of the many.
He knew that Ignorance would not give up its grip on our
souls too easily:

> Heroisms, exceeding those of the past, will be needed
> and will be supplied. We need not fear. We know the
> great heart of humanity.[158]

The Circle Complete

On the whole I am struck by the singularly *little* difference I feel in myself, as I realise it now, from what I was when a boy – say of eighteen or twenty . . . I used to go and sit on the beach at Brighton and dream, and now I sit on the shore of human life and dream practically the same dreams. I remember about the time that I mention – or it may have been a trifle later – coming to the distinct conclusion that there were only two things really worth living for – the glory and beauty of Nature, and the glory and beauty of human love and friendship. And today I still feel the same.[159]

The circle was complete – or perhaps it would be better to say the circle in the spiral, for he did not see death as the end of his union with nature:

So at last passing (the great sea stilled, the raging
ocean) – passing away,
All sorrow left behind, the great intolerable burdens
which men vainly try to carry,
All all abandoned, left there lying –
Suddenly lightened, like a bird that shakes itself free
from the limed twigs,
Soaring, soaring, into joy supernal passing,
Lo! the dead we leave behind and pass to the realms
of the living.[160]

To him, the acceptance of Love was one gate to a vaster state of being, and the acceptance of Death another, perhaps greater. His thoughts on this matter may still be of service to us yet, living in a world where love is still so often about possession and therefore also about exclusion and enmity – where the fear of change (in individuals and states) on the one hand causes the fist to clench, the blow to be struck, the army to march, the bombs to drop, and on the other prevents us from seeing death as but one phase in our evolution.

Edward once remarked that in the first few lines of *Towards Democracy* were the seeds of all he had to say. Perhaps it would be suitable to conclude with those lines:

   The sun, the moon and the stars, the grass, the water
that flows round the earth, and the light air of heaven:
   To You greeting. I too stand behind these and send
you word across them.

   Freedom at last!
   Long sought, long prayed for – ages and ages long:
   The burden to which I continually return, seated
here thick-booted and obvious yet dead and buried and
passed into heaven, unsearchable;
   (How know you indeed but what I have passed into
you?)
   And Joy, beginning but without ending – the journey
of journeys – Thought laid quietly aside:

   These things I, writing, translate for you – I wipe a
mirror and place it in your hands.[161]

Noël Greig
London, June 1984

My Days and Dreams

(excerpts)

My life hitherto (7th July 1890) divides into four pretty
distinct periods – first, my early life up to the age of twenty,
during which time I lived mainly at Brighton, embedded in a
would-be fashionable world which I hated; secondly, the
period from '64 to about '74, during which time I was mostly
at Cambridge, in a more or less intellectual atmosphere;
thirdly, from '74 to '81, when I carried on the Extension
lectures and made acquaintance with the manufacturing
centres and commercial society of the North of England;
and fourthly, for the ten years from '80 and '81 down to the
present time, when I have lived almost entirely among the
working masses, and been largely engaged in manual labour.

It may seem ungrateful to say so, but my abiding
recollection of early days is one of discomfort. Not but that I
had on the whole good times at school, in the classes and in
the games; not but that at home I was lapped in the ease and
attentive service of a well-to-do household, and had a
hundred advantages denied to an ordinary child of the
people; but that after all at home I never felt really at home.
Perhaps I was unduly sensitive; anyhow I felt myself an
alien, an outcast, a failure, and an object of ridicule.

The social life which encircled us at Brighton was
artificial enough; but it was the standard which we children
had to live to. My parents were the best people in the world,
but they could not fly out of the conditions in which they
belonged. I hated the life, was miserable in it – the heartless
conventionalities, silly proprieties – but I never imagined, it
never occurred to me, that there *was* any other life. To be
pursued by the dread of appearances – what people would

say about one's clothes or one's speech – to be always in fear of committing unconscious trespasses of invisible rules – this seemed in my childhood the normal condition of existence; so much so that I never dreamed of escaping from it. I only prayed for a time when grace might be given me to pass by without reproach. I was never a daring or rumbustious child. Timid and sensitive, my spirit was sadly lacking in the inestimable virtue of revolt. I suffered and was stupid enough to think myself in the wrong.

There was a curate at one of the churches to which we used to go – a smooth-haired, carefully shaven, meek young man, probably of feeble mind; but all I knew was that people praised him: such a good-looking, well-mannered fellow he was, and preached such nice sermons! 'Happy Mr Cass,' I used to think, for even now I remember his name – 'Oh, happy Mr Cass, if only I could be like *you* when I grow up.' I was then about fourteen, and I fancy that the mere sight of Cass in his spotless surplice must have worked upon me, for it was about that time or a little later that I began to make up my mind to take Orders. No doubt from the first there was a fatal bias towards religion. I remember distinctly – and it must have been about the same period – thinking as I lay awake in bed at night that if the house were on fire I would save my *prayer-book*! I saw myself in my mind's eye in heroic attitude rushing into my mother's room where the sacred volume lay, and bearing it out through flames and smoke into the street. It was not my mother or sisters that I was going to save . . . but my prayer-book! Alas! what a defect of nature, or of teaching, must have been there!

Curious, the covered underground life that some children lead! I never remember, all those years at Brighton, till I was nineteen or twenty, a single person older than myself who was my confidant. I do not remember a single occasion in which in any trouble or perplexity I was able to go to any one for help or consolation. My mother, firm, just, and courageous as she was, and setting her children an heroic example, belonged to the old school, which thought any manifestation of feeling unbecoming. We early learned to suppress and control emotion, and to fight our own battles alone: in some ways a good training, but liable in the long run to starve the emotional nature. Masters at school in those days did not 'draw boys out'; education was mainly a nipping of buds; older friends outside the family, who may so often play a useful part in the development of boy or girl life, never came – that I remember – to the rescue; and so my abiding recollection of all that time is one of silent concealment and loneliness.

*

Towards the later part of my time at Brighton the natural *épanchement* of youth led me often to seek consolation and an escape from the wounds of daily life in intercourse with Nature. The Brighton social life – with its greetings where no kindness is – was to me chilly in the extreme, and I often used in later years to feel that I 'caught cold' (morally speaking) whenever I returned to it. The scenery and surroundings of Brighton are also bare and chilly enough; and trees, whose friendly covert I have always loved, do not exist there; but the place has two Nature-elements in it – and these two singularly wild and untampered – the Sea and the Downs. We lived within two hundred yards of the sea, and its voice was in our ears night and day. On terrific stormy nights it was a 'grisly joy' to go down to the water's edge at 10 or 11 p.m. – pitchy darkness – feeling one's way with feet or hands, over the stony beach, hardly able to stand for the wind – and to watch the white breakers suddenly leap out of the gulf close upon one – the 'scream of the madden'd beach dragged down by the wave', the booming of the wind, like distant guns, and the occasional light of some vessel labouring for its life in the surge.

But the Downs were my favourite refuge. On sunny days I would wander on over them for miles, not knowing very clearly where I was going – in a strange broody moony state – glad to find some hollow (like that described in Jefferies' *Story of My Heart*) where one could lie secluded for any length of time and see only the clouds and the grasses and an occasional butterfly, or hear the distant bark of a dog or the far rumble of a railway train. The Downs twined themselves with all my thought and speculations of that time. Their chaste subdued gracious outlines and quiet colour have a peculiar charm. Their strongest line is generally some white edge of cliffs or curve of the shore itself, their deepest tint the blue of the sea or occasionally a field of red clover or one overgrown with charlock. For the rest they wear the faint blue-green colour of thin turf through which the chalk almost shows. Over the velvety sward and among the fine herbage cropped by plentiful sheep run innumerable tiny flowers dwarfed by salt wind and scanty soil – thistles, whose chins rest on the ground out of which they grow; patches of sweet thyme which the wild bees love, of pink centaury and thrift and madder and dwarf-broom, and that sweet yellow lotus or bird's-foot trefoil, which runs all over the world, in Siberia and Alps and Himalayas the same, one of the commonest and friendliest of all the flowers that grow. Overhead the lark sings, the clouds drift through the untampered blue, the bee and the butterfly sweep past on the breeze. Three or four miles from Brighton, and one is in a world remote from man. Except an occasional shepherd there is hardly a human to be seen. Here and there in a hollow nestles the tiniest hamlet – an old farmhouse, one or two cottages, a dwarf church faced with rough work of flints, a few trees and a well. Taking its character from the sky – as all chalk and limestone countries largely do – this land has an ethereal beauty in summer weather; but on wintry and gray days it is monotonous and sad. The shepherd then huddles himself in his cloak in the lee of the gorse-bush, the cloudy rack drives over the backs of his sheep, line behind line the Downs stretch, colourless, unbroken by any hint of tree or habitation; the wind whistles among the thin grass stems with a peculiar shrill and mournful pipe, and in its pauses the sullen and distant roar of the sea is heard.

How can I describe, how shall I not recall, the thoughts which came to me as I wandered, towards the close of my school time, over these same hills – the brooding ill-defined, half-shapen thoughts? The Downs were my escape; even in their most chill and lonely moods they were my escape from a worse coldness and loneliness, which, except for a few boy-friends at school, I somehow experienced during all that time. Nature was more to me, I believe, than any human attachment, and the Downs were my Nature. It was among them at a later time that I first began to write a few verses. But at the time I mention, and till quite the end of my school days, I never wrote anything at all. If the thought of writing had occurred to me I should have deemed it, in my then state of mind, monstrous presumption – but I doubt whether the thought ever did occur to me. I did not even read poetry. Mozart and Beethoven were familiar to me, but I must have been eighteen years old before I was roused to any interest in Tennyson (the poet of the day) by a lecture at school on 'In Memoriam'. After that I read 'In Memoriam' and loved it well. This was followed (at Cambridge) by Wordsworth; and then by Shelley, who excited in me the same passionate attachment that he has excited in so many others. After that Whitman dominated me. I do not think any others of the poets – unless Plato should bear that name – have deeply influenced me.

As to friends – that absorbing subject – I can trace the desire for a passionate attachment in my earliest boyhood. But the desire had no expression, no chance of expression. Such things as affection were never spoken about either at home or at school, and I naturally concluded that there was no room for them in the scheme of creation! The glutinous boy-friendships that one formed in classroom or playground were of the usual type: they staved off a greater hunger, but they did not satisfy. On the other hand I worshipped the very ground on which some, generally elder, boys stood; they were heroes for whom I would have done anything. I dreamed about them at night, absorbed them with my eyes in the day, watched them at cricket, loved to press against them unnoticed in a football melly, or even to get accidentally hurt by one of them at hockey, was glad if they just spoke to me or smiled; but never got a word farther with it all. What could I say? Even to one of the masters, I remember, who was a little kind to me, I felt this unworded devotion; but he never helped me over the stile, and so I remained on the farther side.

I often think what a fund of romance, and of intense feeling, there is in this direction latent in so many boys and capable even of heroic expression – and how much will have to be done some day in the matter of directing and giving a constructive outlet to it. Already however there is a great difference in the tone of the public schools themselves on this subject, from what there was twenty-five or thirty years ago. The trouble in schools from bad sexual habits and frivolities arises greatly – though of course not altogether – from the suppression and misdirection of the natural emotions of boy-attachment. I, as a day boy, and one who happened to be rather pure-minded than otherwise, grew up quite free from these evils: though possibly it would have been a good thing if I had had a little more experience of them than I had. As it was, no elder person *ever* spoke to me about sexual matters – no mother, father, brother, monitor or master ever said a word. I picked up the usual information from the talk of my companions, and made up my own mind unbiased by any person or book. I suppose it was in consequence of this that I never saw anything repellent or shameful in sexual acts themselves. From the earliest time when I thought about these things they seemed to me natural – like digestion or any other function – and I remember wondering why people made such a fuss about the mention of them – why they told lies rather than speak the truth, why they were shocked, or why they giggled and stuffed handkerchiefs in their mouths. It was not till (at the age of twenty-five) I read Whitman – and then with a great leap of joy – that I met with the treatment of sex which accorded with my own sentiments.

Nevertheless though these desires were never to me unclean, yet during all that time of later boyhood and early university life they were strangely discounted by that other desire of the heart. I could not think much of sex while the hunger of the heart was unsatisfied – and *that* for the time being occupied all the foreground of my life. Indeed at times it threatened to paralyse my mental and physical faculties. It was like an open wound continually bleeding. I felt starved and unfed, and unable to rest in the chilling contacts of ordinary life. As to the usual attractions set before the eyes of middle-class youth, the hopeless, helpless young ladyisms, or the bolder beauties of the gutter, they were both a detestable boredom to me.

For indeed the life, and with it the character, of the ordinary 'young lady' of that period, and of the sixties generally, was tragic in its emptiness. The little household duties for women, encouraged in an earlier and simpler age, had now gone out of date, while the modern idea of work in the great world was not so much as thought of. In a place like Brighton there were hundreds, perhaps, of households, in which girls were growing up with but one idea in life, that of taking their 'proper place in society'. A few meagre accomplishments – plentiful balls and dinner-parties, theatres and concerts – and to loaf up and down the parade, criticising each other, were the means to bring about this desirable result! There was absolutely nothing else to do or live for. It is curious – but it shows the state of public opinion of that time – to think that my father, who was certainly quite advanced in his ideas, never for a moment contemplated that any of his daughters should learn professional work with a view to their living – and that in consequence he more than once drove himself quite ill with worry. Occasionally it happened that, after a restless night of anxiety over some failure among his investments, and of dread lest he should not be able at his death to leave the girls a competent income, he would come down to breakfast looking a picture of misery. After a time he would break out. 'Ruin impended over the family,' securities were falling, dividends disappearing; there was only one conclusion – 'the girls would have to go out as governesses.' Then silence and gloom would descend on the household. It was true; that was the only resource. There was only one profession possible for a middle-class woman – to be a governess – and to adopt that was to become a *pariah*. But in a little time affairs would brighten up again. Stocks went up, the domestic panic subsided; and dinner-parties and balls were resumed as usual.

As time went by, and I gradually got to know what life really meant, and to realise the situation, it used to make me intensely miserable to return home and see what was going on there. My parents of course were fully occupied, but for the rest there were six or seven servants in the house, and my six sisters had absolutely nothing to do except dabble in paints and music as aforesaid, and wander aimlessly from room to room to see if by any chance 'anything was going on'. Dusting, cooking, sewing, darning – all light household duties were already forestalled; there was not private garden, and if there had been it would have been 'unladylike' to do anything in it; *every* girl could not find an absorbing interest in sol-fa or water-colours; athletics were not invented; every aspiration and outlet, except in the direction of dress and dancing, was blocked; and marriage, with the growing scarcity of men, was becoming every day less likely, or easy to compass. More than once girls of whom I least expected it told me that their lives were miserable 'with nothing on earth to do'. Multiply this picture by thousands and hundreds of thousands all over the country, and it is easy to see how, when the causes of the misery were understood, it led to the powerful growth of the modern 'Women's Movement'.

*

When my father after some hesitation consented to let me go to Cambridge, and asked me which College I would prefer, I said 'Trinity Hall', and for my reason that it was a *gentlemanly* college. My father laughed, as he certainly was justified in doing – and I can only wonder now what sort of animal I was then. At any rate the answer shows that notwithstanding all my sufferings at Brighton I had not yet realised what was the true cause of them. There were however other reasons for my choice. One was that Romer, the last Senior Wrangler, was a 'Hall' man; the other was that the same College was now Head of the River. Both events had brought Trinity Hall into notice.

So thither I went, and found myself immediately in the thick of a boating set. The whole College was given up to boating. Not to row or help in the rowing in some way or other was rank apostasy. A few might read besides, and a few – a dozen or two at most – did so. I boated and talked boating slang; was made stroke of the second boat, and it went down several places; became Secretary of the Boat Club; and for two years wore out the seat of my breeches and the cuticle beneath with incessant aquatic service. At the end of that time I got sadly bored with the business, and gave it up. Indeed I was obliged to give it up; for reading pretty hard for my degree, as I was later on, the two strains together were too much, and my health was breaking down. But so far perhaps boating had not been a bad thing. It was healthy exercise, and brought me in with healthy muscular companions who bothered their heads about no abstruse problems, and for the most part rarely read a book. Fives and rackets too occupied some of my time; but in athletic sports I was not so successful as I had been at school. At Brighton I had been a good high-jumper, having cleared 5 ft. 3 or 4, a good height in those days – but at Cambridge, probably owing to the relaxing quality of the air, I failed to make any mark. Thus, with games and wine parties and boat suppers, life slid easily onward.

Certainly nothing could be more unlike what I had expected. I had imagined a university where folk would talk Latin naturally and where I, lamely taught at school and late coming from loafing in Germany, would be an outcast and an object of contumely. I found myself at the end of the first term easily head of my year in the College examinations. Myself and another. He, Yate, was the son of a country doctor – keen on boating, but a fellow of some originality and thought as well and of singular gentleness and candour. A friendship sprang up between up; and for the next year or two we were always together. In examination honours (such as they were) we were quits, and it was sincerely I believe a matter of indifference to both of us which might win the prize. Then he fell ill of rheumatic fever, and ultimately died without taking his degree – my first experience of loss of this kind.

*

[F]or a couple of years or so after my degree I entered with great zest into this academically intellectual existence – these chit-chat societies, these little supper parties, these lingerings over the wine in combination-room after dinner – where every subject in Heaven and Earth was discussed, with the university man's perfect freedom of thought and utterance, but also with his perfect absence of practical knowledge or of intention to apply his theories to any practical issue. It was helpful no doubt especially as a solvent of old ideas and prejudices; but after a time it began to pall upon me and bore me. There was a vein of what might be called painful earnestness in my character. These talking machines were, many of them, very obnoxious to me. And then of what avail was the brain, when the heart demanded so much, and demanding was still unsatisfied?

Looking back, I think with regard to this last-mentioned matter, that the fault was probably a good deal on my own side. Strong as had been two or three attachments of this and my earlier undergraduate period, and deeply as they had moved me (to a degree indeed which I should be almost ashamed to confess); yet for the most part, owing to my reserved habits, and the self-repressive education I had received – combined with the fatuities of public opinion – I consumed my own smoke, and did not give myself the utterance I ought to have given. By concealing myself I was unfair to my friends, and at the same time suffered torments which I need not have suffered.

As I have already said, during the time shortly after my degree I scribbled a great deal in verse form merely as an outlet to my own feelings, and without much attention to conventionalities of style and rhythms – though of course along the ordinary lines of versification. But now came my introduction to the poet who was destined so deeply to influence my life. It was in the summer of '68, I believe (though it may have been '69), that one day H. D. Warr – one of the Fellows of Trinity Hall, and a very brilliant and amusing man – came into my room with a blue-covered book in his hands (William Rossetti's edition of Whitman's poems) only lately published, and said:–

'Carpenter, what do you think of this?'

I took it from him, looked at it, was puzzled, and asked him what he thought of it.

'Well,' he said, 'I thought a good deal of it at first, but I don't think I can stand any more of it.'

With those words he left me; and I remember lying down then and there on the floor and for half an hour poring, pausing, wondering. I could not make the book out, but I knew at the end of that time that I intended to go on reading it. In a short time I bought a copy for myself, then I got *Democratic Vistas*, and later on (after three or four years) *Leaves of Grass* complete.

From that time forward a profound change set in within me. I remember the long and beautiful summer nights, sometimes in the College garden by the riverside, sometimes sitting at my own window which itself overlooked a little old-fashioned garden enclosed by grey and crumbling walls; sometimes watching the silent and untroubled dawn; and feeling all the time that my life deep down was flowing out and away from the surroundings and traditions amid which I lived – a current of sympathy carrying it westward, across the Atlantic. I wrote to Whitman, obtained his books from him, and occasional postcardial responses. But outwardly, and on the surface, my life went on as usual.

*

But by '71 and '72 I began to feel that continued existence in my surroundings was becoming impossible to me. The tension and dislocation of my life was increasing, and I became aware that a crisis was approaching. In May of the former I had taken a holiday and got away from Cambridge. In October I returned to my lecturing and College work, but not to the church duties; and all '72 I continued on, going through the daily round – but in a torpid, perfunctory manner – feeling probably that I ought to throw it all up, yet without the pluck to do so till I was fairly forced. By the end of '72 I was obviously ill and incapacitated, and when I asked for leave of absence for a couple of terms it was readily granted – my own object in asking (so I put it to myself) being to get quite away and for long enough to be able to estimate my position and future action fairly and deliberately.

The year '73 was an important one for me. Feeling shattered and exhausted and with a big holiday before me, I determined to go to Italy. It was a new life and I may almost say inspiration. I spent two months in Rome, a month in the Bay of Naples, and a month at Florence. I was alone, still alone; but the healing influences of the air and the sunshine were upon me. Amid the bright external life of the day, and the rich records and suggestions of the past, all the questions which had been tormenting me faded away. I *thought* about them no more; but new elements came into my life which decided them for me.

*

It had come on me with great force that I would go and throw in my lot with the mass-people and the manual workers.

*

From the first I was taken with the Sheffield people. Rough in the extreme, twenty or thirty years in date behind other towns, and very uneducated, there was yet a heartiness about them, not without shrewdness, which attracted me. I felt more inclined to take root here than in any of the Northern towns where I had been.

But during all this lecturing period my health had been bad, and getting worse instead of better; and now I was approaching a crisis in regard to it. The state of my nerves was awful; they were really in a quite shattered condition. My eyes, which even in Cambridge days had been weak, kept getting worse. There was no disease or defect – I had been to three first-rate oculists and they all agreed about that. It was simply extreme sensitiveness – probably the optic nerve itself. A strong light from a lamp or candle was quite painful. I could hardly read more than an hour a day – certainly not two hours. It caused a pain in the nerve, which seemed to mount to and disorganise the brain . . .

And behind it all there was that other need – which I have already mentioned more than once – that of my affectional nature, that hunger which had indeed hunted me down since I was a child. I can hardly bear even now to think of my early life, and of the idiotic social reserve and Britannic pretence which prevailed over all that period, and still indeed to a large extent prevails – especially among the so-called well-to-do classes of this country – the denial and systematic ignoring of the obvious facts of the heart and of sex, and the consequent desolation and nerve-ruin of thousands and thousands of women, and even of a considerable number of men. I came home in the summer to Brighton to find my sisters, for the most part unmarried, wearing out their lives and their affectional capacities with nothing to do, and nothing to care for: a little music, a little painting, a walk up and down the Promenade; but the primal needs of life unspoken and unallowed; suffering (as one can now see all this commercial age has been doomed to suffer) from a state of society which has set up gold and gain in the high place of the human heart, and to make more room for these has disowned and dishonoured love. It is curious – and interesting in its queer way – to think that almost the central figure of the drawing-room in that later

Victorian age (and one may see it illustrated in the pages of *Punch* of that period) was a young or middle-aged woman lying supine on a couch – while round her, amiably conveying or consuming tea and coffee, stood a group of quasi-artistic or intellectual men. The conversation ranged, of course, over artistic and literary topics, and the lady did her best to rise to it; but the effort probably did her no good. For the real trouble lay far away. It was of the nature of *hysteria* – and its meaning is best understood by considering the derivation of that word. I had two sisters – who each of them for some twenty years led that supine, and one may say tragic, life; so I had good occasion – beside what may have lain within my own experience – to understand it pretty thoroughly. Certainly the disparity of the sexes and the absolute non-recognition of sexual needs – non-recognition either in life or in thought – weighed terribly hard upon the women of that period.[1]

Another cause, increasing the hardship of disparity, was the growing disinclination of men (of the upper classes) to get married. Partly this arose, no doubt, from their growing realisation of the perils and complications of matrimony; but partly also it arose from an increase in the number of men of what may be called an intermediate type, whose temperament did not lead them very decisively in the direction of marriage – or even led them away from it; men who did not feel the romance in that direction which alone can make marriage attractive, and perhaps justifiable. There have of course been, in all ages, thousands and thousands of women who have not felt that particular sort of romance and attraction towards men, but only to their own kind; and in all ages there have been thousands and thousands of men similarly constituted in the reverse way; but they have been, by the majority, little understood and recognised. Now however it is coming to be seen that they also – both classes – have their part to play in the world.

For my part I have always had excellent and enduring alliances among women, and life would indeed be sadly wanting and impoverished without their friendship and society; but since the days when I sat a boy of nine or ten under the table, apparently playing with my marbles, while my elder sisters and their girl friends were talking freely and unconsciously with each other about some ball of the night before, and their partners in the dances, and their conversations – the workings of the feminine mind and nature have always been perfectly open and clear to me. By a sort of intuition (partly no doubt inborn) I never had any difficulty in following these workings. They enshrined no mystery for me. This fact has always caused me to find women's society interesting; but naturally it did no conduce to headlong adorations and marriage! The romance of my life went elsewhere.

Whether such a state of affairs may be desirable or undesirable, whether it may indicate a high moral nature or a low moral nature, and so forth, are questions which (in a land where *everything* is either moral or immoral) are sure to be asked. But in a sense they are quite beside the mark. They do not alter the fact; and that has always been the same since my earliest days.[2] But it will be evident enough – to any one who takes the trouble to think what these things mean – that to a person of my emotional nature the conditions which brought about – to a comparatively late age – the absence of marriage, or its equivalent, were a fruitful source of trouble and nervous prostration. I realised in my own person some of the sufferings which are endured by an immense number of modern women, especially of the well-to-do classes, as well as by that large class of men of whom I have just spoken, and to whom the name of Uranians is often given.

Certainly my isolation was in a sense my own fault – due partly to reserve and partly to ignorance. When at a later time I broke through this double veil, I soon discovered that others of like temperament to myself were abundant in all directions, and to be found in every class of society; and I need not say that from that time forward life was changed for me. I found sympathy, understanding, love, in a hundred unexpected forms, and my world of the heart became as rich in that which it needed as before it had seemed fruitless and barren.

The Uranian temperament in Man closely resembles the normal temperament of Women in this respect, that in both Love – in some form or other – is the main object of life. In the normal Man, ambition, moneymaking, business, adventure, etc., play their part – love is as a rule a secondary matter. The majority of men (for whom the physical side of sex, if needed, is easily accessible) do not for a moment realise the griefs endured by thousands of girls and women – in the drying up of the well-springs of affection as well as in the crucifixion of their physical needs. But as these sufferings of women, of one kind or another, have been the great inspiring cause and impetus of the Women's Movement – a movement which is already having a great influence in the reorganisation of society; so I do not practically doubt that the similar sufferings of the Uranian class of men are destined in their turn to lead to another wide-reaching social organisation and forward movement in the direction of Art and Human Compassion.

Love's Coming-of-Age

The Sex-Passion

The subject of Sex is difficult to deal with. There is no doubt a natural reticence connected with it. There is also a great deal of prudery. The passion occupies, without being spoken of, a large part of human thought; and words on the subject being so few and inadequate, everything that *is* said is liable to be misunderstood. Violent inferences are made and equivocations surmised, from the simplest remarks; qualified admissions of liberty are interpreted into recommendations of unbridled license; and generally the perspective of literary expression is turned upside down.

There is in fact a vast deal of fetishism in the current treatment of the question. Nor can one altogether be surprised at this when one sees how important Sex is in the scheme of things, and how deeply it has been associated since the earliest times not only with man's personal impulses but even with his religious sentiments and ceremonials.

Next to hunger it is doubtless the most primitive and imperative of our needs. But in modern civilised life Sex enters probably even more into *consciousness* than hunger. For the hunger-needs of the human race are in the later societies fairly well satisfied, but the sex-desires are strongly restrained, both by law and custom, from satisfaction — and so assert themselves all the more in thought.

To find the place of these desires, their utterance, their control, their personal import, their social import, is a tremendous problem to every youth and girl, man and woman.

There are a few of both sexes, doubtless, who hardly feel the passion — who have never been 'in love', and who experience no strong sexual appetite — but these are rare. Practically the passion is a matter of universal experience; and speaking broadly and generally, we may say it is a matter on which it is quite desirable that every adult at some time or other *should* have actual experience. There may be exceptions; but, as said, the instinct lies so deep and is so universal, that for the understanding of life — of one's own life, of that of others, and of human nature in general — as well as for the proper development of one's own capacities, such experience is as a rule needed.

And here in passing I would say that in the social life of the future this need will surely be recognised, and that (while there will be no stigma attaching to voluntary celibacy) the state of enforced celibacy in which vast numbers of women live today will be looked upon as a national wrong, almost as grievous as that of prostitution — of which latter evil indeed it is in some degree the counter-part or necessary accompaniment.

Of course Nature (personifying under this term the more unconscious, even though human, instincts and forces) takes pretty good care in her own way that sex shall not be neglected. She has her own purposes to work out, which in a sense have nothing to do with the individual — her racial purposes. But she acts in the rough, with tremendous sweep and power, and with little adjustment to or consideration for the later developed and more conscious and intelligent ideals of humanity. The youth, deeply infected with the sex-passion, suddenly finds himself in the presence of Titanic forces — the Titanic but sub-conscious forces of his own nature. 'In love' he feels a superhuman impulse — and naturally so, for he identifies himself with cosmic energies and entities, powers that are preparing the future of the race, and whose operations extend over vast regions of space and millennial lapses of time. He sees into the abysmal deeps of his own being, and trembles with a kind of awe at the disclosure. And what he feels concerning himself he feels similarly concerning the one who has inspired his passion. The glances of the two lovers penetrate far beyond the surface, ages down into each other, waking a myriad antenatal dreams.

For the moment he lets himself go, rejoicing in the sense of limitless power beneath him — borne onwards like a man down rapids, too intoxicated with the glory of motion to think of whither he is going; then the next moment he discovers that he is being hurried into impossible situations — situations which his own moral conscience, as well as the moral conscience of Society, embodied in law and custom, will not admit. He finds perhaps that the satisfaction of his imperious impulse is, to all appearances, inconsistent with the welfare of her he loves. His own passion arises before him as a kind of rude giant which he or the race to which he belongs may, Frankenstein-like, have created ages back, but which he now has to dominate or be dominated by; and there declares itself in him the fiercest conflict — that between his far-back Titanic instinctive and sub-conscious nature, and his later-developed, more especially human and moral self.

While the glory of Sex pervades and suffuses all Nature; while the flowers are rayed and starred out towards the sun in the very ecstasy of generation; while the nostrils of the animals dilate, and their forms become instinct, under the passion, with a proud and fiery beauty; while even the human lover is transformed, and in the great splendours of the mountains and the sky perceives something to which he had not the key before — yet it is curious that just here, in Man, we find the magic wand of Nature suddenly broken, and doubt and conflict and division entering in, where a kind of unconscious harmony had erst prevailed.

And the reason of this is not far to seek. For in comparing, as we did a page or two back, the sex-needs and the hunger-needs of the human race we left out of account one great difference, namely, that while food (the object of hunger) has no moral rights of its own,[1] and can be appropriated without misgiving on that score, the object of sex is a person, and cannot be used for private advantage without the most dire infringement of the law of equality. The moment Man rises into any sort of consciousness of the equal rights of others with himself his love-needs open up this terrible problem. His needs are no less — perhaps they are greater — than they were before, but they are stricken with a deadly swound at the thought that there is something even greater than them.

Heine, I think, says somewhere that the man who loves unsuccessfully knows himself to be a god. It is not perhaps till the great current of sexual love is checked and brought into conflict with the other parts of his being that the whole nature of the man, sexual and moral, under the tremendous stress rises into consciousness and reveals in fire its god-like quality. This is the work of the artificer who makes immortal souls — who out of the natural Love evolves even a more perfect love. '*In tutti gli amanti*,' says Giordano Bruno, '*è questo fabro vulcano*' ('in all lovers is this Olympian blacksmith present').

It is the subject of this conflict, or at least differentiation betwen the sexual and the more purely moral and social instincts in man which interests us here. It is clear, I think, that if sex is to be treated rationally, that is, neither superstitiously on the one hand, nor licentiously on the other, we must be willing to admit that both the satisfaction of the passion and the non-satisfaction of it are desirable and beautiful. They both have their results, and man has to reap the fruits which belong to both experiences. May we not say that there is probably some sort of Transmutation of essences continually effected and effectible in the human frame? Lust and Love — the *Aphrodite Pandemos* and the *Aphrodite Ouranios* — are subtly interchangeable. Perhaps the corporeal amatory instinct and the ethereal human yearning for personal union are really and in essence one thing with diverse forms of manifestation. However that may be, it is pretty evident that there is *some* deep relationship between them. It is a matter of common experience that the unrestrained outlet of merely physical desire leaves the nature drained of its higher love-forces; while on the other hand if the physical satisfaction be denied, the body becomes surcharged with waves of emotion — sometimes to an unhealthy and dangerous degree. Yet at times this emotional love may, by reason of its expression being checked or restricted, transform itself into the all-penetrating subtle influence of spiritual love.

Marcus Aurelius quotes a saying of Heraclitus to the effect that the death of earth is to become water (liquefaction), and the death of water is to become air (evaporation), and the death of air is to become fire (combustion). So in the human body are there sensual, emotional, spiritual, and other elements of which it may be said that their death on one plane means their transformation and new birth on other planes.

It will readily be seen that I am not arguing that the lower or more physical manifestations of love should be killed out in order to force the growth of the more spiritual and enduring forms — because Nature in her slow evolutions does not generally countenance such high and mighty methods; but am merely trying to indicate that there are grounds for believing in the transmutability of the various forms of the passion, and grounds for thinking that the sacrifice of a lower phase may sometimes be the only condition on which a higher and more durable phase can be attained; and that therefore Restraint (which is absolutely necessary at times) *has* its compensation.

Any one who has once realised how glorious a thing Love is in its essence, and how indestructible, will hardly need to call anything that leads to it a sacrifice; and he is indeed a master of life who, accepting the grosser desires as they come to his body, and not refusing them, knows how to transform them at will into the most rare and fragrant flowers of human emotion.

Until these subjects are openly put before children and young people with some degree of intelligent and sympathetic handling, it can scarcely be expected that anything but the utmost confusion, in mind and in morals, should reign in matters of Sex. That we should leave our children to pick up their information about the most sacred, the most profound and vital, of all human functions, from the mere gutter, and learn to know it first from the lips of ignorance and vice, seems almost incredible, and certainly indicates the deeply-rooted unbelief and uncleanness of our own thoughts. Yet a child at the age of puberty, with the unfolding of its far-down emotional and sexual nature, is eminently capable of the most sensitive, affectional, and serene appreciation of what Sex means (generally more so, as things are today, than its worldling parent or guardian); and can absorb the teaching, if sympathetically given,

without any shock or disturbance to its sense of shame —
that sense which is so natural and valuable a safeguard of
early youth. To teach the child first, quite openly, its
physical relation to its own mother, its long indwelling in
her body, and the deep and sacred bond of tenderness
between mother and child in consequence; then, after a
time, to explain the relation of fatherhood, and how the love
of the parents for each other was the cause of its own (the
child's) existence: these things are easy and natural — at
least they are so to the young mind — and excite in it no
surprise, or sense of unfitness, but only gratitude and a kind
of tender wonderment.[2] Then, later on, as the special sexual
needs and desires develop, to instruct the girl or boy in the
further details of the matter, and the care and right conduct
of her or his own sexual nature; on the meaning and the
dangers of solitary indulgence — if this habit has been
contracted; on the need of self-control and the presence of
affection in all relations with others, and (without undue
asceticism) on the possibility of deflecting physical desire to
some degree into affectional and emotional channels, and
the great gain so resulting; all these are things which an
ordinary youth of either sex will easily understand and
appreciate, and which may be of priceless value, saving such
an one from years of struggle in foul morasses, and waste of
precious life-strength. Finally, with the maturity of the
moral nature, the supremacy of the pure human relation
should be taught — not the extinguishment of desire, but
the attainment of the real kernel of it, its dedication to the
well-being of another — the evolution of the *human*
element in love, balancing the natural — till at last the
snatching of an unglad pleasure, regardless of the other from
whom it is snatched, or the surrender of one's body to
another, for any reason except that of love, become things
impossible.

Between lovers then a kind of hardy temperance is much
to be recommended — for all reasons, but especially
because it lifts their satisfaction and delight in each other
out of the region of ephemeralities (which too soon turn to
dull indifference and satiety) into the region of more lasting
things — one step nearer at any rate to the Eternal Kingdom.
How intoxicating indeed, how penetrating — like a most

precious wine — is that love which is the sexual transformed by the magic of the will into the emotional and
spiritual! And what a loss on the merest grounds of prudence
and the economy of pleasure is its unbridled waste along
physical channels! So nothing is so much to be dreaded
between lovers as just this — the vulgarisation of love —
and this is the rock upon which marriage so often splits.

There is a kind of illusion about physical desire similar to
that which a child suffers from when, seeing a beautiful
flower, it instantly snatches the same, and destroys in a few
moments the form and fragrance which attracted it. He
only gets the full glory who holds himself back a little, and
truly possesses who is willing if need be not to possess.

On the other hand it must not be pretended that the
physical passions are by their nature unclean, or otherwise
than admirable or desirable in their place. Any attempt to
absolutely disown or despite them, carried out over long
periods either by individuals or bodies of people, only ends
in the *thinning out* of the human nature — by the very
consequent stinting of the supply of its growth-material,
and is liable to stultify itself in time by leading to reaction-
ary excesses. It must never be forgotten that the physical
basis throughout life is of the first importance, and supplies
the nutrition and food-stuff without which the higher
powers cannot exist or at least manifest themselves.
Intimacies founded on intellectual and moral affinities
alone are seldom very deep and lasting; if the physical basis
in any form is quite absent, the acquaintanceship is liable to
die away again like an ill-rooted plant. In many cases
(especially of women) the nature is never really understood
or disclosed till the sex-feeling is touched — however
lightly. Besides it must be remembered that in order for a
perfect intimacy between two people their bodies must by
the nature of the case be free to each other. The bodily
intimacy or endearment may not be the object for which
they come together; but if it is denied, its denial will bar any
real sense of repose and affiance, and make the relation
restless, vague, tentative and unsatisfied.

In these lights it will be seen that what we call asceticism
and what we call libertinism are two sides practically of the
same shield. So long as the tendency towards mere pleasure-

indulgence is strong and uncontrolled, so long will the instinct towards asceticism assert itself — and rightly, else we might speedily find ourselves in headlong Phaethonian career. Asceticism is in its place (as the word would indicate) as an *exercise*; but let it not be looked upon as an end in itself, for that is a mistake of the same kind as going to the opposite extreme. Certainly if the welfare and happiness of the beloved one were always really the main purpose in our minds we should have plenty of occasion for self-control, and an artificial asceticism would not be needed. We look for a time doubtless when the hostility between these two parts of man's unperfected nature will be merged in the perfect love; but at present and until this happens their conflict is certainly one of the most pregnant things in all our experience; and must not by any means be blinked or evaded, but boldly faced. It is in itself almost a sexual act. The mortal nature through it is, so to speak, torn asunder; and through the rent so made in his mortality does it sometimes happen that a new and immortal man is born.

Sex-pleasures afford a kind of type of all pleasure. The dissatisfaction which at times follows on them is the same as follows on all pleasure which is *sought*, and which does not come unsought. The dissatisfaction is not in the nature of pleasure itself but in the nature of *seeking*. In going off in pursuit of things external, the 'I' (since it really has everything and needs nothing) deceives itself, goes out from its true home, tears itself asunder, and admits a gap or rent in its own being. This, it must be supposed, is what is meant by *sin* — the separation or sundering of one's being — and all the pain that goes therewith. It all consists in *seeking* those external things and pleasures; not (a thousand times be it said) in the external things or pleasures themselves. They are all fair and gracious enough; their place is to stand round the throne and offer their homage — rank behind rank in their multitudes — if so be we will accept it. But for us to go out of ourselves to run after *them*, to allow ourselves to be divided and rent in twain by *their* attraction, that is an inversion of the order of heaven.

To this desertion of one's true self sex tempts most strongly, and stands as the type of Maya and the world-illusion; yet the beauty of the loved one and the delight of corporeal union all turn to dust and ashes if bought at the price of disunion and disloyalty in the higher spheres — disloyalty even to the person whose mortal love is sought. The higher and more durable part of man, whirled along in the rapids and whirlpools of desire, experiences tortures the moment it comes to recognise that It is something other than physical. Then comes the struggle to regain its lost Paradise, and the frightful effort of co-ordination between the two natures, by which the centre of consciousness is gradually transferred from the fugitive to the more permanent part, and the mortal and changeable is assigned its due place in the outer chambers and forecourts of the temple.

Pleasure should come as the natural (and indeed inevitable) accompaniment of life, believed in with a kind of free faith, but never sought as the object of life. It is in the inversion of this order that the uncleanness of the senses arises. Sex today throughout the domains of civilisation is thoroughly unclean. Everywhere it is slimed over with the thought of pleasure. Not for joy, not for mere delight in and excess of life, not for pride in the generation of children, not for a symbol and expression of deepest soul-union, does it exist — but for our own gratification. Hence we disown it in our thoughts, and cover it up with false shame and unbelief — knowing well that to seek a social act for a private end is a falsehood. The body itself is kept religiously covered, smothered away from the rush of the great purifying life of Nature, infected with dirt and disease, and a subject for prurient thought and exaggerated lust such as in its naked state it would never provoke. The skin becomes sickly and corrupt, and of a dead leaden white hue, which strangely enough is supposed to be more beautiful than the rich rose-brown, delicately shaded into lighter tints in the less exposed parts, which it would wear if tanned by daily welcome of sun and wind. Sexual embraces themselves seldom receive the benison of Dame Nature, in whose presence alone, under the burning sun or the high canopy of the stars and surrounded by the fragrant atmosphere, their meaning can be fully understood: but take place in stuffy dens of dirty upholstery and are associated with all unbeautiful things.

Even literature, which might have been expected to

preserve some decent expression on this topic, reflects all too clearly by its silence or by its pruriency the prevailing spirit of unbelief; and in order to find any sane faithful strong and calm words on the subject, one has to wade right back through the marshes and bogs of civilised scribbledom, and toil eastward across its arid wastes to the very dawn-hymns of the Aryan races.

In one of the Upanishads of the Vedic sacred books (the Brihadaranyaka Upanishad) there is a fine passage in which instruction is given to the man who desires a noble son as to the prayers which he shall offer to the gods on the occasion of congress with his wife. In primitive simple and serene language it directs him how, at such times, he should pray to the various forms of deity who preside over the operations of Nature: to Vishnu to prepare the womb of the future mother, to Prajápati to watch over the influx of the semen, and to the other gods to nourish the foetus, etc. Nothing could be (I am judging from the only translation I have met with, a Latin one) more composed, serene, simple, and religious in feeling, and well might it be if such instructions were preserved and followed, even today; yet such is the pass we have come to that actually Max Müller in his translations of the Sacred Books of the East appears to have been unable to persuade himself to render these and a few other quite similar passages into English, but gives them in the original Sanskrit! One might have thought that as Professor in the University of Oxford, presumedly *sans peur et sans reproche*, and professedly engaged in making a translation of these books for students, it was his duty and it might have been his delight to make intelligible just such passages as these, which give the pure and pious sentiment of the early world in so perfect a form; unless indeed he thought the sentiment impure and impious — in which case we have indeed a measure of the degradation of the public opinion which must have swayed his mind. As to the only German translation of the Upanishad which I can find, it baulks at the same passages in the same feeble way — repeating *nicht wiederzugeben, nicht wiederzugeben*, over and over again, till at last one can but conclude that the translator is right, and that the simplicity and sacredness of the feeling is in this our time indeed 'not to be reproduced.'

Our public opinion, our literature, our customs, our laws, are saturated with the notion of the uncleanness of Sex, and are so making the conditions of its cleanness more and more difficult. Our children, as said, have to pick up their intelligence on the subject in the gutter. Little boys bathing on the outskirts of our towns are hunted down by idiotic policemen, apparently infuriated by the sight of the naked body, even of childhood. Lately in one of our northern towns, the boys and men bathing in a public pool set apart by the corporation for the purpose, were — though forced to wear some kind of covering — kept till nine o'clock at night before they were allowed to go into the water — lest in the full daylight Mrs Grundy should behold any portion of their bodies! And as for women and girls their disabilities in the matter are most serious.

Till this dirty and dismal sentiment with regard to the human body is removed there can be little hope of anything like a free and gracious public life. With the regeneration of our social ideas the whole conception of Sex as a thing covert and to be ashamed of, marketable and unclean, will have to be regenerated. That inestimable freedom and pride which is the basis of all true manhood and womanhood will have to enter into this most intimate relation to preserve it frank and pure — pure from the damnable commercialism which buys and sells all human things, and from the religious hypocrisy which covers and conceals; and a healthy delight in and cultivation of the body and all its natural functions, and a determination to keep them pure and beautiful, open and sane and free, will have to become a recognised part of national life.

Possibly, and indeed probably, as the sentiment of common life and common interest grows, and the capacity for true companionship increases with the decrease of self-regarding anxiety, the importance of the mere sex-act will dwindle till it comes to be regarded as only one very special-ised factor in the full total of human love. There is no doubt that with the full realisation of affectional union the need of actual bodily congress loses some of its urgency; and it is not difficult to see in our present-day social life that the want of the former is (according to the law of transmutation) one marked cause of the violence and extravagance of the lower passions. But however things may change with the further evolution of man, there is no doubt that first of all the sex-relation must be divested of the sentiment of uncleanness which surrounds it, and rehabilitated again with a sense almost of religious consecration; and this means, as I have said, a free people, proud in the mastery and the divinity of their own lives, and in the beauty and openness of their own bodies.[3]

Sex is the allegory of Love in the physical world. It is from this fact that it derives its immense power. The aim of Love is non-differentiation — absolute union of being; but absolute union can only be found at the centre of existence. Therefore whoever has truly found another has found not only that other, and with that other himself, but has found also a third — who dwells at the centre and holds the plastic material of the universe in the palm of his hand, and is a creator of sensible forms.

Similarly the aim of sex is union and non-differentiation — but on the physical plane — and in the moment when this union is accomplished creation takes place, and the generation (in the plastic material of the sex-elements) of sensible forms.

In the animal and lower human world — and wherever the creature is incapable of realising the perfect love (which is indeed able to transform it into a god) — Nature in the purely physical instincts does the next best thing, that is, she effects a corporeal union and so generates another creature, who by the very process of his generation shall be one step nearer to the universal soul and the realisation of the desired end. Nevertheless the moment the other love and all that goes with it is realised the natural sexual love has to fall into a secondary place — the lover must stand on his feet and not on his head — or else the most dire confusions ensue, and torments aeonian.

Taking all together I think it may fairly be said that the prime object of Sex is *union*, the physical union as the allegory and expression of the real union, and that generation is a secondary object or result of this union. If we go to the lowest material expressions of Sex — as among the protozoic cells — we find that they, the cells, unite together, two into one; and that, as a result of the nutrition that ensues, this joint cell after a time (but not always) breaks up by fission into a number of progeny cells; or if on the other hand we go to the very highest expression of Sex, in the sentiment of Love, we find the latter takes the form chiefly and before all else of a desire for union, and only in lesser degree of a desire for race-propagation.[4]

I mention this because it probably makes a good deal of difference in our estimate of Sex whether the one function or the other is considered primary. There is perhaps a slight tendency among medical and other authorities to overlook the question of the important physical relations and reactions, and even corporeal modifications, which may ensue upon sexual intercourse between two people, and to fix their attention too exclusively upon their childbearing function; but in truth it is probably, I think, from various considerations,[5] that the spermatozoa pass through the tissues and affect the general body of the female, as well as that the male absorbs minutest cells *from* the female; and that generally, even without the actual Sex-act, there is an interchange of vital and ethereal elements — so that it might be said there is a kind of generation taking place *within* each of the persons concerned, through their mutual influence on each other, as well as that more specialised generation which consists in the propagation of the race.

At the last and taking it as a whole one has the same difficulty in dealing with the subject of Love which meets one at every turn in modern life — the monstrous separation of one part of our nature from another — the way in which, no doubt in the necessary course of evolution, we have cut ourselves in twain as it were, and assigned 'right' and 'wrong ', heaven and hell, spiritual and material, and other violent distinctions, to the separate portions. We have eaten of the Tree of Knowledge of good and evil with a vengeance! The Lord has indeed driven us out of Paradise into the domain of that '*fabro vulcano*' who with tremendous hammer-strokes must *hammer the knowledge of good and evil out of us again*. I feel that I owe an apology to the beautiful god for daring even for a moment to think of dissecting him soul from body, and for speaking as if these artificial distinctions were in any wise eternal. Will the man or woman, or race of men and women, never come, to whom love in its various manifestations shall be from the beginning a perfect whole, pure and natural, free and standing sanely on its feet?

Man, the Ungrown

Man, the ordinary human male, is a curious animal. While mastering the world with his pluck, skill, enterprise, he is in matters of Love for the most part a child. The passion plays havoc with him; nor does he ride the Leopard, as Ariadne is fabled to have done.

In this he differs from the other sex; and the difference can be seen in earliest years. When the boy is on his rocking horse, the girl is caressing her doll. When the adolescent youth, burning to master a real quadruped, is still somewhat contemptuous of Love's power, 'sweet seventeen' has already lost and regained her heart several times, and is accomplished in all the finesse of feeling.

To the grown man love remains little more than a plaything. Affairs, politics, fighting, money-making, creative art, constructive industry, are his serious business; the affections are his relaxation; passion is the little fire with which he toys, and which every now and then flares out and burns him up. His affections, his passions, are probably as a rule stronger than woman's; but he never attains to understand them or be master of their craft. With woman all this is reversed.

A man pelts along on his hobby — his business, his career, his latest invention, or what not — forgetful that there is such a thing in the world as the human heart; then all of a sudden he ''falls in love,'', tumbles headlong in the most ludicrous way, fills the air with his cries, struggles frantically like a fly in treacle: and all the time hasn't the faintest idea whether he has been inveigled into the situation, or whether he got there of his own accord, or what he wants now he is there. Suicides, broken hearts, lamentations, and certainly a whole panorama, marvellous in beauty, of lyrical poetry and art, mark the experience of love's distress in Man. Woman in the same plight neither howls nor cries, she does not commit suicide or do anything extravagant, she creates not a single poem or work of art of any account; but she simply goes her way and suffers in silence, shaping her life to the new conditions. Never for a moment does she forget that her one serious object is Love; but never for a moment does she 'give herself away' or lose her head, in the pursuit of that object.

It is perhaps in a kind of revenge for this that man for so many centuries has made woman his serf. Feeling that she really somehow mastered him on the affectional plane, he in revenge on the physical plane has made the most of his superior strength, and of his power over her; or, more probably, not thinking about it at all, he has simply allowed all along the sex-passion (so strong in him) to prompt him to this mastery.

For the sex-passion in man is undoubtedly a force — huge and fateful — which has to be reckoned with. Perhaps (speaking broadly) *all* the passions and powers, the intellect and affections and emotions and all, are really profounder and vaster in Man than in Woman — are more varied, root deeper, and have wider scope; but then the woman has this advantage, that her powers are more co-ordinated, are in harmony with each other, where his are disjointed or in conflict. A girl comes of age sooner than a boy. And the coming-of-age of Love (which harmonises all the faculties in the human being) may take place early in the woman, while in the man it is delayed long and long, perhaps never completely effected. The problem is so much bigger, so much more complex, with him; it takes longer for its solution. Women are sometimes impatient with men on this score; but then they do not see, judging from their own little flock, what a big herd of cattle the man has to bring home.

Anyhow the point is that Man with his great unco-ordinated nature *has* during these later centuries dominated the other sex, and made himself the ruler of society. In consequence of which we naturally have a society made after his pattern — a society advanced in mechanical and intellectual invention, with huge passional and emotional elements, but all involved in whirling confusion and strife — a society ungrown, which on its material side may approve itself a great success, but on its more human and affectional side seems at times an utter failure.

This ungrown, half-baked sort of character is conspicuous in the class of men who organise the modern world — the men of the English-speaking well-to-do class. The boy of this class begins life at a public school. He does not learn much from the masters; but he knocks about among his fellows in cricket and football and athletics, and turns out with an excellent organising capacity and a tolerably firm and reliable grip on the practical and material side of life — qualities which are of first-rate importance, and which give the English ruling classes a similar mission in the world to the Romans of the early empire. A certain standard too (for what it is worth) of schoolboy honour and fairness is thumped into him. It is very narrow and conventional, but at its best rises as high as a conception of self-sacrifice and duty, though never to the conception of love. At the same time a strong and lavish diet and an easy life stimulate his functional energies and his animal passions to a high degree.

Here certainly is some splendid material, and if well pounded into shape, kneaded and baked, might result in a useful upper crust for society. But alas! it remains, or actually degenerates into, a most fatuous dough. The boy never learns anything after he leaves school. He gets no more thumps. He glides easily into the higher walks of the world — backed by his parents' money — into Law or Army or Church or Civil Service or Commerce. He has really no serious fights to fight, or efforts to make, sees next to nothing of actual life; has an easy time, can marry pretty well whom he chooses, or console himself with unmarried joys; and ultimately settles down into the routine and convention of his particular profession — a picture of beefy self-satisfaction. Affection and tenderness of feeling, though latent in him, have never, owing to the unfortunate conditions of his life, been developed; but their place begins to be taken by a rather dreary cynicism. Sex, always strong, still even now in its waning days, retains the first place; and the mature man, having no adequate counterpoise to it in the growth of his sympathetic nature, is fain to find his highest restraints or sanctions in the unripe code of his school-days or the otiose conventions and prejudices of the professional clique to which he belongs.

So it comes about that the men who have the sway of the world today are in the most important matters quite ungrown; they really have never come of age in any adequate sense. Like Ephraim they are 'a cake not turned'. Wherever they turn up: in Lords or Commons, Civil or Military, Law or Church or Medicine, the Judge on the bench, the Bishop, the ruler of India, the exploiter of South Africa, the man who booms a company in the city, or who builds up a great commercial trust and gets a title for supporting a Government: it is much the same. Remove the distinctive insignia of their clique and office, and you find underneath — no more than a public schoolboy. Perhaps, indeed, rather less; for while the schoolboy mind is there, and the schoolboy code of life and honour, the enthusiasm and the promise of youth are gone.

It is certainly very maddening at times to think that the Destinies of the world, the organisation of society, the wonderful scope of possible statesmanship, the mighty issues of trade and industry, the loves of Women, the lives of criminals, the fate of savage nations, should be in the hands of such a set of general nincompoops; men so fatuous that it actually does not hurt them to see the streets crammed with prostitutes by night, or the parks by day with the semi-lifeless bodies of tramps; men, to whom it seems quite natural that our marriage and social institutions should lumber along over the bodies of women, as our commercial institutions grind over the bodies of the poor, and our 'imperial' enterprise over the bodies of barbarian races, destroyed by drink and devilry. But then no doubt the world is made like that. Assuredly it is no wonder that the more go-ahead Women (who have come round to the light by their own way, and through much darkness and suffering) should rise in revolt; or that the Workmen (finding their lives in the hands of those who do not know what life is) should do the same.

Leaving now the Upper and Middle-class man of today, the great representative of modern civilisation, and the triumphant outcome of so many centuries of human progress, to enjoy his distinction – we may turn for a moment to the only other great body of men who are of any importance: the more capable and energetic manual workers.

In the man of this class we have a type superior in many ways to the other. In the first place he knows something of what Life is; from an early age probably he has had to do something towards his own living. Anyhow he has been called upon in a thousand ways to help his parents, or his brothers and sisters, and has developed a fair capacity of sympathy and affection – a thing which can hardly be said of the public schoolboy; while his work, narrow though it may be, has given him a certain definite ability and grasp of actual fact. If, as is now happening in hundreds of thousands of cases, there is superadded to all this some of the general culture which arises from active reading and study, it is clear that the result is going to be considerable. It may not count much today, but it will tomorrow.

On the other hand this class is lamentably wanting in the very point where the other man excels – the organising faculty. Take a workman from the bench, where he has never so to speak had to look beyond his nose, and place him in a position of responsibility and command, and he is completely at sea. He turns out hopelessly slattern and ineffectual, or a martinet or a bully; he has no sense of perspective and stickles absurdly over little points while he lets the great ones go; and it is almost impossible for him to look before and after as he should do, or bring to a proper focus a whole field of considerations. In all this he is a mere child: and evidently by himself unfit to rule the world.

In many respects the newer Women and the Workmen resemble each other. Both have been bullied and sat upon from time immemorial, and are beginning to revolt; both are good at detailed and set or customary work, both are bad at organisation; both are stronger on the emotional than on the intellectual side; and both have an ideal of better things, but do not quite see their way to carry it out. Their best hope perhaps lies in their both getting hold of the Well-to-do Man and thumping him on each side till they get him to organise the world for them. The latter has no ideal, no object, no enthusiasm, of his own. He cannot set himself to work; and consequently he is just made use of by the commercial spirit of the day. It is really lamentable to think how his great organising capacity — which might create a holy Human empire of the world — is simply at present the tool of the Jew and the Speculator. In Parliamentary, Military, Indian, Home or Colonial politics, the quondam public schoolboy is just led by the nose by the money-grubbing interest, to serve its purposes; and half the time has not the sense to see that he is being so led.

It might seem that it would be the greatest blessing and benefit to the man of this class to find him an ideal to work to. Certainly it is his only real and conceivable function to form an alliance with the two other great classes of the modern nations — the women and the workmen — and organise for them. Whether he will see it so, we know not; but if this might come about great things would happen in the world.

Woman, the Serf

A half-grown man is of course a tyrant. And so it has come about that the rule of Man in the world has for many ages meant the serfdom of Woman.

Far back in History, at a time when in the early societies the thought of inequality had hardly arisen, it would appear that the female in her own way — as sole authenticator of birth and parentage, as guardian of the household, as inventress of agriculture and the peaceful arts, as priestess or prophetess or sharer in the councils of the tribe — was as powerful as man in his, and sometimes even more so. But from thence, down to today, what centuries of repression, of slavehood, of dumbness and obscurity have been her lot!

There is much to show that the greed of Private Property was the old Serpent which brought about the fall of our first parents; for as this sentiment — the chief incentive to modern Civilisation — rose and spread with a kind of contagion over the advancing races of mankind, the human Male, bitten by it, not only claimed possession of everything he could lay hands upon, but ended by enslaving and appropriating his own mate, his second self — reducing her also to a mere chattel, a slave and a plaything.

Certainly it is curious that, with whatever occasional exceptions, the periods of man's ascendancy have been the periods of so much sadness and degradation of women. He, all through, more and more calmly assuming that it must be her province to live and work for him; shutting her more and more into the seclusion of the boudoir and the harem, or down to the drudgery of the hearth; confining her body, her mind; playing always upon her sex-nature, accentuating always that — as though she were indeed nought else but sex; yet furious if her feelings were not always obedient to his desire; arrogating to himself a masculine licence, yet revenging the least unfaithfulness on her part by casting her out into the scorned life of the prostitute; and granting her more and more but one choice in life – to be a free woman, and to die, unsexed, in the gutter; or for creature-comforts and a good name to sell herself, soul and body, into life-long bondage. While she, more and more, has accepted as inevitable the situation; and moved sad-eyed, to her patient and uncomplaining work, to the narrow sphere and petty details of household labour and life, of patience and self-effacement, of tenderness and love, little noticed and less understood; or twisted herself into a ridiculous mime of fashion and frivolity, if so she might find a use for her empty head, and some favour with her lord; her own real impulses and character, her own talents and genius, all the while smothered away, and blighted, her brain dwarfed, and her outlook on the world marred by falsity and ignorance.

Such, or something like it, has been the fate of woman through the centuries. And if, like man, she had been light-armed for her own defence, it might have been possible to say it was her own fault that she allowed all this to take place; but when we remember that she all the while has had to bear the great and speechless burden of Sex — to be herself the ark and cradle of the Race down the ages — then we may perhaps understand what a tragedy it has all been.

For the fulfilment of sex is a relief and a condensation to the Man. He goes his way, and, so to speak, thinks no more about it. But to the Woman it is the culmination of her life, her profound and secret mission to humanity, of incomparable import and delicacy.

It is difficult, of course, for men to understand the depth and sacredness of the mother-feeling in woman − its joys and hopes, its leaden weight of cares and anxieties. The burden of pregnancy and gestation, the deep inner solicitude and despondency, the fears that all may not be well, the indrawing and absorption of her life into the life of the child, the increasing effort to attend to anything else, to care for anything else; her willingness even to die if only the child may be born safe: these are things which man − except it be occasionally in his role as artist or inventor − does but faintly imagine. Then, later on, the dedication to the young life or lives, the years of daylong and nightlong labour and forethought, in which the very thought of self is effaced, of tender service for which there is no recognition, nor ever will or can be − except in the far future; the sacrifice of personal interests and expansions in the ever-narrowing round of domestic duty; and in the end the sad wonderment and grievous unfulfilled yearning as one by one the growing boy and girl push their way into the world and disavow their home-ties and dependence; the sundering of heartstrings even as the navel-cord had to be sundered before: for these things, too, Woman can hope but little sympathy and understanding from the other sex.

But this fact, of man's non-perception of it, does not make the tragedy less. Far back from out the brows of Greek goddess, and Sibyll, and Norse and German seeress and prophetess, over all this petty civilisation look the grand untamed eyes of a primal woman the equal and the mate of man; and in sad plight should we be if we might not already, lighting up the horizon from East and West and South and North, discern the answering looks of those new comers who, as the period of woman's enslavement is passing away, send glances of recognition across the ages to their elder sisters.

After all, and underneath all the falsities of this period, may we not say that there is a deep and permanent relation between the sexes, which must inevitably assert itself again?

To this relation the physiological differences perhaps afford the key. In woman — modern science has shown — the more fundamental and primitive nervous centres, and the great sympathetic and vaso-motor system of nerves generally, are developed to a greater extent than in man; in woman the whole structure and life rallies more closely and obviously round the sexual function than in man; and, as a general rule, in the evolution of the human race, as well as of the lower races, the female is less subject to variation and is more constant to and conservative of the type of the race than the male.[1] With these physiological differences are naturally allied the facts that, of the two, Woman is the more primitive, the more intuitive, the more emotional. If not so large and cosmic in her scope, the great unconscious processes of Nature lie somewhere nearer to her; to her, sex is a deep and sacred instinct, carrying with it a sense of natural purity, nor does she often experience that divorce between the sentiment of Love and the physical passion which is so common with men, and which causes them to be aware of a grossness and a conflict in their own natures; she is, or should be, the interpreter of Love to man, and in some degree his guide in sexual matters. More, since she keeps to the great lines of evolution and is less biased and influenced by the momentary currents of the day; since her life is bound up with the life of the child; since in a way she is nearer the child herself, and nearer to the savage; it is to her that Man, after his excursions and wanderings, mental and physical, continually tends to return as to his primitive home and resting-place, to restore his balance, to find his centre of life, and to draw stores of energy and inspiration for fresh conquests of the outer world. 'In women men find beings who have not wandered so far as they have from the typical life of earth's creatures; women are for men the human embodiments of the restful responsiveness of Nature. To every man, as Michelet has put it, the woman whom he loves is as the Earth was to her legendary son; he has but to fall down and kiss her breast and he is strong again.'[2]

If it be true that by natural and physiological right Woman

stands in some such primitive relationship to Man, then we may expect this relationship to emerge again into clear and reasonable light in the course of time; though it does not of course follow that a relationship founded on physiological distinctions is *absolutely* permanent — since these latter may themselves vary to some degree. That a more natural and sensible relation of some kind between the sexes is actually coming to birth, few who care to read the signs of the times can well doubt. For the moment, however, and by way of parenthesis before looking to the future, we have to consider a little more in detail the present position of women under civilisation. Not that the consideration will be altogether gracious and satisfactory, but that it may — we are fain to hope — afford us some hints for the future.

It was perhaps not altogether unnatural that Man's craze for property and individual ownership should have culminated in the enslavement of woman — his most precious and beloved object. But the consequence of this absurdity was a whole series of other absurdities. What between insincere flattery and rose-water adorations on the one hand, and serfdom and neglect on the other, woman was, as Havelock Ellis says, treated as 'a cross between an angel and an idiot'. And after a time, adapting herself to the treatment, she really became something between an angel and an idiot — a bundle of weak and flabby sentiments, combined with a wholly undeveloped brain. Moreover by being continually specialised and specialised in the sexual and domestic direction, she lost touch with the actual world, and grew, one may say, into a separate species from man — so that in the later civilisations the males and females, except when the sex-attraction has compelled them as it were to come together, have been wont to congregate in separate herds, and talk languages each unintelligible to the other. Says the author of the *Woman's Question*: 'I admit there is no room for pharisaical self-laudation here. The brawling mass of *man*kind on a race-course or the stock-exchange is degrading enough in all conscience. Yet this even is hardly so painful as the sight which meets our eyes between three and four in the afternoon in any fashionable London street. Hundreds of women — mere dolls — gazing intently into shop-windows at various bits of coloured ribbon. . . . Perhaps nothing is more disheartening than this, except the mob of women in these very same streets between twelve and one at night.'

The 'lady', the household drudge, and the prostitute, are the three main types of woman resulting in our modern civilisation from the process of the past — and it is hard to know which is the most wretched, which is the most wronged, and which is the most unlike that which in her own heart every true woman would desire to be.

In some sense the 'lady' of the period which is just beginning to pass away is the most characteristic product of Commercialism. The sense of Private Property, arising and joining with the 'angel and idiot' theory, turned Woman more and more — especially of course among the possessing classes — into an emblem of possession — a mere doll, an empty idol, a brag of the man's exclusive right in the sex — till at last, as her vain splendours increased and her real usefulness diminished, she ultimated into the 'perfect lady'. But let every woman who piques and preens herself to the fulfilment of this ideal in her own person, remember what is the cost and what is the meaning of her quest: the covert enslavement to, and the covert contempt of Man.

The instinct of helpful personal service is so strong in women, and such a deep-rooted part of their natures, that to be treated as a mere target for other people's worship and service — especially when this is tainted with insincerity — must be most obnoxious to them. To think that women still exist by hundreds and hundreds of thousands, women with hearts and hands formed for love and helpfulness, who are brought up as 'ladies' and have to spend their lives listening to the idiotic platitudes of the Middle-class Man, and 'waited upon' by wage-bought domestics, is enough to make one shudder. The modern 'gentleman' is bad enough, but the 'lady' of bourgeois-dom, literally 'crucified twixt a smile and whimper', prostituted to a life which in her heart she hates — with its petty ideals, its narrow horizon, and its empty honours – is indeed a pitiful spectacle.

In Baronial times the household centered round the Hall, where the baron sat supreme; today it centres round the room where the lady reigns. The 'with' is withdrawn from the withdrawing-room, and that apartment has become the most important of all. Yet there is an effect of mockery in the homage paid to the new sovereign; and, as far as her rule is actual, a doubt whether she is really qualified yet for the position. The contrast between the two societies, the Feudal and the Commercial, is not inaptly represented by this domestic change. The former society was rude and rough, but generous and straightforward; the latter is polished and nice, but full of littleness and *finesse*. The Drawing-room, with its feeble manners and effects of curtains and embroidery, gives its tone to our lives nowadays. But we look forward to a time when this room also will cease to be the centre of the house, and another — perhaps the Commonroom — will take its place.

Below a certain level in society — the distinctively commercial — there are no drawing-rooms. Among the working masses, where the woman is of indispensable importance in daily life, and is not sequestered as an idol, there is no room specially set apart for her worship — a curious change takes place in her nominal position, and whereas in the supernal sphere she sits in state and has her tea and bread and butter brought to her by obsequious males, in the cottage, the men take their ease and are served by the women. The customs of the cottage, however, are rooted in a natural division of labour by which the man undertakes the outdoor, and the woman the indoor work; and there is, I think, quite as much real respect shown to her here as in the drawing-room.

In the cottage, nevertheless, the unfortunate one falls into the second pit that is prepared for her — that of the household drudge; and here she leads a life which, if it has more honesty and reality in it than that of the 'lady', is one of abject slavery. Few men again realise, or trouble themselves to realise, what a life this of the working housewife is. They are accustomed to look upon their own employment, whatever it may be, as 'work' (perhaps because it brings with it 'wages'); the woman's they regard as a kind of pastime. They forget what monotonous drudgery it really means, and yet what incessant forethought and care; they forget that the woman has no eight hours day, that her work is always staring her in the face, and waiting for her, even on into the night; that the body is wearied, and the mind narrowed down, 'scratched to death by rats and mice' in a perpetual round of petty cares. For not only does civilisation and multifarious invention (including smoke) make the burden of domestic life immensely complex, but the point is that each housewife has to sustain this burden to herself in lonely effort. What a sight, in any of our great towns, to enter into the cottages or tenements which form the endless rows of suburban streets, and to find in each one a working wife struggling alone in semi-darkness and seclusion with the toils of an entire separate household — with meals to be planned and provided, with bread to be baked, clothes to be washed and mended, children to be kept in order, a husband to be humoured, and a house to be swept and dusted; herself wearied and worried, debilitated with confinement and want of fresh air, and low-spirited for want of change and society! How futile! and how dreary!

There remains the third alternative for women; nor can it be wondered at that some deliberately choose a life of prostitution as their only escape from the existence of the lady or the drudge. Yet what a choice it is! On the one hand is the caged Woman, and on the other is the free: and which to choose? 'How can there be a doubt,' says one, 'surely freedom is always best.' Then there falls a hush. 'Ah!' says society, pointing with its finger, 'but a free *Woman*!'

And yet is it possible for Woman ever to be worthy her name, unless she is free?

Today, or up to today, just as the wage-worker has had no means of livelihood except by the sale of his bodily labor, so woman has had no means of livelihood except by the surrender of her bodily sex. She could dispose of it to one man for life, and have in return the respect of society and the caged existence of the lady or the drudge, or she could sell it night by night and be a 'free woman', scorned of the world and portioned to die in the gutter. In either case (if she really thinks about the matter at all) she must lose her self-respect. What a choice, what a frightful choice! — and this has been the fate of Woman for how long?

If, as a consequence of all this, woman has gone down hill, there is no doubt that man has gravitated too. (Or was it really that Jack fell down first, and 'Jill came tumbling after'?) Anyhow I think that nothing can be more clear — and this I believe should be taken as the basis of any discussion on the relation of the sexes — than that whatever injures the one sex injures the other; and that whatever defects or partialities may be found in the one must from the nature of the case be tallied by corresponding defects and partialities in the other. The two halves of the human race are comple-mentary, and it is useless for one to attempt to glorify itself at the expense of the other. As in Olive Schreiner's allegory of Woman ('Three Dreams in a Desert'), man and woman are bound together by a vital band, and the one cannot move a step in advance of the other.

If we were called upon to characterise these mutual defects (inbred partly by the false property relation) we should be inclined to say they were brutality and conceit on the one hand, and *finesse* and subtlety on the other. Man, as owner, has tended to become arrogant and callous and egotistic; woman, as the owned, slavish and crafty and unreal.

As a matter of fact, and allowing that sweeping general-isations of this kind are open to a good many exceptions, we do find (at any rate in the British Isles) a most wonderful and celestial indifference to anything but their own affairs amongst the 'lords of creation', an indifference so ingrained and constitutional that it is rarely conscious of itself, and which assumes quite easily and naturally that the weaker sex exists for the purpose of playing the foil, so to speak, to the chief actor in life's drama. Nor does the fact that this indifference is tempered, from time to time, by a little gallantry afford much consolation — as may be imagined — to the woman who perceives that the gallantry is inspired by nothing more than a passing sex-desire.

On the other hand Jill has come tumbling after pretty quickly, and has tumbled to the conclusion that though she cannot sway her lord by force, she may easily make use of him by craft. *Finesse*, developed through scores of generations, combined with the skilful use of the glamour belonging to her sex, have given her an extraordinary faculty of carrying out her own purposes, often through the most difficult passes, without ever exposing her hand. Possibly the knowledge of this forms one reason why women distrust each other so much more than men distrust each other.

Certainly one of the rarest of God's creatures is a truly undesigning female, but — when dowered with intellect such as might seem to justify it in being designing — one of the most admirable and beautiful!

Looking a little deeper, and below the superficial contrast which an unsatisfactory relation between the sexes has doubtless created, one seems to discern some of those more vital and deep-rooted differentiations spoken of on an earlier page. It is a commonly received opinion that woman tends more to intuition and man to logic;[3] and certainly the male mind seems better able to deal with abstractions and generalisations, and the female mind with the personal and the detailed and the concrete. And while this difference may be in part attributable to the artificial confinement of women to the domestic sphere, there is probably something more organic in it than that. At any rate it gives to Woman some of her best qualities — a quick and immediate perception, appreciation of character, tact, and a kind of artistic sense in the ordering of her own life, so that you do not see the tags and unravelled ends which appear in man's conduct. While the man is blundering about, fighting with himself, hesitating, doubting, weighing, trying vainly to co-ordinate all the elements of his nature, the woman (often no doubt in a smaller sphere) moves serene and prompt to her ends. Her actions are characterised by grace and finality; she is more at unity with herself; and she has the inestimable advantage of living in a world of persons — which may well seem so much more important and full of interest than that of things.

On the other hand, this want of the power of generalisation has made it difficult for women (at any rate up to to-day) to emerge from a small circle of interests, and to look at things from the point of view of public advantage and good. While her sympathies for individuals are keen and quick, abstract and general ideas such as those of Justice, Truth, and the like have been difficult of appreciation to her; and her deficiency in logic has made it almost impossible to act upon her through the brain. A man, if he is on the wrong track, can be argued with; but with a woman of this type, if her motives are nefarious, there is no means of changing them by appeal to her reason, or to the general sense of

Justice and Right — and unless controlled by the stronger sway of a determined personal will (of a man) her career is liable to be pretty bad.

Generally it will be admitted, as we are dealing with points of mental and moral difference between the sexes, Man has developed the more active, and Woman the more passive qualities; and it is pretty obvious, here too, that this difference is not only due to centuries of social inequality and of property-marriage, but roots back in some degree to the very nature of their respective sexual functions. That there are permanent complementary distinctions between the male and female, dating first perhaps from sex, and thence spreading over the whole natures, physical, mental and moral, of each, no one can reasonably doubt. These distinctions have, however, we contend, been strangely accentuated and exaggerated during the historic period — till at last a point of maximum divergence and absolute misunderstanding has been reached. But that point is behind us now.

Woman in Freedom

It is clear enough, from what has been said, that what Woman most needs today, and is mostly seeking for, is a basis of independence for her life. Nor is her position likely to be improved until she is able to face man on an equality; to find, self-balanced, her natural relation to him; and to dispose of herself and of her sex perfectly freely, and not as a thrall must do.

Doubtless if man were an ideal creature his mate might be secure of equal and considerate treatment from him without having to insist upon an absolute economic independence; but as that is only too obviously not the case there is nothing left for her today but to unfold the war-flag of her 'rights', and (dull and tiresome as it may be) to go through a whole weary round of battles till peace is concluded again upon a better understanding.

Yet it must never be forgotten that nothing short of large social changes, stretching beyond the sphere of women only, can bring about the complete emancipation of the latter. Not till our whole commercial system, with its barter and sale of human labour and human love for gain, is done away, and not till a whole new code of ideals and customs of life has come in, will women really be free. They must remember that their cause is also the cause of the oppressed labourer over the whole earth, and the labourer has to remember that his cause is theirs.[1]

And since Motherhood is, after all, woman's great and incomparable work, people will come to see that a sane maternity is one of the very first things to be considered — and that really, though not the only consideration, it is a work which if properly fulfilled *does* involve the broadest and largest culture. Perhaps this might seem to some only too obvious; yet when for a moment we glance around at the current ideals, when we see what Whitman calls 'the incredible holds and webs of silliness, millinery and every kind of dyspeptic depletion' in which women themselves live, when we see the absolute want of training for motherhood and the increasing physical incapacity for it, and even the feminine censure of those who pass through the ordeal too easily, we begin to realise how little the recent notion of what woman should be is associated with the healthy fulfilment of her most perfect work. A woman capable at all points to bear children, to guard them, to teach them, to turn them out strong and healthy citizens of the great world, stands at the farthest remove from the finnikin doll or the meek drudge whom man by a kind of false sexual selection has through many centuries evolved as his ideal.

The nervous and sexual systems of women today, ruined amongst the rich by a life and occupations which stimulate the emotional sensibilities without ever giving the strength and hardiness which flow from healthy and regular industry, and often ruined among the poor by excessive labour carried on under most unhealthy conditions, make real wifehood and motherhood things almost unknown. 'Injudicious training,' says Bebel, 'miserable social conditions (food, dwelling, occupation) produce weak, bloodless,

nervous beings, incapable of fulfilling the duties of matrimony. The consequences are menstrual troubles[2] and
disturbances in the various organs connected with sexual
functions, rendering maternity dangerous or impossible.
Instead of a healthy, cheerful companion, a capable mother,
a helpmate equal to the calls made upon her activity, the
husband has a nervous excitable wife, permanently under
the doctor's hands, and too fragile to bear the slightest
draught or noise.'

The Modern Woman sees plainly enough that no decent
advance for her sex is possible until this whole question is
fairly faced — involving, as of course it will do, a life very
different from her present one, far more in the open air, with
real bodily exercise and development, some amount of
regular manual work, a knowledge of the laws of health and
physiology, an altogether wider mental outlook, and greater
self-reliance and nature-hardihood. But when once these
things are granted, she sees that she will no longer be the
serf, but the equal, the mate, and the comrade of Man.

Before any such new conception it is obvious enough that
the poor little pinched ideal of the 'lady', which has ruled
society so long, will fade away into distance and obscurity.
People may rail at the new developments, but what, it may
be asked, *can* any decently sensible woman think of her
present position — of the mock salutations and heroic
politeness of the conventional male — with their suggestion
of an empty homage to weakness and incapacity; of the
unwritten law which condemns her, if occupying any place
in society, to bridle in her chin and use an affected speech in
order that it may be patent to everybody that she is *not* free;
which forbids natural and spontaneous gesture as unbecoming and suspicious — and indeed in any public place as liable
to the attention of the policeman; what can she think of the
perpetual lies under which she has to live — too numerous
to be recorded; except that all these things are intolerable?
Rather than remain in such a coil the modern woman is
sensible enough to see that she must face the stigma of
doing things 'unlady-like'; and that only by facing it can she
win her true place in the world, and a real comradeship with
the only class of man who is capable of such a thing —
namely, the man who is willing not to be 'a gentleman'.

That a new code of manners between the sexes, founded
not on covert lust but on open and mutual helpfulness, has
got to come in, is obvious enough. The cry of equality need
not like a red rag infuriate the Philistine bull. That woman
is in general muscularly weaker than man, and that there
are certain kinds of effort, even mental, for which she is less
fitted — as there are other kinds of effort for which she is
more fitted — may easily be granted; but this only means, in
the language of all good manners, that there are special ways
in which men can assist women, as there are special ways in
which women can assist men. Anything which goes beyond
this, and the friendly exchange of equal services, and which
assumes, in the conventionalities of the private household
or the public place, that the female claims a general indulgence (because of her general incapacity) is an offence —
against the encouragement of which women themselves
will no doubt be on their guard.

I say the signs of revolt on the part of the lady class —
revolt long delayed but now spreading all along the line —
are evident enough. When, however, we come to the second
type of woman mentioned in the preceding pages, the
working-wife, we — naturally enough — do not find much
conscious movement. The life of the household drudge is
too like that of a slave, too much consumed in mere toil, too
little illuminated by any knowledge, for her to rise of herself
to any other conception of existence. Nevertheless it is not
difficult to see that general and social changes are working
to bring about her liberation also. Improved house-
construction, public bakeries and laundries, and so forth,
and, what is much more important, a more rational and
simple and healthful notion of food and furniture, are
tending very largely to reduce the labours of Housework and
Cookery; and conservative though women are in their
habits, when these changes are brought to their doors they
cannot but see the advantage of them. Public institutions
too are more and more taking over the responsibilities and
the cost of educating and rearing children; and even here and
there we may discern a drift towards the amalgamation of
households, which by introducing a common life and
division of labour among the women-folk will probably do
much to cheer and lighten their lot. None of these changes,

however, will be of any great use unless or until they wake the overworked woman herself to see and insist on her rights to a better life, and until they force from the man a frank acknowledgment of her claim. And surely here and there the man himself will do something to educate his mate to this point. We see no reason indeed why he should not assist in some part of the domestic work, and thus contribute his share of labour and intelligence to the conduct of the house; nor why the woman – being thus relieved – should not occasionally, and when desirable, find salaried work outside, and so contribute to the maintenance of the family, and to her own security and sense of independence. The over-differentiation of the labours of the sexes today is at once a perpetuation of the servitude of women and a cause of misunderstanding between her and man, and of lack of interest in each other's doings.

The third type of woman, the prostitute, provides us with that question which – according to Bebel – is the sphinx-riddle that modern society cannot solve, and yet which unsolved threatens society's destruction. The commercial prostitution of love is the last outcome of our whole social system, and its most clear condemnation. It flaunts in our streets, it hides itself in the garment of respectability under the name of matrimony, it eats in actual physical disease and death right through our midst; it is fed by the oppression and the ignorance of women, by their poverty and denied means of livelihood, and by the hypocritical puritanism which forbids them by millions not only to gratify but even to speak of their natural desires; and it is encouraged by the callousness of an age which has accustomed men to buy and sell for money every most precious thing – even the life-long labour of their brothers, therefore why not also the very bodies of their sisters?

Here there is no solution *except* the freedom of woman – which means of course also the freedom of the masses of the people, men and women, and the ceasing altogether of economic slavery. There is no solution which will not include the redemption of the terms 'free woman' and 'free love' to their *true* and rightful significance. Let every woman whose heart bleeds for the sufferings of her sex, hasten to declare herself and to constitute herself as far as she possibly can, a free woman. Let her accept the term with all the odium that belongs to it; let her insist on her right to speak, dress, think, act, and above all to use her sex, as she deems best; let her face the scorn and the ridicule; let her 'lose her own life' if she likes; assured that only so can come deliverance, and that only when the free woman is honoured will the prostitute cease to exist. And let every man who really would respect his counterpart, entreat her also to act so; let him never by word or deed tempt her to grant as a bargain what can only be precious as a gift; let him see her with pleasure stand a little aloof; let him help her to gain her feet; so at last, by what slight sacrifices on his part such a course may involve, may it dawn upon him that he has gained a real companion and helpmate on life's journey.

The whole evil of commercial prostitution arises out of the domination of Man in matters of sex. Better indeed were a Saturnalia of *free* men and women than the spectacle which as it is our great cities present at night. Here in Sex, the woman's instincts are, as a rule, so clean, so direct, so well-rooted in the needs of the race, that except for man's domination they would scarcely have suffered this perversion. Sex in man is an unorganised passion, an individual need or impetus; but in woman it may more properly be termed a constructive instinct, with the larger signification that that involves. Even more than man should woman be 'free' to work out the problem of her sex-relations as may commend itself best to her — hampered as little as possible by legal, conventional, or economic considerations, and relying chiefly on her own native sense and tact in the matter. Once thus free — free from the mere cash-nexus to a husband, from the money-slavery of the streets, from the nameless terrors of social opinion, and from the threats of the choice of perpetual virginity or perpetual bondage — would she not indeed choose her career (whether that of wife and mother, or that of free companion, or one of single-blessedness) far better for herself than it is chosen *for* her to-day — regarding really in some degree the needs of society, and the welfare of children, and the sincerity and durability of her relations to her lovers, and less the petty motives of profit and fear?

The point is that the whole conception of a nobler

Womanhood for the future has to proceed candidly from this basis of her complete freedom as to the disposal of her sex, and from the healthy conviction that, with whatever individual aberrations, she will on the whole use that freedom rationally and well. And surely this — in view too of some decent education of the young on sexual matters — is not too great a demand to make on our faith in women. If it is, then indeed we are undone — for short of this we can only retain them in servitude, and society in its form of the hell on earth which it largely is today.

Refreshing therefore in its way is the spirit of revolt which is spreading on all sides. Let us hope such revolt will continue. If it lead here and there to strained and false situations, or to temporary misunderstandings — still, declared enmity is better than unreal acquiescence. Too long have women acted the part of mere appendages to the male, suppressing their own individuality and fostering his self-conceit. In order to have souls of their own they must free themselves, and greatly by their own efforts. They must learn to fight. Whitman in his poem 'A woman waits for me', draws a picture of a woman who stands in the sharpest possible contrast with the feeble bourgeois ideal — a woman who can 'swim, row, ride, wrestle, shoot, run, strike, retreat, defend herself', etc.; and Bebel, in his book on *Woman*, while pointing out that in Sparta, 'where the greatest attention was paid to the physical development of both sexes, boys and girls went about naked till they had reached the age of puberty, and were trained together in bodily exercises, games and wrestling,' complains that nowadays 'the notion that women require strength, courage and resolution is regarded as very heterodox.' But the truth is that qualities of courage and independence are not agreeable in a slave, and that is why man during all these centuries has consistently discountenanced them — till at last the female herself has come to consider them 'unwomanly'. Yet this last epithet is absurd; for if tenderness is the crown and glory of woman, nothing can be more certain than that true tenderness is only found in strong and courageous natures; the tenderness of a servile person is no tenderness at all.

It has not escaped the attention of thinkers on these subjects that the rise of Women into freedom and larger social life here alluded to — and already indeed indicated by the march of events — is likely to have a profound influence on the future of our race. It is pointed out that among most of the higher animals, and indeed among many of the early races of mankind, the males have been selected by the females on account of their prowess or superior strength or beauty, and this has led to the evolution in the males and in the race at large of a type which (in a dim and unconscious manner) was the ideal of the female.[3] But as soon as in the history of mankind the property-love set in, and woman became the chattel of man, this action ceased. She, being no longer free, could not possibly choose man, but rather the opposite took place, and man began to select woman for the characteristics pleasing to *him*. The latter now adorned herself to gratify his taste, and the female type and consequently the type of the whole race have been correspondingly affected. With the return of woman to freedom the ideal of the female may again resume its sway. It is possible indeed that the more dignified and serious attitude of women towards sex may give to sexual selection when exercised by them a nobler influence than when exercised by the males. Anyhow it is not difficult to see that women really free would never countenance for their mates the many mean and unclean types of men who today seem to have things all their own way, nor consent to have children by such men; nor is it difficult to imagine that the feminine influence might thus sway to the evolution of a more manly and dignified race than has been disclosed in these last days of commercial civilisation!

The Modern Woman with her clubs, her debates, her politics, her freedom of action and costume, is forming a public opinion of her own at an amazing rate; and seems to be preparing to 'spank' and even thump the Middle-class Man in real earnest! What exactly evolution may be preparing for us, we do not know, but apparently some lively sparring matches between the sexes. Of course all will not be smooth sailing. The women of the new movement are naturally largely drawn from those in whom the maternal instinct is not especially strong; also from those in whom the sexual instinct is not preponderant. Such women do not altogether represent their sex; some are rather mannish in temperament; some are 'homogenic', that is, inclined to attachments to their own, rather than to the opposite sex; some are ultra-rationalising and brain-cultured; to many, children are more or less a bore; to others, man's sex-passion is a mere impertinence, which they do not understand, and whose place they consequently misjudge. It would not do to say that the majority of the new movement are thus out of line, but there is no doubt that a large number are; and the course of their progress will be correspondingly curvilinear.

Perhaps the deficiency in maternal instinct would seem the most serious imputation. But then, who knows (as we have said) what evolution is preparing? Sometimes it seems possible that a new sex is on the make — like the feminine neuters of Ants and Bees — not adapted for child-bearing, but with a marvellous and perfect instinct for social service, indispensable for the maintenance of the common life. Certainly most of those who are freeing themselves — often with serious struggles — from the 'lady' chrysalis are fired with an ardent social enthusiasm; and if they may person-ally differ in some respects from the average of their sex, it is certain that their efforts will result in a tremendous improvement in the general position of their more common-place sisters.

If it should turn out that a certain fraction of the feminine sex should for one reason or another not devote itself to the work of maternity, still the influence of this section would react on the others to render their notion of motherhood far more dignified than before. There is not much doubt that in the future this most important of human labours will be carried on with a degree of conscious intelligence hitherto unknown, and such as will raise it from the fulfilment of a mere instinct to the completion of a splendid social purpose. To save the souls of children as well as their bodies, to raise heroic as well as prosperous citizens, will surely be the desire and the work of the mothers of our race.[4]

It will perhaps be said that after going about to show (as in the previous chapter) the deficiency of women hitherto in the matter of the generalising faculty, it is somewhat incon-sistent to express any great hope that they will ever take much active interest in the general social life to which they belong; but indeed the answer to this is that they are already beginning to do so. The social enthusiasm and activity shown by women in Britain, Russia, and the United States is so great and well-rooted that it is impossible to believe it a mere ephemeral event; and though in the older of these countries it is at present confined to the more wealthy classes, we can augur from that . — according to a well-known principle — that it will in time spread downwards to the women of the nation.

Important as is the tendency of women in the countries mentioned to higher education and brain development, I think it is evident that the widening and socialisation of their interests is not taking place so much through mere study of books and the passing of examinations in political economy and other sciences, as through the extended actual experience which the life of the day is bringing to them. Certainly the book-studies are important and must not be neglected; but above all is it imperative (and men, if they are to have any direct sway in the future destinies of the other sex, must look to it) that women, so long confined to the narrowest mere routine and limited circle of domestic life, should see and get experience, all they can, of the actual world. The theory, happily now exploded, of keeping them 'innocent' through sheer ignorance partakes too much of the 'angel and idiot' view. To see the life of slum and palace and workshop, to enter into the trades and professions, to become doctors, nurses, and so forth, to have to look after themselves and to hold their own as against men, to travel, to meet with sexual experience, to work together in trade-unions, to join in social and political uprisings and rebellions, etc., is what women want just now. And it is evident enough that at any rate among the more prosperous sections in this country such a movement is going on apace. If the existence of the enormous hordes of unattached females that we find living on interest and dividends today is a blemish from a Socialistic point of view; if we find them on the prowl all over the country, filling the theatres and concert-rooms and public entertainments in the proportion of three to one male, besetting the trains, swarming on to the tops of the buses, dodging on bicycles under the horses' heads, making speeches at street corners, blocking the very pavements in the front of fashionable shops, we must not forget that for the objects we have just sketched, even this class is going the most direct way to work, and laying in stores of experience, which will make it impossible for it ever to return to the petty life of times gone by.

At the last, and after centuries of misunderstanding and association of triviality and superficiality with the female sex, it will perhaps dawn upon the world that the truth really lies in an opposite direction — that, in a sense, there is something more deep-lying fundamental and primitive in the woman nature than in that of the man; that instead of being the over-sensitive hysterical creature that civilisation has too often made her, she is essentially of calm large and acceptive even though emotional temperament. 'Her shape arises,' says Walt Whitman,

> She less guarded than ever, yet more guarded than
> ever,
> The gross and soil'd she moves among do not make
> her gross and soil'd,
> She knows the thoughts as she passes, nothing is
> concealed from her,
> She is none the less considerate or friendly therefor,
> She is the best belov'd, it is without exception; she
> has no reason to fear, and she does not fear.

The Greek goddesses look down and across the ages to the very outposts beyond civilisation; and already from far America, Australia, Africa, Norway, Russia, as even in our midst from those who have crossed the border-line of all class and caste, glance forth the features of a grander type — fearless and untamed — the primal merging into the future Woman; who, combining broad sense with sensibility, the passion for Nature with the love of Man, and commanding indeed the details of life, yet risen out of localism and convention, will help us to undo the bands of death which encircle the present society, and open the doors to a new and wider life.

Marriage: a Retrospect

Of the great mystery of human Love, and that most intimate personal relation of two souls to each other – perhaps the firmest, most basic and indissoluble fact (after our own existence) that we know; of that strange sense – often, perhaps generally, instantaneous – of long precedent familiarity and kinship, that deep reliance on and acceptation of another in his or her entirety; of the tremendous strength of the chain which thus at times will bind two hearts in lifelong dedication and devotion, persuading and indeed not seldom compelling the persons concerned to the sacrifice of some of the other elements in their lives and characters; and, withal, of a certain inscrutable veiledness from each other which so frequently accompanies the relation of the opposite sexes, and which forms at once the abiding charm, and the pain, sometimes the tragedy, of their union; of this palpitating winged living thing, which one may perhaps call the real Marriage – I would say but little; for indeed it is only fitting or possible to speak of it by indirect language and suggestion, nor may one venture to rudely drag it from its sanctuary into the light of the common gaze.

Compared with this, the actual marriage, in its squalid perversity as we too often have occasion of knowing it, is as the wretched idol of the savage to the reality which it is supposed to represent; and one seems to hear the Aristophanic laughter of the gods as they contemplate man's little clay image of the Heavenly Love – which, cracked in the fire of daily life, he is fain to bind together with rusty hoops of law, and parchment bonds, lest it should crumble and fall to pieces altogether.

The whole subject, wide as life itself – as Heaven and Hell – eludes anything like adequate treatment, and we need make no apology for narrowing down our considerations here to just a few practical points; and if we cannot navigate upward into the very heart of the matter – namely, into the causes which make some people love each other with a true and perfect love, and others unite in obedience to but a counterfeit passion — yet we may fairly, I imagine, study some of the conditions which give to actual marriage its present form, or which in the future are likely to provide real affection with a more satisfactory expression than it has as a rule today.

As long as man is only half-grown, and woman is a serf or a parasite, it can hardly be expected that Marriage should be particularly successful. Two people come together, who know but little of each other, who have been brought up along different lines, who certainly do not understand each other's nature; whose mental interests and occupations are different, whose worldly interest and advantage are also different; to one of whom the subject of sex is probably a sealed book, to the other perhaps a book whose most dismal page has been opened first. The man needs an outlet for his passion; the girl is looking for a 'home' and a proprietor. A glamour of illusion descends upon the two, and drives them into each other's arms. It envelopes in a gracious and misty halo all their differences and misapprehensions. They marry without misgiving; and their hearts overflow with gratitude to the white-surpliced old gentleman who reads the service over them.

But at a later hour, and with calmer thought, they begin to realise that it is a life-sentence which he has so suavely passed upon them — not reducible (as in the case of ordinary convicts) even to a term of 20 years. The brief burst of their first satisfaction has been followed by satiety on the physical plane, then by mere vacuity of affection, then by boredom, and even nausea. The girl, full perhaps of a tender emotion, and missing the sympathy and consolation she expected in the man's love, only to find its more materialistic side — 'This, this then is what I am wanted for;' the man, who looked for a companion, finding he can rouse no mortal interest in his wife's mind save in the most exasperating trivialities; — whatever the cause may be, a veil has fallen from before their faces, and there they sit, held together now by the least honourable interests, the interests which they themselves can least respect, but to which Law and Religion lend all their weight. The monetary dependence of the woman, the mere sex-needs of the man, the fear of public opinion, all form motives, and motives of the meanest kind, for maintaining the seeming tie; and the relation of the two hardens down into a dull neutrality, in which lives and characters are narrowed and blunted, and deceit becomes the common weapon which guards divided interests.

A sad picture! and of course in this case a portrayal deliberately of the seamy side of the matter. But who shall say what agonies are often gone through in those first few years of married life? Anyhow, this is the sort of problem which we have to face today, and which shows its actuality by the amazing rate at which it is breaking out in literature on all sides.

It may be said — and often of course is said — that such cases as these only prove that marriage was entered into under the influence of a passing glamour and delusion, and that there was not much real devotion to begin with. And no doubt there is truth enough in such remarks. But — we may say in reply — because two people make a mistake in youth, to condemn them, for that reason, to lifelong suffering and mutual degradation, or to see them so condemned, without proposing any hope or way of deliverance, but with the one word 'serves you right' on the lips, is a course which can commend itself only to the grimmest and dullest Calvinist. Whatever safeguards against a too frivolous view of the relationship may be proposed by the good sense of society in the future, it is certain that the time has gone past when Marriage can continue to be regarded as a supernatural institution to whose maintenance human bodies and souls must be indiscriminately sacrificed; a humaner, wiser, and less panic-stricken treatment of the subject must set in; and if there are difficulties in the way they must be met by patient and calm consideration of human welfare — superior to any law, however ancient and respectable.

I take it then, that without disguising the fact that the question is a complex one, and that our conclusions may be only very tentative, we have to consider as rationally as we conveniently can, first, some of the drawbacks or defects of the present marriage customs, and secondly such improvements in these as may seem feasible.

And with regard to the former, one of the most important

points — which we have already touched on — is the extra-ordinary absence of any allusion to these subjects in the teaching of young folk. In a day when every possible study seems to be crammed into the school curriculum, it is curious that the one matter which is of supreme importance to the individual and the community is most carefully ignored. That one ought to be able to distinguish a passing sex-spell from a true comradeship and devotion is no doubt a very sapient remark; but since it is a thing which mature folk often fail to do, how young things with no experience of their own or hint from others should be expected to do it is not easy to understand. The search for a fitting mate, espe-cially among the more sensitive and highly-organised types of mankind, is a very complex affair; and it is really monstrous that the girl or youth should have to set out — as they mostly have to do today — on this difficult quest without a word of help as to the choice of the way or the very real doubts and perplexities that beset it.

If the pair whom we have supposed as about to be married had been brought up in almost any tribe of savages, they would a few years previously have gone through regular offices of initiation into manhood and womanhood, during which time ceremonies (possibly indecent in our eyes) would at any rate have made many misapprehensions impossible. As it is, the civilised girl is led to the 'altar' often in uttermost ignorance and misunderstanding as to the nature of the sacrificial rites about to be consummated. The youth too is ignorant in his way. Perhaps he is unaware that love in the female is, in a sense, more diffused than in the male, less specially sexual: that it dwells longer in caresses and embraces, and determines itself more slowly towards the reproductive system. Impatient, he injures and horrifies his partner, and unconsciously perhaps aggravates the very hysterical tendency which marriage might and should have allayed.[1]

Among the middle and well-to-do classes especially, the conditions of high civilisation, by inducing an overfed masculinity in the males and a nervous and hysterical tendency in the females,[2] increase the difficulties mentioned; and it is among the 'classes' too that the special evils exist of sex-starvation and sex-ignorance on the one hand, and of mere licentiousness on the other.

Among the comparatively uncivilised mass of the people, where a good deal of familiarity between the sexes takes place before marriage, and where probably there is less ignorance on the one side and less licentiousness on the other, these ills are not so prominent. But here too the need for some sensible teaching is clear; and sheer neglect of the law of Transmutation, or sheer want of self-control, are liable to make the proletarian union brutish enough.

So far with regard to difficulties arising from personal ignorance and inexperience. But stretching beyond and around all these are those others that arise from the special property-relation between the two sexes, and from deep-lying historic and economic causes generally. The long historic serfdom of woman, creeping down into the moral and intellectual natures of the two sexes, has exaggerated the naturally complementary relation of the male and the female into an absurd caricature of strength on the one hand and dependence on the other. This is well seen in the ordinary marriage-relation of the common-prayer-book type. The frail and delicate female is supposed to cling round the sturdy husband's form, or to depend from his arm in graceful incapacity; and the spectator is called upon to admire the charming effect of the union — as of the ivy with the oak — forgetful of the terrible moral, namely, that (in the case of the trees at any rate) it is really a death-struggle which is going on, in which either the oak must perish suffocated in the embraces of its partner, or in order to free the former into anything like healthy development the ivy must be sacrificed.

Too often of course of such marriages the egoism, lordship and physical satisfaction of the man are the chief motive causes. The woman is practically sacrificed to the part of the maintenance of these male virtues. It is for her to spend her days in little forgotten details of labour and anxiety for the sake of the man's superior comfort and importance, to give up her needs to his whims, to 'humour' him in all ways she can; it is for her to wipe her mind clear of all opinions in order that she may hold it up as a kind of mirror in which he may behold reflected his lordly self; and it is for her to sacrifice even her physical health and natural instincts in deference to what is called her 'duty' to her husband.

How bitterly *alone* many such a woman feels! She has dreamed of being folded in the arms of a strong man, and surrendering herself, her life, her mind, her all, to his service. Of course it is an unhealthy dream, an illusion, a mere luxury of love; and it is destined to be dashed. She has to learn that self-surrender may be just as great a crime as self-assertion. She finds that her very willingness to be sacrificed only fosters in the man, perhaps for his own self-defence, the egotism and coldness that so cruelly wound her.

For how often does he with keen prevision see that if he gives way from his coldness the clinging dependent creature will infallibly overgrow and smother him! − that she will cut her woman-friends, will throw aside all her own interests and pursuits in order to 'devote' herself to him, and affording no sturdy character of her own in which *he* can take any interest, will hang the festoons of her affection on every ramification of his wretched life − nor leave him a corner free − till he perishes from all manhood and social or heroic uses into a mere matrimonial clothespeg, a warning and a wonderment to passers by!

However, as an alternative, it sometimes happens that the Woman, too wise to sacrifice her own life indiscriminately to the egoism of her husband, and not caring for the 'festoon' method, adopts the middle course of *appearing* to minister to him while really pursuing her own purposes. She cultivates the gentle science of indirectness. While holding up a mirror for the Man to admire himself in, *behind that mirror* she goes her own way and carries out her own designs, separate from him; and while sacrificing her body to his wants, she does so quite deliberately and for a definite reason, namely, because she has found out that she can so get a shelter for herself and her children, and can solve the problem of that maintenance which society has hitherto denied to her in her own right. For indeed by a cruel fate women have been placed in exactly that position where the sacrifice of their self-respect for base motives has easily passed beyond a temptation into being a necessity. They have had to live, and have too often only been able to do so by selling themselves into bondage to the man. Willing or unwilling, overworked or dying, they have had to bear children to the caprice of their lords; and in this serf-life their very natures have been blunted; they have lost — what indeed should be the very glory and crown of woman's being — the perfect freedom and the purity of their love.[3]

At this whole spectacle of woman's degradation the human male has looked on with stupid and open-mouthed indifference — as an ox might look on at a drowning ox-herd — not even dimly divining that his own fate was somehow involved. He has calmly and obliviously watched the woman drift farther and farther away from him, till at last, with the loss of an intelligent and mutual understanding between the sexes, Love with unequal wings has fallen lamed to the ground. Yet it would be idle to deny that even in such a state of affairs as that depicted, men and women have in the past and do often even now find some degree of satisfaction — simply indeed because their types of characters are such as belong to, and have been evolved in accordance with, this relation.

Today, however, there are thousands of women — and everyday more thousands — to whom such a lopsided alliance is detestable; who are determined that they will no longer endure the arrogant lordship and egoism of men, nor countenance in themselves or other women the craft and servility which are the necessary complements of the relation; who see too clearly in the oak-and-ivy marriage its parasitism on the one hand and strangulation on the other to be sensible of any picturesqueness; who feel too that they have capacities and powers of their own which need space and liberty, and some degree of sympathy and help, for their unfolding; and who believe that they have work to do in the world, as important in its own way as any that men do in theirs. Such women have broken into open warfare — not against marriage, but against a marriage which makes true and equal love an impossibility. They feel that as long as women are economically dependent they *cannot* stand up for themselves and insist on those rights which men from stupidity and selfishness will not voluntarily grant them.

On the other hand there are thousands — and one would hope every day more thousands — of men who (whatever their forerunners may have thought) do *not* desire or think it delightful to have a glass continually held up for them to admire themselves in; who look for a partner in whose life and pursuits they can find some interests, rather than for one who has no interest but in them; who think perhaps that they would rather minister than be (like a monkey fed with nuts in a cage) the melancholy object of another person's ministrations; and who at any rate feel that love, in order to be love at all, must be absolutely open and sincere, and free from any sentiment of dependence or inequality. They see that the present cramped condition of women is not only the cause of the false relation between the sexes, but that it is the fruitful source — through its debarment of any common interests — of that fatal boredom of which we have spoken, and which is the bugbear of marriage; and they would gladly surrender all of that masterhood and authority which is supposed to be their due, if they could only get in return something like a frank and level comradeship.

Thus while we see in the present inequality of the sexes an undoubted source of marriage troubles and unsatisfactory alliances, we see also forces at work which are tending to reaction, and to bringing the two nearer again to each other — so that while differentiated they will not perhaps in the future be quite so *much* differentiated as now but only to a degree which will enhance and adorn, instead of destroy, their sense of mutual sympathy.

There is another point which ought to be considered as contributing to the ill-success of many marriages, and which no doubt is closely connected with that just discussed — but which deserves separate treatment. I mean the harshness of the line, the kind of 'ring-fence', which social opinion (at any rate in this country) draws round the married pair with respect to their relations to outsiders. On the one hand, and within the fence, society allows practically the utmost passional excess or indulgence, and condones it; on the other hand (I am speaking of the middling bulk of the people, not of the extreme aristocratic and slum classes) beyond that limit, the slightest familiarity, or any expression of affection which might by any possibility be interpreted as deriving from sexual feeling, is sternly anathematised. Marriage, by a kind of absurd fiction, is represented as an oasis situated in the midst of an arid desert

— in which latter, it is pretended, neither of the two parties is so fortunate as to find any objects of real affectional interest. If they do they have carefully to conceal the same from the other party.

The result of this convention is obvious enough. The married pair, thus *driven* as well as drawn into closest continual contact with each other, are put through an ordeal which might well cause the stoutest affection to quail. To have to spend all your life with another person is severe; but to have all outside personal interests, except of the most abstract kind, debarred, and if there happens to be any natural jealousy in the case, to have it tenfold increased by public interference, is terrible; and yet unless the contracting parties are fortunate enough to be, both of them, of such a temperament that they are capable of strong attachments to persons of their own sex — and this does not always exclude jealousy — such must be their fate.

It is hardly necessary to say, not only how dull a place this makes the home, but also how narrowing it acts on the lives of the married pair. However appropriate the union may be in itself it cannot be good that it should degenerate — as it tends to degenerate so often, and where man and wife are most faithful to each other — into a mere *égoisme à deux*. And right enough no doubt as a great number of such unions actually are, it must be confessed that the bourgeois marriage as a rule, and just in its most successful and pious and respectable form, carries with it an odious sense of Stuffiness and narrowness, moral and intellectual; and that the type of Family which it provides is too often like that which is disclosed when on turning over a large stone we disturb an insect Home that seldom sees the light.

But in cases where the marriage does not happen to be particularly successful or unsuccessful, when perhaps a true but not overpoweringly intense affection is satiated at a needlessly early stage by the continual and unrelieved impingement of the two personalities on each other, then the boredom resulting is something frightful to contemplate — and all the more so because of the genuine affection behind it, which contemplates with horror its own suicide. The weary couples that may be seen at seaside places and pleasure resorts — the respectable working-man with his wife trailing along by his side, or the highly respectable stock-jobber arm-in-arm with his better and larger half — their blank faces, utter want of any common topic of conversation which has not been exhausted a thousand times already, and their obvious relief when the hour comes which will take them back to their several and divided occupations — these illustrate sufficiently what I mean. The curious thing is that jealousy (accentuated as it is by social opinion) sometimes increases in exact proportion to mutual boredom; and there are thousands of cases of married couples leading a cat-and-dog life, and knowing that they weary each other to distraction, who for that very reason dread all the more to lose sight of each other, and thus never get a chance of that holiday from their own society, and renewal of outside interests, which would make a real good time for them possible.

Thus the sharpness of the line which society draws around the pair, and the kind of fatal snap-of-the-lock with which marriage suddenly cuts them off from the world, not only precluding the two from sexual, but even from any openly affectional relations with outsiders, and corroborating the selfish sense of monopoly which each has in the other — these things lead inevitably to the narrowing down of lives, and the blunting of general human interests, to intense mutual ennui, and when (as an escape from these evils) outside relations are covertly indulged in, to prolonged and systematic deceit.

From all which the only conclusion seems to be that marriage must be either alive or dead. As a dead thing it can of course be petrified into a hard and fast formula, but if it is to be a living bond, that living bond must be trusted to, to hold the lovers together; nor be too forcibly stiffened and contracted by private jealousy and public censorship, lest the thing that it would preserve for us perish so, and cease altogether to be beautiful. It is the same with this as with everything else. If we would have a living thing, we must give that thing some degree of liberty — even though liberty bring with it risk. If we would debar all liberty and all risk, then we can have only the mummy and dead husk of the thing.

Thus far I have had the somewhat invidious task, but

perhaps necessary as a preliminary one, of dwelling on the defects and drawbacks of the present marriage system. I am sensible that, with due discretion, some things might have been said, which have not been said, in its praise; its successful, instead of its unsuccessful, instances might have been cited; and taking for granted the dependence of women, and other points which have already been sufficiently discussed, it might have been possible to show that the bourgeois arrangement was on the whole as satisfactory as could be expected. But such a course would neither have been sincere nor have served any practical purpose. In view of the actually changing relations between the sexes, it is obvious that changes in the form of the marriage institution are impending, and the questions which are really pressing on folks' mind are: What are those changes going to be? and, Of what kind do we wish them to be?

Marriage: a Forecast

In answer to the last question it is not improbable that the casual reader might suppose the writer of these pages to be in favour of a general and indiscriminate loosening of all ties — for indeed it is always easy to draw a large inference even from the simplest expression.

But such a conclusion would be a mistake. There is little doubt, I think, that the compulsion of the marriage-tie (whether moral, social, or merely legal) acts beneficially in a considerable number of cases — though it is obvious that the more the compelling force takes a moral or social form and the less purely legal it is, the better; and that any changes which led to a cheap and continual transfer of affections from one object to another would be disastrous both to the character and happiness of a population. While we cannot help seeing that the marriage-relation — in order to become the indwelling-place of Love — must be made far more *free* than it is at present, we may also recognise that a certain amount of external pressure is not (as things are at least) without its uses: that, for instance, it tends on the whole to concentrate affectional experience and romance on one object, and that though this may mean a loss at times in breadth it means a gain in depth and intensity; that, in many cases, if it were not for some kind of bond, the two parties, after their first passion for each other was past, and when the unavoidable period of friction had set in, might in a moment of irritation easily fly apart, whereas being forced for a while to tolerate each other's defects they learn thereby one of the most useful lessons of life — a certain forebearance and gentleness, which as time goes on not unfrequently deepens again into a more satisfying sort of love than the first — a love founded indeed on the first physical intimacy, but concentrated and strengthened by years of linked experience, of twined associations, of shared labours and of mutual forgiveness; and in the third place that the existence of a distinct tie or pledge discredits the easily-current idea that mere pleasure-seeking is to be the object of the association of the sexes — a phantasmal and delusive notion, which if it once got its head, and the bit between its teeth, might soon dash the car of human advance in ruin to the ground.

But having said thus much, it is obvious that external public opinion and pressure are looked upon only as having an *educational* value; and the question arises whether there is beneath this any *reality* of marriage which will ultimately emerge and make itself felt, enabling men and women to order their relations to each other, and to walk freely, unhampered by props or pressures from without.

And it would hardly be worth while writing on this subject, if one did not believe in some such reality. Practically I do not doubt that the more people think about these matters, and the more experience they have, the more they must ever come to feel that there *is* such a thing as a permanent and life-long union — perhaps a many-life-long union — founded on some deep elements of attachment and congruity in character; and the more they must come to prize the constancy and loyalty which rivets such unions, in comparison with the fickle passion which tends to dissipate them.

In all men who have reached a certain grade of evolution, and certainly in almost all women, the deep rousing of the sexual nature carries with it a romance and tender emotional yearning towards the object of affection, which lasts on and is not forgotten, even when the sexual attraction has ceased to be strongly felt. This, in favourable cases, forms the basis of what may almost be called an amalgamated personality. That there should exist one other person in the world towards whom all openness of interchange should establish itself, from whom there should be no concealment; whose body should be as dear to one, in every part, as one's own; with whom there should be no sense of Mine or Thine, in property or possession; into whose mind one's thoughts should naturally flow, as it were to know themselves and to receive a new illumination; and between whom and oneself there should be a spontaneous rebound of sympathy in all the joys and sorrows and experiences of life; such is perhaps one of the dearest wishes of the soul. It is obvious however that this state of affairs cannot be reached at a single leap, but must be the gradual result of years of intertwined memory and affection. For such a union Love must lay the foundation, but patience and gentle consideration and self-control must work unremittingly to perfect the structure. At length each lover comes to know the complexion of the other's mind, the wants, bodily and mental, the needs, the regrets, the satisfactions of the other, almost as his or her own — and without prejudice in favour of self rather than in favour of the other; above all, both parties come to know in course of time, and after perhaps some doubts and trials, that the great want, the great need, which holds them together, is not going to fade away into thin air; but is going to become stronger and more indefeasible as the years go on. There falls a sweet, an irresistible, trust over their relation to each other, which consecrates as it were the double life, making both feel that nothing can now divide; and robbing each of all desire to remain, when death has indeed (or at least in outer semblance) removed the other.[1]

So perfect and gracious a union — even if not always realised — is still, I say, the *bona fide* desire of most of those who have ever thought about such matters. It obviously yields far more and more enduring joy and satisfaction in life than any number of frivolous relationships. It commends itself to the common sense, so to speak, of the modern mind — and does not require, for its proof, the artificial authority of Church and State. At the same time it is equally evident — and a child could understand this — that it requires some rational forbearance and self-control for its realisation, and it is quite intelligible too, as already said, that there may be cases in which some outside pressure, of social opinion at least, if not of actual law, may be helpful for the supplementing or reinforcement of the weak personal self-control of those concerned.

The modern Monogamic Marriage however, certified and sanctioned by Church and State, though apparently directed to this ideal, has for the most part fallen short of it. For in constituting — as in a vast number of cases — a union resting on *nothing* but the outside pressure of Church and State, it constituted a thing obviously and by its nature bad and degrading; while in its more successful instances by a too great exclusiveness it has condemned itself to a fatal narrowness and stuffiness.

Looking back to the historical and physiological aspects of the question it might of course be contended — and probably with some truth — that the human male is, by his nature and needs, polygamous. Nor is it necessary to suppose that polygamy in certain countries and races is by any means so degrading or unsuccessful an institution as some folk would have it to be.[2] But, as Letourneau in his *Evolution of Marriage* points out, the progress of society in the past has on the whole been from confusion to distinction; and we may fairly suppose that with the progress of our own race (for each race no doubt has its special genius in such matters), and as the spiritual and emotional sides of man develop in relation to the physical, there is probably a tendency for our deeper alliances to become more unitary. Though it might be said, that the growing complexity of man's nature would be likely to lead him into more rather than fewer relationships, yet on the other hand it is obvious that as the depth and subtlety of any attachment that will really hold him increases, so does such attachment become more permanent and durable, and less likely to be realised in a number of persons. Woman, on the other hand, cannot be said to be by her physical nature polyandrous as man is polygynous. Though of course there are plenty of examples of women living in a state of polyandry both among savage and civilised peoples, yet her more limited sexual needs, and her long periods of gestation, render one mate physically sufficient for her; while her more clinging affectional nature perhaps accentuates her capacity of absorption in the one.

In both man and woman then we may say that we find a distinct tendency towards the formation of this double unit of wedded life (I hardly like to use the word Monogamy on account if its sad associations) — and while we do not want to stamp such natural unions with any false irrevocability or dogmatic exclusiveness, what we do want is a recognition today of the tendency to their formations as a natural *fact*, independent of any artificial laws, just as one might believe in the natural bias of two atoms of certain different chemical substances to form a permanent compound atom or molecule.

It might not be so very difficult to get quite young people to understand this — to understand that even though they may have to contend with some superfluity of passion in early years, yet that the most deeply-rooted desire within them will probably in the end point to a permanent union with one mate; and that towards this end they must be prepared to use self-control against the aimless straying of their passions, and patience and tenderness towards the realisation of the union when its time comes. Probably most youths and girls, at the age of romance, would easily appreciate this position; and it would bring to them a much more effective and natural idea of the sacredness of Marriage than they ever get from the artificial thunder of the Church and the State on the subject.

No doubt the suggestion of the mere possibility of any added freedom of choice and experience in the relations of the sexes will be very alarming to some people — but it is so, I think, not because they are at all ignorant that men already take to themselves considerable latitude, and that a distinct part of the undoubted evils that accompany that latitude springs from the fact that it is not recognised; not because they are ignorant that a vast number of respectable women and girls suffer frightful calamities and anguish by reason of the utter *inexperience* of sex in which they are brought up and have to live; but because such good people assume that any the least loosening of the formal barriers between the sexes must mean (and must be meant to mean) an utter dissolution of all ties, and the reign of mere licentiousness. They are convinced that nothing but the most unyielding and indeed exasperating strait-jacket can save society from madness and ruin.

To those, however, who can look facts in the face, and who see that as a matter of fact the *reality* of Marriage is coming more and more to be considered in the public mind in comparison with its *formalities*, the first thought will probably be one of congratulation that after such ages of treatment as a mere formality there should be any sense of the reality of the tie left; and the second will be the question how to give this reality its natural form and expression. Having satisfied ourselves that the formation of a more or less permanent double unit is − for our race and time − on the whole the natural and ascendant law of sex-union, slowly and with whatever exceptions establishing and enforcing itself independently of any artificial enactments that exist, then we shall not feel called upon to tear our hair or rend our garments at the prospect of added freedom for the operation of this force, but shall rather be anxious to consider how it may best *be* freed and given room for its reasonable development and growth.

I shall therefore devote the rest of this chapter to this question. And it will probably seem (looking back to what has already been said) that the points which most need consideration, as means to this end, are (1) the furtherance of the freedom and self-dependence of women; (2) the provision of some rational teaching, of heart and of head, for both sexes during the period of youth; (3) the recognition in marriage itself of a freer, more companionable, and less pettily exclusive relationship; and (4) the abrogation or modification of the present odious law which binds people together for *life*, without scruple, and in the most artificial and ill-sorted unions.

It must be admitted that the first point (1) is of basic

importance. As true Freedom cannot be without Love so true Love cannot be without Freedom. You cannot truly give yourself to another, unless you are master or mistress of yourself to begin with. Not only has the general *custom* of the self-dependence and self-ownership of women, in moral, social, and economic respects, to be gradually introduced, but the Law has to be altered in a variety of cases where it lags behind the public conscience in these matters — as in actual marriage, where it still leaves woman uncertain as to her rights over her own body, or in politics, where it still denies to her a voice in the framing of the statutes which are to bind her.

With regard to (2) hardly any one at this time of day would seriously doubt the desirability of giving adequate teaching to boys and girls. That is a point on which we have sufficiently touched, and which need not be farther discussed here. But beyond this it is important, and especially perhaps, as things stand now, for girls — that each youth or girl should personally see enough of the other sex at an early period to be able to form some kind of judgment of his or her relation to that sex and to sex-matters generally. It is monstrous that the first case of sex-glamour — the true nature of which would be exposed by a little experience — should, perhaps for two people, decide the destinies of a lifetime. Yet the more the sexes are kept apart, the more overwhelming does this glamour become, and the more ignorance is there, on either side, as to its nature. No doubt it is one of the great advantages of co-education of the sexes, that it tends to diminish these evils. Co-education, games and sports to some extent in common, and the doing away with the absurd superstition that because Corydon and Phyllis happen to kiss each other sitting on a gate, therefore they must live together all their lives, would soon mend matters considerably. Nor would a reasonable familiarity of this kind between the sexes in youth necessarily mean an increase of casual or clandestine sex-relations. But even if casualties did occur they would not be the fatal and unpardonable sins that they now — at least for girls — are considered to be. Though the recognition of anything like common pre-matrimonial sex-intercourse would probably be foreign to the temper of a northern nation; yet it is open to question whether Society here, in its mortal and fetishistic dread of the thing, has not, by keeping the youth of both sexes in ignorance and darkness and seclusion from each other, created worse ills and suffering than it has prevented, and whether, by giving sexual acts so feverish an importance, it has not intensified the particular evil that it dreaded, rather than abated it.

In the next place (3) we come to the establishment in marriage itself of a freer and broader and more healthy relationship than generally exists at the present time. Attractive in some ways as the ideal of the exclusive attachment is, it runs the fatal risk, as we have already pointed out, of lapsing into a mere stagnant double selfishness. But, after all, Love is fed not by what it takes, but by what it gives; and the love of man and wife too must be fed by the love they give to others. If they cannot come out of their secluded haven to reach a hand to others, or even to give some boon of affection to those who need it more than themselves, or if they mistrust each other in doing so, then assuredly they are not very well fitted to live together.

A marriage, so free, so spontaneous, that it would allow of wide excursions of the pair from each other, in common or even in separate objects of work and interest, and yet would hold them all the time in the bond of absolute sympathy, would by its very freedom be all the more poignantly attractive, and by its very scope and breadth all the richer and more vital — would be in a sense indestructible; like the relation of two suns which, revolving in fluent and rebounding curves, only recede from each other in order to return again with renewed swiftness into close proximity — and which together blend their rays into the glory of one double star.

It has been the inability to see and understand this very simple truth that has largely contributed to the failure of the Monogamic union. The narrow physical passion of jealousy, the petty sense of private property in another person, social opinion, and legal enactments, have all converged to choke and suffocate wedded love in egoism, lust, and meanness. But surely it is not very difficult (for those who believe in the real thing) to imagine so sincere and natural a trust between man and wife that neither would be greatly alarmed at the other's friendship with a third person, nor conclude at once that it meant mere infidelity — or difficult even to imagine that such a friendship might be hailed as a gain by both parties. And if it is quite impossible (to some people) to see in such intimacies anything but a confusion of all sex-relations and a chaos of mere animal desire, we can only reply that this view exposes with fatal precision the kind of thoughts which our present marriage-system engenders. In order to suppose a rational marriage at all one must credit the parties concerned with *some* modicum of real affection, candour, common sense and self-control.

Withal seeing the remarkable and immense *variety* of love in human nature, when the feeling is really touched — how the love-offering of one person's soul and body is entirely different from that of another person's so much so as almost to require another name — how one passion is predominantly physical, and another predominantly emotional, and another contemplative, or spiritual, or practical, or sentimental; how in one case it is jealous and exclusive and in another hospitable and free, and so forth — it seems rash to lay down any very hard and fast general laws for the marriage-relation, or to insist that a real and honourable affection can only exist under this or that special form. It is probably through this fact of the variety of love that it does remain possible, in some cases, for married people to have intimacies with outsiders, and yet to continue perfectly true to each other; and in rare instances for triune and other such relations to be permanently maintained.

We now come to the last consideration, namely (4) the modification of the present law of marriage. It is pretty clear that people will not much longer consent to pledge themselves irrevocably for life as at present. And indeed there are already plentiful indications of a growing change of practice. The more people come to recognise the sacredness and naturalness of the real union, the less will they be willing to bar themselves from this by a lifelong and artificial contract made in their salad days. Hitherto the great bulwark of the existing institution has been the dependence of Women, which has given each woman a direct and most material interest in keeping up the supposed sanctity of the bond — and which has prevented a man of any generosity from proposing an alteration which would have the appearance of freeing himself at the cost of the woman; but as this fact of the dependence of women gradually dissolves out, and as the great fact of the spiritual nature of the true Marriage crystalises into more clearness — so will the formal bonds which bar the formation of the latter gradually break away and become of small import.

Love when felt at all deeply has an element of transcendentalism in it, which makes it the most natural thing in the world for the two lovers — even though drawn together by a passing sex-attraction — to swear eternal troth to each other; but there is something quite diabolic and mephistophelean in the practice of the Law, which creeping up behind, as it were, at this critical moment, and overhearing the two thus pledge themselves, claps its book together with a triumphant bang, and exclaims: 'There now you're married and done for, for the rest of your natural lives.'

What actual changes in Law and Custom the collective sense of society will bring about is a matter which in its detail we cannot of course foresee or determine. But that the drift will be, and must be, towards greater freedom, is pretty clear. Ideally speaking it is plain that anything like a perfect union must have perfect freedom for its condition; and while it is quite supposable that a lover might out of the fulness of his heart *make* promises and give pledges, it is really almost inconceivable that anyone having that delicate and proud sense which marks deep feeling, could possibly *demand* a promise from his loved one. As there is undoubtedly a certain natural reticence in sex, so perhaps the most decent thing in true Marriage would be to say nothing, make no promises — either for a year or a lifetime. Promises are bad at any time, and when the heart is full silence befits it best. Practically, however, since a love of this kind is slow to be realised, since social custom is slow to change, and since the partial dependence and slavery of Women must yet for a while continue, it is likely for such period that formal contracts of some kind will still be made; only these (it may be hoped) will lose their irrevocable and rigid character, and become in some degree adapted to the needs of the contracting parties.

Such contracts might of course, if adopted, be very

various in respect to conjugal rights, conditions of termination, division of property, responsibility for and rights over children, etc. In some cases[3] possibly they might be looked upon as preliminary to a later and more permanent alliance; in others they would provide, for disastrous marriages, a remedy free from the inordinate scandals of the present Divorce Courts. It may, however, be said that rather than adopt any new system of contracts, public opinion in this country would tend to a simple facilitation of Divorce, and that if the latter were made (with due provision for the children) to depend on mutual consent, it would become little more than an affair of registration, and the scandals of the proceeding would be avoided. In any case we think that marriage-contracts, if existing at all, must tend more and more to become matters of private arrangement as far as the relations of husband and wife are concerned, and that this is likely to happen in proportion as woman becomes more free, and therefore more competent to act in her own right. It would be felt intolerable, in any decently constituted society, that the old blunderbuss of the Law should interfere in the delicate relations of wedded life. As it is today the situation is most absurd. On the one hand, having been constituted from times back in favour of the male, the Law still gives to the husband barbarous rights over the person of his spouse; on the other hand, to compensate for this, it rushes in with the farcicalities of Breach of Promise; and in any case, having once pronounced its benediction over a pair — however hateful the alliance may turn out to be to both parties, and however obvious its failure to the whole world — the stupid old thing blinks owlishly on at its own work, and professes itself totally unable to undo the knot which once it tied!

The only point where there is a permanent ground for State-interference — and where indeed there is no doubt that the public authority should in some way make itself felt — is in the matter of the children resulting from any alliance. Here the relation of the pair ceases to be private and becomes social; and the interests of the child itself, and of the nation whose future citizen the child is, have to be safeguarded. Any contracts, or any proposals of divorce, before they could be sanctioned by the public authority, would have to contain satisfactory provisions for the care and maintenance of the children in such casualties as might ensue; nor ought there to be maintained any legal distinction between 'natural' and 'legitimate' children, since it is clear that whatever individuals or society at large may, in the former case, think of the conduct of the parents, no disability should on that account accrue to the child, nor should the parents (if identifiable) be able to escape their full responsibility for bringing it into the world. If those good people who make such a terrific outcry against folk entering into married life without going through all the abracadabra of the Law, *on account of the children*, would try and get the law altered so as to give illegitimate children the same *status* and claim on their parents as legitimate children, it would show more genuinely for their anxiety about the children, and would really be doing something in the interests of positive morality.

If it be objected that private contracts, or such facilitations of Divorce as here spoken of, would simply lead to frivolous experimental relationships entered into and broken off *ad infinitum*, it must be remembered that the responsibility for due rearing and maintenance of children must give serious pause to such a career; and that to suppose that any great mass of the people would find their good in a kind of matrimonial game of General Post is to suppose that the mass of the people have really never acquired or been taught the rudiments of common sense in such matters — is to suppose a case for which there would hardly be a parallel in the customs of any nation or tribe that we know of.

In conclusion, it is evident that no very great change for the better in marriage-relations can take place except as the accompaniment of deep-lying changes in Society at large; and that alterations in the Law alone will effect but a limited improvement. Indeed it is not very likely, as long as the present commercial order of society lasts, that the existing Marriage-laws — founded as they are on the idea of property — *will* be very radically altered, though they may be to some extent. More likely is it that, underneath the law, the common practice will slide forward into newer customs. With the rise of the new society, which is already outlining itself within the structure of the old, many of the difficulties and bugbears, that at present seem to stand in the way of a more healthy relation between the sexes, will of themselves disappear.

It must be acknowledged, however, that though a gradual broadening out and humanising of Law and Custom are quite necessary, it cannot fairly be charged against these ancient tyrants that they are responsible for *all* the troubles connected with sex. There are millions of people today who never could marry happily – however favourable the conditions might be – simply because their natures do not contain in sufficient strength the elements of loving surrender to another; and, as long as the human heart is what it is, there will be natural tragedies arising from the willingness or unwillingness of one person to release another when the former finds that his or her love is not returned.[4] While it is quite necessary that these natural tragedies should not be complicated and multiplied by needless legal interference – complicated into the numberless artificial tragedies which are so exasperating when represented on the stage or in romance, and so saddening when witnessed in real life – still we may acknowledge that, short of the millennium, they will always be with us, and that no institution of marriage alone, or absence of institution, will rid us of them. That entire and unswerving refusal to 'cage' another person, or to accept an affection not perfectly free and spontaneous, which will, we are fain to think, be always more and more the mark of human love, must inevitably bring its own price of mortal suffering with it; yet the Love so gained, whether in the individual or in society, will be found in the end to be worth the pang – and as far beyond the other love, as is the wild bird of Paradise that comes to feed out of our hands unbidden more lovely than the prisoner we shut with draggled wings behind the bars. Love is doubtless the last and most difficult lesson that humanity has to learn; in a sense it underlies all the others. Perhaps the time has come for the modern nations when, ceasing to be children, they may even try to learn it.

Love's Ultimate Meaning

'Silence is golden.' And in human love-affairs especially may
one venture to say that this is true. One often thinks what
divine and beautiful creatures — men and women — there
are all around, how loving and loveable, how gracious in
their charm, how grand in their destiny! — if indeed they
could only be persuaded to remain within that magic circle
of silence. And then alas! one of these divinities begins to
talk — and it is like the fair woman in the fable, out of
whose mouth, whenever she opened it, there jumped a
mouse! The shock is almost more than one can bear. Not
that the shock proceeds from the ignorance displayed — for
the animals and even the angels are deliciously ignorant —
but from the revelations which speech unconsciously makes
of certain states of soul — from the strange *falsity* which is
too often heard in the words, and in the very tones of the
voice.

But Love burns this falsity away. That is why love — even
rude and rampant and outrageous love — does more for the
moralising of poor humanity than a hundred thousand
Sunday schools. It cleans the little human soul from the
clustered lies in which it has nested itself — from the petty
conceits and deceits and cowardices and covert meannesses
— and all the things that fly from the tip of the tongue
directly the mouth opens. It burns and cleans them away,
and leaves the lover speechless — but approximately
honest!

Love is an art, and the greatest of the Arts — and the truth
of it cannot be said in words; that is, in any direct use of
words. You may write a sonnet, of course, to your mistress's
eyebrow; but that is work, that is doing something; it is or is
trying to be, a work of Art — and anyhow your mistress is
not obliged to read it! Or you may take a more decisive line
to express your feelings — by slaying your rival, for
instance, with a sword. That is allowable. But to bore the
lady with protestations, and to demand definite replies (that

is, to tell lies yourself, and to compel her to tell lies), is both foolish and wicked.

The expression of Love is a great art, and it needs man's highest ingenuity and capacity to become skilled in it — but in the public mind it is an art utterly neglected and despised, and it is only by a very few (and those not always the most 'respectable') that it is really cultivated. It is a great art, for the same reason that the expression of Beauty is a great art — for the reason that Love itself (like Beauty) belongs to another plane of existence than the plane of ordinary life and speech.

Speech is man's great prerogative, which differentiates him from the other creatures, and of which he is, especially during the Civilisation period, so proud. The animals do not use it, because they have not arrived at the need of it; the angels do not use it, because they have passed beyond the need. It belongs to the second stage of human consciousness, that which is founded on self-consciousness — on the rooted consciousness of the self as something solitary, apart from others, even antagonistic to them, the centre (strange contradiction in terms!) even among millions of other centres, to which everything has to be referred. The whole of ordinary speech proceeds, and has proceeded, from this kind of self-consciousness — is generated from it, describes it, analyses it, pictures it forth and expresses it — and in the upshot is just as muddled and illusive and unsatisfactory as the thing it proceeds from. And *Love*, which is *not* founded on that kind of self-consciousness — which is in fact the denial of self-centration — has no use for it. Love can only say what it wants by the language of life, action, song, sacrifice, ravishment, death, and the great panorama of creation.

Self-consciousness is fatal to love. The self-conscious lover never 'arrives'. The woman looks at him — and then she looks at something more interesting. And so too the whole modern period of commercial civilisation and Christianity has been fatal to love; for both these great movements have concentrated the thoughts of men on their own individual salvation — Christianity on the salvation of their souls, and commercialism on the salvation of their money-bags. They have bred the self-regarding consciousness in the highest degree; and so — though they may have had their uses and their parts to play in the history of mankind, they have been fatal to the communal spirit in society, and they have been fatal to the glad expression of the soul in private life.

Self-consciousness is fatal to love, which is the true expression of the soul. And it is curious how (for some occult reason) the whole treatment of the subject in our modern world drives it along this painful mirror-lined ravine — how the child is brought up in ignorance and darkness, amid averted faces and frowns, and always the thought of self and its own wickedness is thrust upon it, and never the good and the beauty of the loved one; how the same attitude continues into years of maturity; how somehow self-forgetting heroisms for the sake of love are made difficult in modern life; how even the act of intercourse itself, instead of taking place in the open air — in touch with the great and abounding life of Nature — is generally consummated in closed and stuffy rooms, the symbols of mental darkness and morbidity, and the breeding-ground of the pettier elements of human nature.[1]

We have said that for any lasting alliance, or really big and satisfactory love-affair, plenty of *time* should be given. Perhaps it is a good rule (if any rule in such matters can be good) never to act until one is practically compelled by one's feelings to do so. At any rate, the opposite policy — that of letting off steam, or giving expression to one's sentiments, at the slightest pressure — is an obvious mistake. It gives no chance for the depths to be stirred, or the big forces to come into play. Some degree, too, of self-repression and holding back on the part of the man gives time, as we have said, for the woman's love-feelings to unfold and define themselves. But there is a limit here, and even sympathy and consideration are not always in place with love. There is something bigger — titanic, elemental — which must also have its way. And, after all, Force (if only appropriately used) is the greatest of compliments. I think every woman, in her heart of hearts, *wishes* to be ravished; but naturally it must be by the right man. This is the compliment which is the most grateful of all to receive, because it is most sincere; and this is the compliment which is the most difficult of all to pay — because nothing but the finest instinct can decide when it is appropriate; and if by chance it is inappropriate the cause is *ipso facto* ruined.

Nature prizes strength and power; and so likewise does love, which moves in the heart of Nature and shares her secrets. To regard Love as a kind of refined and delicate altruism is, as we have already hinted, drivelling nonsense. To the lover in general violence is more endurable than indifference; and many lovers are of such temperament that blows and kicks (actual or metaphorical) stimulate and increase their ardour. Even Ovid — who must have been something of a gay dog in his day — says, '*non nisi laesus amo.*'* There is a feeling that at all costs one must come to close quarters with the beloved — if not in the mimic battles of sex, then in quite serious and hostile encounters. To reach the other one somehow, to leave one's mark, one's impress on the beloved — or *vice versa* to *be* reached and to *feel* the impress — is a necessity. I sometimes think that this is the explanation of those strange cases in which a man, mad with love, and unable to satisfy his passion, *kills* the girl he loves. I don't think it is hypothetical jealousy of a possible other lover. I think it is something much more direct than that — the blind urge to reach her very actual self, even if it be only with a knife or bullet. I am sure that this is the explanation of those many cases of unhappily married folk who everlastingly nag at each other, and yet will not on any account part company. They cannot love each other properly, and yet they cannot leave each other alone. A strange madness urges them into continual contact and collision.

But yet possibly there is even something more in the whole thing, on and beyond what is here indicated. In the extraordinary and often agonising experiences attending the matter of 'falling in love', great changes, as we have already suggested, are being wrought in the human being. Astounding inner convulsions and conversions take place — rejections of old habits, adoptions of new ones. The presence of the beloved exercises this magical selective and reconstructive influence — and that independently to a large degree of whether the relation is a happy and 'successful' one, or whether it is contrary and unsuccessful. The main thing is contact, and the coming of one person into touch with the other.

We have seen,* in the case of the Protozoa, the amazing fact of the 'maturation-divisions' and the 'extrusion of polar bodies' as a preparation for conjugation — how, when the two cells which are about to unite approach each other, changes take place already before they come into contact, and half the chromatin elements from one cell are expelled, and half the chromatin elements also from the other. What the exact nature of this division and extrusion may be is a thing not yet known, but there seems every reason to believe that it is of such a character as to leave the residual elements on both sides complementary to one another — so that when united they shall restore the total attributes of the race-life, only perhaps in a new and unprecedented combination. The Protozoa in fact 'prepare' themselves for conjugation and realisation of the race-life, by casting out certain elements which would interfere with this realisation. And we may well ask ourselves whether in the case of Man the convulsions and conversions of which we have spoken have not the same purpose and result, or something much resembling it. Whatever really takes place in the unseen world in the case of human Love, we cannot but be persuaded that it is something of very far-reaching and long-lasting import; and to find that the process should often involve great pain to the little mortals concerned seems readily conceivable and by no means unnatural.

The complementary nature of love is a thing which has often been pointed out — how the dark marries the fair, the tall the short, the active the lethargic, and so forth. Schopenhauer, in his *Welt als Wille und Vorstellung* has made a special study of this subject. Plato, Darwin, and others have alluded to it. It seems as if, in Love, the creature — to use Dante Rosetti's expression — feels a 'poignant thirst and exquisite hunger' for that other one who will supply the elements wanting in himself, who will restore the balance, and fill up the round of the race ideal. And as every one of us is eccentric and out of balance and perfection on one side or another, so it almost seems as if for every one there must be, on the other side, a complementary character to be found — who needs *something* at any rate of what *we* can supply. And this consideration may yield us the motto — however painfully conscious we may be of our own weaknesses and deficiencies and follies and vices and general ungainliness — the motto of 'Never despair!' Innocent folk, whose studies of this subject have been chiefly perhaps derived from penny novelettes — are sometimes inclined to think that love is a stereotyped affair occurring in a certain pattern and under certain conditions between the ages of 18 and 35; and that if you are not between these ages and are not fortunate enough to have a good complexion and a nicely formed aquiline nose, you may as well abandon hope. They suppose that there is a certain thing called a Man, and another certain thing called a Woman, and that the combination of these two forms a third quite stereotyped thing called Marriage, *and there is an end of it*.

But by some kind of Providential arrangement it appears that the actual facts are very different — that there are really hundreds of thousands of different kinds of men, and hundreds of thousands of different kinds of women, and consequently thousands of millions of different kinds of marriage; that there are no limits of grace or comeliness, or of character and accomplishment, or even of infirmity or age, within which love is obliged to move; and that there is no defect, of body or mind, which is of necessity a bar — which may not even (to some special other person) become an object of attraction. Thus it is that the ugly and deformed have no great difficulty in finding their mates — as a visit to the seaside on a bank-holiday speedily convinces us; a squint may be a positive attraction to some, as it is said to have been to the philosopher Descartes, and marks of smallpox indispensable to others;[2] while I have read of a case somewhere, where the man was immediately stirred to romance by the sight of a wooden leg in a woman![3]

But apart from these extreme instances which may be due to special causes, the general principle of compensation through opposites is very obvious and marked. The fluffy and absurd little woman is selected by a tall and statuesque grenadier; the tall and statuesque lady is made love to by a man who has to stand on a chair to kiss her; the society elegant takes to a snuffy and preposterous professor; the bookish scholar (as in *Jude the Obscure*) to a mere whore; the clever beauty (as in *L'homme qui rit*) to a grinning clown; and of course the 'wicked' man is always saved by the saintly woman. The masculine, virago-like woman, on the other hand, finds a man who positively *likes* being beaten with a stick; and the miaowling, aimlessly amiable female gets a bully for a husband (and one can only say, 'Serve them both right')... Finally, the well-formed aquiline nose insists on marrying a pug nose — and this apparently quite regardless of what the other bodily and mental parts may be, or what they may want.

Everyone knows cases of quite young men who only love women of really advanced age, beyond the limit of child-birth; and these are curious because they seem to point to impelling forces in love beyond and independent of genera-tion and race-perpetuation, and therefore lying outside of the Schopenhauerian explanations. And similarly we all know cases of young girls who are deadly earnest in their affection for quite old men, men who might well be their fathers or grandfathers, but hardly, one would think, their husbands. In these cases it looks as if the young thing needs and seeks a parent as well as a lover — the two in one, combined. And where such love is returned, it is returned in a kind of protective love, rather than an amative love — or at any rate as a love in which the protective and amative characters are closely united.

Similarly there are numbers of cases in which mature or quite grown men and women only love (passionately and devotedly) boys and girls of immature age — their love for them ceasing from its ardour and intensity when the objects of devotion reach the age, say, of twenty or twenty-one. And in many of these cases the love is ardently returned. Here, again, it is evidently not a case of generation or race-perpetuation, but simply of compensation — the young thing requiring the help and protection of the older, and the older requiring an outlet for the protective instinct — a case of exchange of essences and qualities which (if at all decently and sensibly managed) might well go to the building up of a full and well-rounded life on either side.

In all these cases (and the above are of course only samples out of thousands) we seem to see an effort of the race-life to restore its total quality — to restore it through the operation of love — either by completing and rounding out the life of the individuals concerned, or by uniting some of their characteristics in the progeny. I say 'seem to see', because we cannot well suppose that this gives a *complete* account of the matter, or that it explains the whole meaning of Love; but it at any rate suggests an important aspect of the question. The full quality of the race-life is always building itself up and restoring itself in this manner. A process of Regeneration is always going on. And this process, as suggested before, is more fundamental even that Generation — or it is a process of which Generation is only one department.

Regeneration is the key to the meaning of love — to be in the first place born again *in* some one else or *through* some one else; in the second place only, to be born again through a child. As in the Protozoa, so among human beings, generation alone can hardly be looked upon as the primary object of conjugation; for, among the latter, out of myriads of unions vast numbers are as a matter of fact infertile, and a considerable percentage (as indicated above) are quite *necessarily* infertile, and yet these infertile unions are quite as close, and the love concerned in them quite as intense and penetrating, as in the case of the fertile one. 'If a girl were free to choose according to her inclinations,' says Florence Farr in an eloquent plea for the economic independence of women,[4] 'there is practically no doubt that she would choose the right father for her child, however badly she might choose a life-long companion for herself.' In this passage the authoress seems to suggest (perhaps following Schopenhauer) that the generation of a perfect child is the one main even though unconscious purpose of love-union, and that the individual parent-lives may instinctively be sacrificed for this object. And there no doubt is so far truth in this, that the tremendous forces of love often pay little respect to the worldly conveniences and compatibilities of the lovers themselves, and that often (as indeed also among the Protozoa) the parent's life is rudely and ruthlessly sacrificed for the birth of the next generation. Still, even so, I think the statement as put here is risky, both as a matter of fact and as a matter of theory. Would it not be more correct or less risky to say: 'If a girl were free to choose, she would choose the man who most completely compensated and rounded out her own qualities, physical and mental (and *so* would be likely to get her a fine babe), even though he might not prove the best of companions'?

It is curious, as we have suggested before, how married folk often quarrel to desperation on the surface, and yet seem to have a deep and permanent hold on each other — returning together again even after separation. It seems in these cases as if they mutually obtained a stimulus from each other, even by their strife, which they could not get elsewhere. *Irae amantium redintegratio amoris.* [*] The idea, too, that the great and primal object of union is to be sought in *the next generation* has something unsatisfactory about it. Why not in *this* generation? Why should the blessedness of mankind always be deferred to posterity? It is not merely, I take it, the *perpetuation* of the race which is the purpose of love, but the perfection of the race, the completeness and adequacy of its self-expression, which love may make possible to-day just as well as to-morrow. Ellen Key, in that fine book, *Liebe und Ehe*,[5] expresses this well when she says: 'Love seeks union, not only in connection with the creation of a new being, but also because two beings *through one another* may become a new being, and a greater than either could be of itself alone.'

The complementary nature of sex-attraction was made much of by that youthful genius Otto Weininger, who in his book, *Sex and Character*,[6] has a chapter on the laws of Sexual Attraction; in which, in the true German manner, he not only gives an algebraic formula for the different types of men and women, but a formula also for the force of attraction between any two given individuals — which latter of course becomes infinite when the two individuals are exactly complementary to each other! Dr. Magnus Hirschfeld, in his very interesting work, *Die Transvestiten*,[7] goes even more into detail than does Weininger on the subject of the variations of human type in special regard to sex-characteristics. Sex-characteristics, he explains, may be divided into four groups, of which two are physiological, namely the primary characteristics (the sex organs and adjuncts) and the secondary (the hair, the voice, the breasts, and so forth); and two are psychological or related (like love-sentiment, mental habit, dress, and so forth). Each of the four groups includes about four different elements; so that altogether he tabulates sixteen elements in the human being — each of which may vary independently of the other fifteen, and take on at least three possible forms, either distinctly masculine, distinctly feminine, or intermediate. Calculating up the number of different types which these variations would thus give rise to, he arrives at the figure 43,046,721! — which figure, I think we may say, we need not analyse further, since it is certainly quite large enough for all practical purposes! And really though we may mock a little at these fanciful divisions and dissections of human nature, they do help us to realise the enormous, the astounding number of varieties of which it is susceptible. And if again we consider that among the supposed forty-three millions each variety would have its counter type or complementary individual, then we realise the enormous number of perfect unions which would be theoretically possible, and the enormous number of distinct and different ways in which the race-life could thus find adequate and admirable expression for itself.

However, we are here getting into a somewhat abstract region. To return to the practical, the complementary idea certainly seems to account for much of human union; for though there are but few cases in which the qualities of the uniting parties are really quite complementary to each other, yet it is obvious that each person tends to seek and admire attributes in the other which he himself possesses only in small degree. At the same time, it must not be forgotten that *some* common qualities and common ground are necessary as a basis for affection, and that sympathy and agreement in like interests and habits are at least as powerful a bond as admiration of opposites. It sometimes happens that there are immense romances between people of quite different classes and habits of life, or of quite different race and colour; and they see, for the moment, flaming ideals and wonder-worlds in each other. But unions in such cases are doubtful and dangerous, because so often the common ground of sympathy and mutual understanding will be too limited; and hereditary instincts and influences, deep-lying and deep-working, will call the wanderers away, even from the star which they seek to follow.

Sympathy with and understanding of the person one lives with must be cultivated to the last degree possible, because it is a condition of any real and permanent alliance. And it may even go so far (and should go so far) as a frank understanding and tolerance of such person's *other* loves. After all, it seldom happens, with any one who has more than one or two great interests in life, that he finds a mate who can sympathise with or understand them all. In that case a certain portion of his personality is left out in the cold, as it were; and if this is an important portion it seems perfectly natural for him to seek for a mate or a lover on that side too. Two such loves are often perfectly compatible and reconcilable — though naturally one will be the dominant love, and the other subsidiary, and if such secondary loves are good-humouredly tolerated and admitted, the effect will generally be to confirm the first and original alliance all the more.

All this, however, does not mean that a man can well be 'in love' with two women, for instance, at the same time. To love is a very different thing from being 'in love'; and the latter indicates a torrent-rush of feeling which necessarily can only move towards one person at a time. (A standing flood of water may embrace and surround several islands, but it cannot very well *flow* in more than one direction at once.) But this torrent-rush does not last forever, and in due time it subsides into the quiescent and lake-like stage — unless indeed it runs itself out and disappears altogether.

Against this running out and disappearance it is part of the Art of Love to be able to guard. It has sometimes been argued that familiarity is of necessity fatal; and that it is useless to contend against this sinister tendency implanted in the very nature of love itself. But this contention contains only a very partial truth. It is true that in physical love there is a certain physical polarity which, like electric polarity, tends to equate itself by contact. The exchange of essences — which we saw as a chief phenomenon of conjugation, from the protozoa upwards — completes itself in any given case after a given time; and after that becomes comparatively quiescent. The same with the exchange of mental essences. Two people, after years, cease to exchange their views and opinions with the same vitality as at first; they lose their snap and crackle with regard to each other — and naturally, because they now know each other's minds perfectly, and have perhaps modified them mutually to the point of likeness. But this only means, or should mean in a healthy case, that their interest in each other has passed into another plane, that the *venue* of Love has been removed to another court. If something has been lost in respect of the physical rush and torrent, and something in respect of the mental breeze and sparkle, great things have been gained in the ever-widening assurance and confidence of spiritual unity, and a kind of lake-like calm which indeed reflects the heavens. And under all, still in the depths, one may be conscious of a subtle flow and interchange, yet going on between the two personalities and relating itself to some deep and unseen movements far down in the heart of Nature.

Of course for this continuance and permanence of love there must be a certain amount of continence, not only physical, but on the emotional plane as well. Anything like nausea, created by excess on either of these planes, has to be avoided. New subjects of interest, and points of contact, must be sought; temporary absences rather encouraged than depreciated; and lesser loves, as we have already hinted, not turned into gages of battle. Few things, in fact, endear one to a partner so much as the sense that one can freely confide to him or her one's *affaires de coeur*; and when a man and wife have reached this point of confidence in their relation to each other, it may fairly then be said (however shocking this may sound to the orthodox) that their union is permanent and assured.

Nothing can, in the longer enduring values of love, well take the place of some such chivalrous mutual consideration which reaches the finest fibres of the heart, and offers a perfect freedom even there. Ellen Key — to quote her *Ueber Liebe und Ehe*[8] again — says, 'Fidelity [in love] can never be promised, but may be *won afresh* every day', and she continues, 'It is sad that this truth — which was clear enough to the chivalrous sentiment of the old courts of Love — must still today be insisted on. One of the reasons, in fact, which these courts gave, why love was not compatible with Marriage, was "that the wife could never expect from her husband the fine consideration that the Lover is bound to exhibit, because the latter only receives as a favour what the husband takes as his right."' To preserve love through years and years with this halo of romance still about it, and this tenderness of devotion which means a daily renewed gift of freedom, is indeed a great Art. It is a great and difficult Art, but one which is assuredly 'worth while'.

The passion altogether, and in all its aspects, is a wonderful thing; and perhaps, as remarked before, the less said about it, the better! When people — I would say — come (not without clatter) and offer you their hearts, do not pay *too* much attention. What they offer may be genuine, or it may not — they themselves probably do not know. Nor do *you* also fall into a like mistake, offering something which you have not the power to give — or to withhold. Silence and Time alone avail. These things lie on the knees of the gods; which place — though it may seem, as someone has said, 'rather cold and uncomfortable' — is perhaps the best place for them.

The Free Society

Taking, finally, a somewhat wider outlook over the whole subject of the most intimate human relations than was feasible in the foregoing chapters, we may make a few general remarks.

One of the great difficulties in the way of arriving at any general understanding on questions of sex — and one which we have already had occasion to note — is the extraordinary diversity of feeling and temperament which exists in these matters. Needless to say, this is increased by the reserve, natural or artificial, which so seldom allows people to express their sentiments quite freely. In the great ocean there are so many currents, cold and warm, fresh, and salt, and brackish; and each one thinks that the current in which he lives is the whole ocean. The man of the world hardly understands, certainly does not sympathise with, the recluse or ascetic — and the want of appreciation is generally returned; the maternal, the sexual, and the philanthropic woman, are all somewhat unintelligible to each other; the average male and the average female approach the great passion from totally different sides, and are continually at odds over it; and again both of these great sections of humanity fail entirely to understand that other and well-marked class of persons, spoken of in the last chapter,* whose love-attraction is (inborn) towards their own sex; and indeed hardly recognise the existence of such a class, although as a matter of fact it is a large and important one in every community. In fact, all these differences have hitherto been so little the subject of impartial study that we are still amazingly in the dark about them.

When we look back to History, and the various customs of the world in different races and tribes and at different periods of time, we seem to see these natural divergencies of human temperament reflected in the extraordinary diversity of practices that have obtained and been recognised. We see that, in some cases, the worship of sex took its place beside the worship of the gods; and — what appears equally strange — that the orgiastic rites and saturnalia of the early world were intimately connected with religious feeling; we find that, in other cases, asceticism and chastity and every denial of the flesh were glorified and looked upon as providing the only way to the heavenly kingdom; we discover that marriage has been instituted and defined and sanctioned in endless forms, each looked upon as the only moral and possible form in its own time and country; and that the position of women under these different conditions has varied in the most remarkable way — that in some of the primitive societies where group-marriages[1] of one kind or another prevailed their dignity and influence were of the highest; that under some forms of Monogamy, as among the Nagas of Bengal,[2] women have been abjectly degraded, while under other forms, as in Ancient Egypt and the later Roman Empire, they have been treated with respect, and so forth. We cannot fail, I say, to recognise the enormous diversity of practice which has existed over the world in this matter of the relations of the sexes; nor, I may add, can we venture — if we possess any sense of humanity — to put our finger down finally on any one custom or institution, and say, Here alone is the right way.

On the contrary, it seems to me probable that, broadly speaking, a really free Society will accept and make use of all that has gone before. If, as we have suggested, historical forms and customs are the indication of tendencies and instincts which still exist among us, then the question is, not the extinction of these tendencies, but the finding of the right place and really rational expression for them. That the various customs of past social life do subsist on beneath the surface of modern society, we know well enough; and it seems likely that society in the future will have to recognise and to a certain extent transform these. In fact, in recognising it will inevitably transform, for it will bring them out from darkness into light, and from the old conditions and surroundings of the past societies into the new conditions of the modern. Polygamy, for instance, or some related form of union, supposing it really did spontaneously and naturally arise in a society which gave perfect freedom and independence to women in their relation to men, would be completely different in character from the old-world polygamy, and would cease to act as a degrading influence on women, since it would be the spontaneous expression of their attachment to each other and to a common husband; Monogamy, under similar circumstances, would lose its narrowness and stuffiness; and the life of the Hetaira, that is of the woman who chooses to be the companion of more than one man might not be without dignity, honour, and sincere attachment.

Again it is easy to see, if the sense of cleanness in sex ever does come in, if the physical body ever becomes clean (which it certainly is not now-a-days), clean and beautiful and accepted, within and without — and this of course it can only be through a totally changed method of life, through pure and clean food, nakedness to a large extent, and a kind of saturation with the free air and light of heaven; and if the mental and moral relation ever becomes clean, which can only be with the freedom of woman and the sincerity of man, and so forth; it is easy to see how entirely all this would alter our criticism of the various sex-relations, and our estimate of their place and fitness.

In the wild and even bacchanalian festivals of all the earlier nations, there was an element of Nature-sex-mysticism which has become lost in modern times, or quite unclean and depraved; yet we cannot but see that this element is a vital and deep-lying one in humanity, and in some form or other will probably reassert itself. On the other hand, in the Monkish and other ascetic movements of Christian or pre-Christian times, with their efforts towards a proud ascendancy over the body, there was (commonly sneered at though it may be in the modern West) an equally vital and important truth,[3] which will have to be rehabilitated. The practices of former races and times, however anomalous they may sometimes appear to us, were after all in the main the expression of needs and desires which *had* their place in human nature, and which still for the most part have their place there, even though overlaid and suppressed beneath existing convention; and who knows, in all the stifled longings of thousands and thousands of hearts, how the great broad soul of Humanity — which reaches to and accepts all times and races — is still ever asserting herself and swelling against the petty bonds of this or that age? The nearer Society comes to its freedom and majority the more lovingly will it embrace this great soul within it, and recognising in all the customs of the past the partial efforts of that soul to its own fulfilment will refuse to deny them, but rather seek, by acceptance and reunion, to transform and illumine them all.

Possibly, to some, these remarks will only suggest a return to general confusion and promiscuity; and of course to such people they will seem inconsistent with what has been said before on the subject of the real Marriage and the tendency of human beings, as society evolves, to seek more and more sincerely a lifelong union with their chosen mate; but no one who thinks twice about the matter could well make this mistake. For the latter tendency, that namely 'from confusion to distinction',is in reality the tendency of all evolution, and cannot be set aside. It is in the very nature of Love that as it realises its own aim it should rivet always more and more towards a durable and distinct relationship, nor rest till the permanent mate and equal is found. As human beings progress their relations to each other must become much *more* definite and distinct instead of less so — and there is no likelihood of society in its onward march lapsing backward, so to speak, to formlessness again.

But it is just the advantage of this onward movement towards definiteness that it allows — as in the evolution of all organic life — of more and more *differentiation* as the life rises higher in the scale of existence. If society should at any future time recognise — as we think likely it will do — the variety of needs of the human heart and of human beings, it will not therefore confuse them, but will see that these different needs indicate different functions, all of which may have their place and purpose. If it has the good sense to tolerate a Nature-festival now and then, and a certain amount of animalism let loose, it will not be so foolish as to be unable to distinguish this from the deep delight and happiness of a permanent spiritual mating; or if it recognises in some case, a woman's temporary alliance with a man for the sake of obtaining a much-needed child, it will not therefore be so silly as to mark her down for life as a common harlot. It will allow in fact that there *are* different forms and functions of the love-sentiment, and while really believing that a lifelong comradeship (possibly with little of the sexual in it) is the most satisfying form, will see that a cast-iron Marriage-custom which, as today, expects two people either to live eternally in the same house and sit on opposite sides of the same table, or else to be strangers to each other — and which only recognises two sorts of intimacy, orthodox and criminal, wedded and adulterous — is itself the source of perpetual confusion and misapprehension.

No doubt the Freedom of Society in this sense, and the possibility of a human life which shall be the fluid and ever-responsive embodiment of true Love in all its variety and manifestation, goes with the Freedom of Society in the economic sense. When mankind has solved the industrial problem so far that the products of our huge mechanical forces have become a common heritage, and no man or woman is the property-slave of another, then some of the causes which compel prostitution, property-marriage, and other perversions of affection, will have disappeared; and in such economically free society human unions may at last take place according to their own inner and true laws.

Hitherto we have hardly thought whether there were any inner laws or not; our thoughts have been fixed on the outer; and the Science of Love, if it may so be called, has been strangely neglected. Yet if, putting aside for the moment all convention and custom, one will look quietly within himself, he will perceive that there are most distinct and inviolable inner forces, binding him by different ties to different people, and with different and inevitable results according to the quality and the nature of the affection bestowed – that there is in fact in that world of the heart a kind of cosmical harmony and variety, and an order almost astronomical.

This is noticeably true of what may be called the planetary law of distances in the relation of people to one another. For of some of the circle of one's acquaintance it may be said that one loves them cordially at a hundred miles' distance; of others that they are dear friends at a mile; while others again are indispensable far nearer than that. If by any chance the friend whose planetary distance is a mile is forced into close quarters, the only result is a violent development of repulsion and centrifugal force, by which probably he is carried even beyond his normal distance, till such time as he settles down into his right place; while on the other hand if we are separated for a season from one who by right is very near and who we know belongs to us, we can bide our time, knowing that the forces of return will increase with the separation. How marked and definite these personal distances are may be gathered from considering how largely the art of life consists in finding and *keeping* them, and how much trouble arises from their confusion, and from the way in which we often only find them out after much blundering and suffering and mutual recrimination.

So marked indeed are these and other such laws that they sometimes suggest that there really is a cosmic world of souls, to which we all belong — a world of souls whose relations are eternal and clearly-defined; and that our terrestrial relations are merely the working-out and expression of far antecedent and unmodifiable facts — an idea which for many people is corroborated by the curious way in which, often at the very first sight, they become aware of their exact relation to a newcomer. In some cases this brings with it a strange sense of previous intimacy, hard to explain; and in other cases, not so intimate, it still will seem to fix almost instantaneously the exact propinquity of the relation

— so that though in succeeding years, or even decades of years, the mutual acquaintanceship may work itself out with all sorts of interesting and even unexpected developments and episodes, yet this *mean distance* does not vary during the whole time, so to speak, by a single hair's breadth.

Is it possible, we may ask (in the light of such experiences), that there really *is* a Free Society in another and deeper sense than that hitherto suggested — a society to which we all in our inmost selves consciously or unconsciously belong — the Rose of souls that Dante beheld in Paradise, whose every petal is an individual, and an individual only through its union with all the rest — the early Church's dream, of an eternal Fellowship in heaven and on earth — the Prototype of all the brotherhoods and communities that exist on this or any planet; and that the innumerable selves of men, united in the one Self, members of it and of one another (like the members of the body) stand in eternal and glorious relationship bound indissolubly together? We know of course that the reality of things cannot be adequately expressed by such phrases as these, or by any phrases, yet possibly some such conception comes as near the truth as any *one* conception can; and, making use of it, we may think that our earthly relations are a continual attempt — through much blindness and ineffectualness and failure — to feel after and to find these true and permanent relations to others.

Surely in some subtle way if one person sincerely love another, heart and soul, that other becomes a part of the lover, indissolubly wrought into his being.[4] Mentally the two grow and become compact together. No thought that the lover thinks, no scene that he looks on, but the impress of his loved one in some way is on it — so that as long as he exists (here or anywhere) with his most intimate self that other is threaded and twined inseparable. So clinging is the relation. Perhaps in the outer world we do not always see such relations quite clear, and we think when death or other cause removes the visible form from us that the hour of parting has come. But in the inner world it is clear enough, and we divine that we and our mate are only two little petals that grow near each other on the great Flower of

Eternity; and that it is because we are near each other in that unchanging world, that in the world of change our mortal selves are drawn together, and will be drawn always, wherever and whenever they may meet.

But since the petals of the immortal Flower are by myriads and myriads, so have we endless lessons of soul-relationship to learn — some most intimate, others doubtless less so, but all fair and perfect — so soon as we have discovered *what* these relationships really are, and are in no confusion of mind about them. For even those that are most distant are desirable, and have the germ of love in them, so soon as they are touched by the spirit of Truth (which means the fearless statement of the life which is in us, in poise against the similar statement of life in others); since, indeed, the spirit of Truth *is* the life of the whole, and only the other side of that Love which binds the whole together.

Looking at things in this light it would seem to us that the ideal of terrestrial society for which we naturally strive is that which would embody best these enduring and deep-seated relations of human souls; and that every society, as far as it is human and capable of holding together, is in its degree a reflection of the celestial City. Never is the essential, real, Society quite embodied in any mundane Utopia, but ever through human history is it working unconsciously in the midst of moral affairs and impelling towards an expression of itself.

At any rate, and however all this may be, the conclusion is that the *inner* laws in these matters — the inner laws of the sex-passion, of love, and of all human relationship — must gradually appear and take the lead, since they alone are the powers which can create and uphold a rational society; and that the outer laws — since they are dead and lifeless things — must inevitably disappear.

Real love is only possible in the freedom of society; and freedom is only possible when love is a reality. The subjecttion of sex-relations to legal conventions is an intolerable bondage, but of course it is a bondage inescapable as long as people are slaves to a merely physical desire. The two slaveries in fact form a sort of natural counterpoise, the one to the other. When love becomes sufficient of a reality to hold the sex-passion as its powerful yet willing servant, the absurdity of Law will be at an end.

Surely it is not too much to suppose that a reasonable society will be capable of seeing these and other such things; that it will neither on the one hand submit to a cast-iron system depriving it of all grace and freedom of movement, nor on the other hand be in danger of falling into swamps of promiscuity; but that it will have the sense to recognise and establish the innumerable and delicate distinctions of relation which build up the fabric of a complex social organism. It will understand perhaps that sincere Love is, as we have said, a real fact and its own justification, and that however various or anomalous or unusual may be the circumstances and combinations under which it appears, it demands and has to be treated by society with the utmost respect and reverence — as a law unto itself, probably the deepest and most intimate law of human life, which only in the most exceptional cases, if at all, may public institutions venture to interfere with.

In all these matters it is surprising today what children we are — how we take the innumerable flowers and try to snip and shape all their petals and leaves to one sorry pattern, or how with a kind of grossness we snatch at and destroy in a few moments the bloom and beauty which are rightfully undying. Perhaps it will only be for a society more fully grown than ours to understand the wealth and variety of affectional possibilities which it has within itself, and the full enchantment of the many relations in which the romance of love by a tender discrimination and aesthetic continence is preserved for years and decades of years in, as it were, a state of evergrowing perfection.

Remarks and Notes

On Jealousy

A great disturber of the celestial order of Love is Jealousy —
that brand of physical passion which carried over into the
emotional regions of the mind will sometimes rage there
like a burning fire. One may distinguish two kinds of
jealousy, a natural and an artificial. The first arises perhaps
from the real uniqueness of the relationship between two
persons — at any rate as it appears to one of them — and the
endeavour to stamp this uniqueness on the whole relationship, sexual and moral — especially on the sexual relationship. This kind of jealousy seems in a sense natural and
normal, at any rate for a period; but when the personal
relation between the two parties has been fully and confes-
sedly established, and is no more endangered, the feeling
does often I think (equally naturally) die away; and may do
so quite well without damaging the intimacy and uniqueness of the alliance. This jealousy is felt with terrible keen-
ness and intensity by lovers before the consummation of
their passion, and perhaps for a year or two afterwards —
though it may be protracted rather indefinitely in the case
where the alliance, on one side at any rate, is not quite
satisfactory.

The other kind of jealousy rests on the sense of property,
and is the kind that is often felt by the average husband and
wife long after honeymooning days — by the husband not
because of his especial devotion to his partner, but because
he is furious at the idea of her disposing as she likes with
what he considers *his property*; and by the wife because she
is terrified at the thought that her matrimonial clothes-peg,
from which depend all her worldly prospects, may vanish
away or become the peg for another woman's clothes. This
kind of jealousy is more especially the product of immediate
social conditions, and is in that sense artificial. Though
probably not quite so heart-rendering as the other, it is often
passionate enough, and lasts on indefinitely, like a chronic
disease.

In early times, with the more communistic feeling of primitive societies, and with customs (like group-marriage) which allowed some latitude in sex-relation, jealousy though strong was not probably a very great force. But with the growth of individualism in life and love, with the rise of the sense of property under civilisation and the accentuation of every personal feeling in what may be called the *cellular* state of society, the passion became one of fearful and convulsive power and fury; as is borne witness to by numberless dramas and poems and romances of the historical period. In the communism and humanism of the future, as the sense of property declines, and as Love rises more and more out of mere blind confusion with the sex-act, we may fairly hope that the artificial jealousy will disappear altogether, and that the other form of the passion will subside again into a comparatively reasonable human emotion.

On the Family

A change somewhat similar to that in the position of Jealousy has taken place in the role of the Family during the progress of society into and through the period of civilisation. In the primitive human association the Family was large in extent, and in outline vague; the boundaries of kinship, in cases where the woman might have several husbands, or the husband several wives, were hard to trace; paternal feeling was little or not at all developed; and the whole institution rested on the maternal instinct of care for the young. In the middle societies of civilisation, and with monogamic arrangements, the Family grew exceedingly definite in form and circumscribed in extent. The growth of property and competition, and the cellular system of society, developed a kind of warfare between the units of which society was composed. These units were families. The essential communism and fraternity of society at large was dwarfed now and contracted into the limits of the family; and this institution acquired an extraordinary importance from the fact that it alone kept alive and showed in miniature (intensified by the darkness and chaos and warfare outside) the sacred fire of human fraternity. So great was this importance in fact that the Holy Family became one of the central religious conceptions of the civilised period, and it was commonly thought that society owed its existence to the Family — instead of, as was the case, the truth being the reverse, namely that the Family was the condensation of the principle which had previously existed, though diffused and unconscious, throughout society.

The third and future stage is of course easy to see — that is, the expansion again of the conception of the family *consciously* into the fraternity and communism of society. It is obvious that as this takes place the family will once more lose its definition of outline and merge more and more again with the larger social groups in which it is embedded — but not into the old barbaric society in which the conception of human fellowship lay diffused and only dimly auroral, but into the newer society in which it shall be clear and all-illuminating as the sun.

Thus the Family institution in its present form and as far as that form may be said to be artificial will doubtless pass away. Nevertheless there remains of course, and must remain, its natural or physiological basis — namely the actual physical relation of the parents to each other and to the child. One perhaps of the most valuable results of the Monogamic family institution under civilisation has been the development of the paternal feeling for the child, which in primitive society was so weak. Today the love of man and wife for each other is riveted, as it never was in ancient days, by the tender beauty of the child-face, in which each parent sees with strange emotion his own features blended with the features of his loved one — the actual realisation of that union which the lovers so desired, and which yet so often seemed to them after all *not* consummated. The little prolongation of oneself, carrying in its eyes the star-look of another's love, and descending a stranger into the world to face a destiny all its own, touches the most personal and mortal-close feelings (as well as perhaps the most impersonal) of the heart. And while to-day this sight often reconciles husband and wife to the legal chains which perforce hold them together, in a Free Society, we may hope, it will more often be the sign and seal of a love which neither requires nor allows any kind of mechanical bond.

On Preventive Checks to Population

This is no doubt a complex and difficult subject. Nature from far back time has provided in the most determined and obstinate way for the perpetuation of organic life, and has endowed animals, and even plants, with a strong sexual instinct. By natural selection this instinct tends, it would seem, to be accentuated; and in the higher animals and man it sometimes attains a pitch almost of ferocity. In civilised man this effect is further increased by the intensity of *consciousness*, which reflects desire on itself, as well as by collateral conditions of life and luxury.

In the animal and plant world generally, and up to the realm of Man, Nature appears to be perfectly lavish in the matter, and careless of the waste of seed and of life that may ensue, provided her object of race-propagation is attained; and naturally when the time arrives that Man, objecting to this waste, faces up to the problem, he finds it no easy one to solve.

And not only Man (the male) objects to lower Nature's methods of producing superfluous individuals only to kill them off again in the struggle for existence; but Woman objects to being a mere machine for perpetual reproduction.

For meeting this difficulty, the only way commonly proposed — short of continence and self-control almost amounting to total abstinence — is the adoption of some kind of artificial preventatives to conception. But it must be acknowledged that artificial checks to population are for the most part very unsatisfactory. Their uncertainty, their desperate matter-of-factness, so fatal to real feeling, the probability that they are in one way or another dangerous or harmful, and then their one-sidedness, since here — as so often in matters of sex — the man's satisfaction is largely at the cost of the woman: all these things are against them. One method however, that which consists in selecting, for sexual congress, a certain part of the woman's monthly cycle, can hardly be called artificial, and is altogether the least open to the objections cited. Its success truly is not absolutely certain, but is perhaps sufficiently nearly so for the general purpose of regulating the family; and if the method involves some self-control, it does not at any rate make an impracticable demand in that direction.

There is also another method which, while it may seem at first to demand considerable self-control, does really perhaps in the end yield fuller satisfaction than any. Late authors have pointed out that a distinction can and should be made between sexual intercourse for the definite purpose of race-propagation and sexual intercourse for simple union — that, in fact, the methods are different. Mrs. A. B. Stockham, in her little book *Karezza* (Progress Publishing Co., Chicago), dwells on this subject. She indicates that for the latter purpose, i.e., union, there may be complete and indeed prolonged bodily conjunction; but the whole process being kept (by the use of a certain amount of physical control) on the emotional plane and the plane of endearment and affection, there need be no actual emission, and the final orgasm may be avoided. 'Given abundant time and mutual reciprocity, the interchange becomes satisfactory and complete without emission or crisis by either party.' The result of this is really a more complete *soul-union*, a strange and intoxicating exchange of life, and transmutation of elements. 'The whole being of each is submerged in the other, and an exquisite exaltation experienced. . . . In the course of an hour the physical tension subsides, the spiritual exaltation increases, and not uncommonly visions of a transcendent life are seen, and consciousness of new powers experienced.' This 'gives to the sexual relation an office entirely distinct from the propagative act — it is a union on the affectional plane, but at the same time it is a preparation for best possible conditions of procreation.'

The importance of this distinction of the generative act from the act of union or conjunction can hardly be overrated. The two things have hitherto been undifferentiated. Though it may not be easy at once to establish the mental and other conditions necessary for the latter, yet they can be established; and the result is an avoidance of waste, and a great economy of vital forces — on the one side a more profound, helpful and satisfying union, and on the other a greater energy for procreation, when that is desired. We cannot help thinking that it is along this line that the solution of the marriage and population problem will, in time, be found. The overhanging dread of undesired childbirth, which so oppresses the life of many a young mother, will be removed; and marriage will be liberated at last from the tyranny of a brute need into the free and pleasurable exercise of a human and intelligent relationship.

The Intermediate Sex

'There are transitional forms between the metals and non-metals; between chemical combinations and simple mixtures, between animals and plants, between phanerogams and cryptogams, and between mammals and birds. . . The improbability may henceforth be taken for granted of finding in Nature a sharp cleavage between all that is masculine on the one side and all that is feminine on the other; or that any living being is so simple in this respect that it can be put wholly on one side, or wholly on the other, of the line.'

O. Weininger

1. Introductory

The subject dealt with in this book is one of great, and one may say growing, importance. Whether it is that the present period is one of large increase in the numbers of men and women of an intermediate or mixed temperament, or whether it merely is that it is a period in which more than usual attention happens to be accorded to them, the fact certainly remains that the subject has great actuality and is pressing upon us from all sides. It is recognised that anyhow the number of persons occupying an intermediate position between the two sexes is very great, that they play a considerable part in general society, and that they necessarily present and embody many problems which, both for their own sakes and that of society, demand solution. The literature of the question has in consequence already grown to be very extensive, especially on the Continent, and includes a great quantity of scientific works, medical treatises, literary essays, romances, historical novels, poetry, etc. And it is now generally admitted that some knowledge and enlightened understanding of the subject is greatly needed for the use of certain classes — as, for instance, medical men, teachers, parents, magistrates, judges, and the like.

That there are distinctions and gradations of Soul-material in relation to Sex — that the inner psychical affections and affinities shade off and graduate, in a vast number of instances, most subtly from male to female, and not always in obvious correspondence with the outer bodily sex — is a thing evident enough to anyone who considers the subject; nor could any good purpose well be served by ignoring this fact — even if it were possible to do so. It is easy of course (as some do) to classify all these mixed or inter-mediate types as *bad*. It is also easy (as some do) to argue that just because they combine opposite qualities they are likely to be *good* and valuable. But the subtleties and complexities of Naure cannot be despatched in this off-hand manner. The great probability is that, as in any other class of human beings, there will be among these too, good and bad, high and low, worthy and unworthy — some perhaps exhibiting through their double temperament a rare and beautiful flower of humanity, others a perverse and tangled ruin.

Before the facts of Nature we have to preserve a certain humility and reverence; nor rush in with our preconceived and obstinate assumptions. Though these gradations of human type have always, and among all peoples, been more or less known and recognised, yet their frequency today, or even the concentration of attention on them, may be the indication of some important change actually in progress. We do *not* know, in fact, what possible evolutions are to come, or what new forms, of permanent place and value, are being already slowly differentiated from the surrounding mass of humanity. It may be that, as at some past period of evolution the worker-bee was without doubt differentiated from the two ordinary bee-sexes, so at the present time certain new types of human kind may be emerging, which will have an important part to play in the societies of the future — even though for the moment their appearance is attended by a good deal of confusion and misapprehension. It may be so; or it may not. We do not know; and the best attitude we can adopt is one of sincere and dispassionate observation of facts.

Of course wherever this subject touches on the domain of love we may expect difficult queries to arise. Yet it is here probably that the noblest work of the intermediate sex or sexes will be accomplished, as well as the greatest errors committed. It seems almost a law of Nature that new and important movements should be misunderstood and vilified — even though afterwards they may be widely approved or admitted to honour. Such movements are always envisaged first from whatever aspect they may possibly present, of ludicrous or contemptible. The early Christians, in the eyes of Romans, were chiefly known as the perpetrators of obscure rites and crimes in the darkness of the catacombs. Modern Socialism was for a long time supposed to be an affair of daggers and dynamite; and even now there are thousands of good people ignorant enough to believe that it simply means 'divide up all around, and each take his threepenny bit.' Vegetarians were supposed to be a feeble and brainless set of cabbage-eaters. The Women's movement, so vast in its scope and importance, was nothing but an absurd attempt to make women 'the apes of men'. An so on without end; the accusation in each case being some tag or last fag-end of fact, caught up by ignorance, and coloured by prejudice. So commonplace is it to misunderstand, so easy to misrepresent.

That the Uranian temperament, especially in regard to its affectional side, is not without faults must naturally be allowed; but that it has been grossly and absurdly misunderstood is certain. With a good deal of experience in the matter, I think one may safely say that the defect of the male Uranian, or Urning,[1] is *not* sensuality — but rather *sentimentality*. The lower, more ordinary types of Urning are often terribly sentimental; the superior types strangely, almost incredibly emotional; but neither *as a rule* (though of course there must be exceptions) are so sensual as the average normal man.

This immense capacity of emotional love represents of course a great driving force. Whether in the individual or in society, love is eminently creative. It is their great genius for attachment which gives to the best Uranian types their penetrating influence and activity, and which often makes them beloved and accepted far and wide even by those who know nothing of their inner mind. How many so-called philanthropists of the best kind (we need not mention names) have been inspired by the Uranian temperament, the world will probably never know. And in all walks of life the great number and influence of folk of this disposition, and the distinguished place they already occupy, is only realised by those who are more or less behind the scenes. It is probably also that it is this genius for emotional love which gives to the Uranians their remarkable *youthfulness*.

Anyhow, with their extraordinary gift for, and experience in, affairs of the heart — from the double point of view, both of the man and of the woman — it is not difficult to see that these people have a special work to do as reconcilers and interpreters of the two sexes to each other. Of this I have spoken at more length below (chaps. 2 and 5). It is probable that the superior Urnings will become, in affairs of the heart, to a large extent the teachers of future society; and if so that their influence will tend to the realisation and expression of an attachment less exclusively sensual than the average of today, and to the diffusion of this in all directions.

While at any rate not presuming to speak with authority on so difficult a subject, I plead for the necessity of a patient consideration of it, for the due recognition of the types of character concerned, and for some endeavour to give them their fitting place and sphere of usefulness in the general scheme of society.

One thing by way of introductory explanation. The word Love is commonly used in so general and almost indiscriminate a fashion as to denote sometimes physical instincts and acts, and sometimes the most intimate and profound feelings; and in this way a good deal of misunderstanding is caused. In this book (unless there be exceptions in the Appendix) the word is used to denote the inner devotion of one person to another; and when anything else is meant — as, for instance, sexual relations and actions — this is clearly stated and expressed.

2. *The Intermediate Sex*

'Urning men and women, on whose book of life Nature has
written her new word which sounds so strange to us, bear
such storm and stress within them, such ferment and fluctuation, so much complex material having its outlet only
towards the future; their individualities are so rich and many-
sided, and withal so little understood, that it is impossible to
characterise them adequately in a few sentences.'

Otto de Joux

In late years (and since the arrival of the New Woman
amongst us) many things in the relation of men and women
to each other have altered, or at any rate become clearer.
The growing sense of equality in habits and customs —
university studies, art, music, politics, the bicycle, etc. —
all these things have brought about a *rapprochement*
between the sexes. If the modern woman is a little more
masculine in some ways than her predecessor, the modern
man (it is to be hoped), while by no means effeminate, is a
little more sensitive in temperament and artistic in feeling
than the original John Bull. It is beginning to be recognised
that the sexes do not or should not normally form two
groups hopelessly isolated in habit and feeling from each
other, but that they rather represent the two poles of *one*
group — which is the human race; so that while certainly
the extreme specimens at either pole are vastly divergent,
there are great numbers in the middle region who (though
differing corporeally as men and women) are by emotion and
temperament very near to each other.[1] We all know women
with a strong dash of the masculine temperament, and we all
know men whose almost feminine sensibility and intuition
seem to belie their bodily form. Nature, it might appear, in
mixing the elements which go to compose each individual,
does not always keep her two groups of ingredients — which
represent the two sexes — properly apart, but often throws
them crosswise in a somewhat baffling manner, now this
way and now that; yet wisely, we must think — for if a
severe distinction of elements were always maintained the
two sexes would soon drift into far latitudes and absolutely

cease to understand each other. As it is, there are some remarkable and (we think) indispensable types of character in whom there is such a union or balance of the feminine and masculine qualities that these people become to a great extent the interpreters of men and women to each other.

There is another point which has become clearer of late. For as people are beginning to see that the sexes form in a certain sense a continuous group, so they are beginning to see that Love and Friendship — which have been so often set apart from each other as things distinct — are in reality closely related and shade imperceptibly into each other. Women are beginning to demand that Marriage shall mean Friendship as well as Passion; that a comrade-like Equality shall be included in the word Love; and it is recognised that from the one extreme of a 'Platonic' friendship (generally between persons of the same sex) up to the other extreme of passionate love (generally between persons of opposite sex) no hard and fast line can at any point be drawn effectively separating the different kinds of attachment. We know, in fact, of Friendships so romantic in sentiment that they verge into love; we know of Loves so intellectual and spiritual that they hardly dwell in the sphere of Passion.

A moment's thought will show that the general conceptions indicated above — if anywhere near the truth — point to an immense diversity of human temperament and character in matters relating to sex and love; but though such diversity has probably always existed, it has only in comparatively recent times become a subject of study.

More than thirty years ago, however, an Austrian writer, K. H. Ulrichs, drew attention in a series of pamphlets (*Memnon, Ara Spei, Inclusa*, etc.) to the existence of a class of people who strongly illustrate the above remarks, and with whom spécially this paper is concerned. He pointed out that there were people born in such a position — as it were on the dividing line between the sexes — that while belonging distinctly to one sex as far as their bodies are concerned they may be said to belong *mentally* and *emotionally* to the other; that there were men, for instance, who might be described as of feminine soul enclosed in a male body (*anima muliebris in corpore virili inclusa*), or in other cases, women whose definition would be just the reverse. And he maintained that this doubleness of nature was to a great extent proved by the special direction of their love-sentiment. For in such cases, as indeed might be expected, the (apparently) masculine person instead of forming a love-union with a female tended to contract romantic friendships with one of his own sex; while the apparently feminine would, instead of marrying in the usual way, devote herself to the love of another feminine.

People of this kind (i.e., having this special variation of the love-sentiment) he called Urnings;[2] and though we are not obliged to accept his theory about the crosswise connection between 'soul' and 'body', since at best these words are somewhat vague and indefinite; yet his work was important because it was one of the first attempts, in modern times, to recognise the existence of what might be called an Intermediate sex, and to give at any rate *some* explanation of it.[3]

Since that time the subject has been widely studied and written about by scientific men and others, especially on the Continent (though in England it is still comparatively unknown), and by means of an extended observation of present-day cases, as well as the indirect testimony of the history and literature of times past, quite a body of general conclusions has been arrived at — of which I propose in the following pages to give some slight account.

Contrary to the general impression, one of the first points that emerges from this study is that 'Urnings,' or Uranians, are by no means so very rare; but that they form, beneath the surface of society, a large class. It remains difficult, however, to get an exact statement of their numbers; and this for more than one reason: partly because, owing to the want of any general understanding of their case, these folk tend to conceal their true feelings from all but their own kind, and indeed often deliberately act in such a manner as to lead the world astray — (whence it arises that a normal man living in a certain society will often refuse to believe that there is a single Urning in the circle of his acquaintance, while one of the latter, or one that understands the nature, living in the same society, can count perhaps a score or more) — and partly because it is indubitable that the numbers do vary very greatly, not only in different countries but even in different classes in the same country. The consequence of all this being that we have estimates differing very widely from each other. Dr Grabowsky, a well-known writer in Germany, quotes figures (which we think must be exaggerated) as high as one man in every 22, while Dr Albert Moll (*Die Conträre Sexualempfindung*, chap. 3) gives estimates varying from 1 in every 50 to as low as 1 in every 500.[4] These figures apply to such as are exclusively of the said nature, i.e., to those whose deepest feelings of love and friendship go out only to persons of their own sex. Of course, if in addition are included those double-natured people (of whom there is a great number) who experience the normal attachment, with the homogenic tendency in less or greater degree superadded, the estimates must be greatly higher.

In the second place it emerges (also contary to the general impression) that men and women of the exclusively Uranian type are by no means necessarily morbid in any way — unless, indeed, their peculiar temperament be pronounced in itself morbid. Formerly it was assumed as a matter of course, that the type was merely a result of disease and degeneration; but now with the examination of the actual facts it appears that, on the contrary, many are fine, healthy specimens of their sex, muscular and well-developed in body, of powerful brain, high standard of conduct, and with nothing abnormal or morbid of any kind observable in their physical structure or constitution. This is of course not true of all, and there still remain a certain number of cases of weakly type to support the neuropathic view. Yet it is very noticeable that this view is much less insisted on by the later writers than by the earlier. It is also worth noticing that it is now acknowledged that even in the most healthy cases the special affectional temperament of the 'Intermediate' is, as a rule, ineradicable; so much so that when (as in not a few instances) such men and women, from social or other considerations, have forced themselves to marry and even have children, they have still not been able to overcome their own bias, or the leaning after all of their life-attachment to some friend of their own sex.

This subject, though obviously one of considerable interest and importance, has been hitherto, as I have pointed out, but little discussed in this country, partly owing to a certain amount of doubt and distrust which has, not unnaturally perhaps, surrounded it. And certainly if the men and women born with the tendency in question were only exceedingly rare, though it would not be fair on that account to ignore them, yet it would hardly be necessary to dwell at great length on their case. But as the class is really, on any computation, numerous, it becomes a duty for society not only to understand them but to help them to understand themselves.

For there is no doubt that in any cases people of this kind suffer a great deal from their own temperament — and yet, after all, it is possible that they may have an important part to play in the evolution of the race. Anyone who realises what Love is, the dedication of the heart, so profound, so absorbing, so mysterious, so imperative, and always just in the noblest natures so strong, cannot fail to see how difficult, how tragic even, must often be the fate of those whose deepest feelings are destined from the earliest days to be a riddle and a stumbling-block, unexplained to themselves, passed over in silence by others.[5] To call people of such temperament 'morbid', and so forth, is of no use. Such a term is, in fact, absurdly inapplicable to many, who are among the most active, the most amiable and accepted members of society; besides, it forms no solution of the problem in question, and only amounts to marking down for disparagement a fellow-creature who has already considerable difficulties to contend with. Says Dr Moll, 'Anyone who has seen many Urnings will probably admit that they form a by no means enervated human group; on the contrary, one finds powerful, healthy-looking folk among them', but in the very next sentence he says that they 'suffer severely' from the way they are regarded; and in the manifesto of a considerable community of such people in Germany occur these words, 'The rays of sunshine in the night of our existence are so rare, that we are responsive and deeply grateful for the least movement, for every single voice that speaks in our favour in the forum of mankind.'[6]

In dealing with this class of folk, then, while I do not deny that they present a difficult problem, I think that just for that very reason their case needs discussion. It would be a great mistake to suppose that their attachments are necessarily sexual, or connected with sexual acts. On the contrary (as abundant evidence shows), they are often purely emotional in their character; and to confuse Uranians (as is so often done) with libertines having no law but curiosity in self-indulgence is to do them a great wrong. At the same time, it is evident that their special temperament may sometimes cause them difficulty in regard to their sexual relations. Into this subject we need not just now enter. But we may point out how hard it is, especially for the young among them, that a veil of complete silence should be drawn over the subject, leading to the most painful misunderstandings, and perversions and confusions of mind; and that there should be no hint of guidance; nor any recognition of the solitary and really serious inner struggles they may have to face! If the problem is a difficult one — as it undoubtedly is — the fate of those people is already hard who have to meet it in their own persons, without their suffering in addition from the refusal of society to give them any help. It is partly for these reasons, and to throw a little light where it may be needed, that I have thought it might be advisable in this paper to give a few general characteristics of the Intermediate types.

As indicated then already, in bodily structure there is, as a rule, nothing to distinguish the subjects of our discussion from ordinary men and women; but if we take the general mental characteristics it appears from almost universal testimony that the male tends to be of a rather gentle, emotional disposition — with defects, if such exist, in the direction of subtlety, evasiveness, timidity, vanity, etc.; while the female is just the opposite, fiery, active, bold and truthful, with defects running to brusqueness and coarseness. Moreover, the mind of the former is generally intuitive and instinctive in its perceptions, with more or less of artistic feeling; while the mind of the latter is more logical, scientific, and precise than usual with the normal woman. So marked indeed are these general characteristics that sometimes by means of them (though not an infallible guide) the nature of the boy or girl can be detected in childhood, before full development has taken place; and needless to say it may often be very important to be able to do this.

It was no doubt in consequence of the observation of these signs that K. H. Ulrichs proposed his theory; and though the theory, as we have said, does not by any means meet *all* the facts, still it is perhaps not without merit, and may be worth bearing in mind.

In the case, for instance, of a woman of this temperament (defined we suppose as 'a male soul in a female body') the theory helps us to understand how it might be possible for her to fall *bona fide* in love with another woman. Krafft-Ebing gives[7] the case of a lady (A.), 28 years of age, who fell deeply in love with a younger one (B.). 'I loved her divinely,' she said. They lived together, and the union lasted four years, but was then broken by the marriage of B. A. suffered in consequence from frightful depression; but in the end — though without real love — got married herself. Her depression however only increased and deepened into illness. The doctors, when consulted, said that all would be well if she could only have a child. The husband, who loved his wife sincerely, could not understand her enigmatic behaviour. She was friendly to him, suffered his caresses, but for days afterwards remained 'dull, exhausted, plagued with irritation of the spine, and nervous'. Presently a journey of the married pair led to another meeting with the female friend — who had now been wedded (but also unhappily) for three years. 'Both ladies trembled with joy and excitement as they fell into each other's arms, and were thenceforth inseparable. The man found that this friendship relation was a singular one, and hastened the departure. When the opportunity occurred, he convinced himself from the correspondence between his wife and her "friend" that their letters were exactly like those of two lovers.'

It appears that the loves of such women are often very intense, and (as also in the case of male Urnings) life-long.[8] Both classes feel themselves blessed when they love happily. Nevertheless, to many of them it is a painful fact that — in consequence of their peculiar temperament — they are, though fond of children, not in the position to found a family.

We have so far limited ourselves to some very general characteristics of the Intermediate race. It may help to clear and fix our ideas if we now describe more in detail, first, what may be called the extreme and exaggerated types of the race, and then the more normal and perfect types. By doing so we shall get a more definite and concrete view of our subject.

In the first place, then, the extreme specimens — as in most cases of extremes — are not particularly attractive, sometimes quite the reverse. In the male of this kind we have a distinctly effeminate type, sentimental, lackadaisical, mincing in gait and manners, something of a chatterbox, skilful at the needle and in woman's work, sometimes taking pleasure in dressing in woman's clothes; his figure not unfrequently betraying a tendency towards the feminine, large at the hips, supple, not muscular, the face wanting in hair, the voice inclining to be high-pitched, etc.; while his dwelling-room is orderly in the extreme, even natty, and choice of decoration and perfume. His affection, too, is often feminine in character, clinging, dependent and jealous, as of one desiring to be loved almost more than to love.[9]

On the other hand, as the extreme type of the homogenic female, we have a rather markedly aggressive person, of strong passions, masculine manners and movements, practical in the conduct of life, sensuous rather than sentimental in love, often untidy, and *outré* in attire;[10] her figure muscular, her voice rather low in pitch; her dwelling-room decorated with sporting-scenes, pistols, etc., and not without a suspicion of the fragrant weed in the atmosphere; while her love (generally to rather soft and feminine specimens of her own sex) is often a sort of furor, similar to the ordinary masculine love, and at times almost uncontrollable.

These are types which, on account of their salience, everyone will recognise more or less. Naturally, when they occur they excite a good deal of attention, and it is not an uncommon impression that most persons of the homogenic nature belong to either one or other of these classes. But in reality, of course, these extreme developments are rare, and for the most part the temperament in question is embodied in men and women of quite normal and unsensational exterior. Speaking of this subject and the connection between effeminateness and the homogenic nature in men,

Dr Moll says: 'It is, however, as well to point out at the outset that effeminacy does not by any means show itself in all Urnings. Though one may find this or that indication in a great number of cases, yet it cannot be denied that a very large percentage, perhaps by far the majority of them, do *not* exhibit pronounced Effeminacy.' And it may be supposed that we may draw the same conclusion with regard to women of this class — namely, that the majority of them do not exhibit pronounced masculine habits. In fact, while these extreme cases are of the greatest value from a scientific point of view as marking tendencies and limits of development in certain directions, it would be a serious mistake to look upon them as representative cases of the whole phases of human evolution concerned.

If now we come to what may be called the more normal type of the Uranian man, we find a man who, while possessing thoroughly masculine powers of mind and body, combines with them the tenderer and more emotional soul-nature of the woman — and sometimes to a remarkable degree. Such men, as said, are often muscular and well-built, and not distinguishable in exterior structure and the carriage of body from others of their own sex; but emotionally they are extremely complex, tender, sensitive, pitiful and loving, 'full of storm and stress, of ferment and fluctuation' of the heart; the logical faculty may or may not, in their case, be well-developed, but intuition is always strong; like women they read characters at a glance, and know, without knowing how, what is passing in the minds of others; for nursing and waiting on the needs of others they have often a peculiar gift; at the bottom lies the artist-nature, with the artist's sensibility and perception. Such an one is often a dreamer, of brooding, reserved habits, often a musician, or a man of culture, courted in society, which nevertheless does not understand him — though sometimes a child of the people, without any culture, but almost always with a peculiar inborn refinement. De Joux, who speaks on the whole favourably of Uranian men and women, says of the former: 'They are enthusiastic for poetry and music, are often eminently skilful in the fine arts, and are overcome with emotion and sympathy at the least sad occurrence. Their sensitiveness, their endless tenderness for children, their love of flowers, their great pity for beggars and crippled folk are truly womanly.' And in another passage he indicates the artist-nature, when he says: 'The nerve-system of many an Urning is the finest and the most complicated musical instrument in the service of the interior personality that can be imagined.'

It would seem probable that the attachment of such an one is of a tender and profound character; indeed, it is possible that in this class of men we have the love senti-ment in one of its most perfect forms — a form in which from the necessities of the situation the sensuous element, though present, is exquisitely subordinated to the spiritual. Says one writer on this subject, a Swiss, 'Happy indeed is that man who has won a real Urning for his friend — he walks on roses, without ever having to fear the thorns'; and he adds, 'Can there ever be a more perfect sick-nurse than an Urning?' And though these are *ex parte* utterances, we may believe that there is an appreciable grain of truth in them. Another writer, quoted by De Joux, speaks to somewhat the same effect, and may perhaps be received in a similar spirit. 'We form,' he says, 'a peculiar aristocracy of modest spirits, of good and refined habit, and in many masculine circles are the representatives of the higher mental and artistic element. In us dreamers and enthusiasts lies the continual counterpoise to the sheer masculine portion of society — inclining, as it always does, to mere restless greed of gain and material sensual pleasures.'

That men of this kind despise women, though a not uncommon belief, is one which hardly appears to be justified. Indeed, though naturally not inclined to 'fall in love' in this direction, such men are by their nature drawn rather near to women, and it would seem that they often feel a singular appreciation and understanding of the emotional needs and destinies of the other sex, leading in many cases to a genuine though what is called 'Platonic' friendship. There is little doubt that they are often instinc-tively sought after by women, who, without suspecting the real cause, are conscious of a sympathetic chord in the homogenic which they miss in the normal man. To quote De Joux once more: 'It would be a mistake to suppose that all Urnings must be woman-haters. Quite the contrary.

They are not seldom the faithfulest friends, the truest allies, and most convinced defenders of women.'

To come now to the more normal and perfect specimens of the homogenic *woman*, we find a type in which the body is thoroughly feminine and gracious, with the rondure and fulness of the female form, and the continence and aptness of its movements, but in which the inner nature is to a great extent masculine; a temperament active, brave, originative, somewhat decisive, not too emotional; fond of out-door life, of games and sports, of science, politics, or even business; good at organisation, and well-pleased with positions of responsibility, sometimes indeed making an excellent and generous leader. Such a woman, it is easily seen, from her special combination of qualities, is often fitted for remarkable work, in professional life, or as manageress of institutions, or even as ruler of a country. Her love goes out to younger and more feminine natures than her own; it is a powerful passion, almost of heroic type, and capable of inspiring to great deeds; and when held duly in leash may sometimes become an invaluable force in the teaching and training of girlhood, or in the creation of a school of thought or action among women. Many a Santa Clara, or abbess-founder of religious houses, has probably been a woman of this type; and in all times such women — not being bound to men by the ordinary ties — have been able to work the more freely for the interests of their sex, a cause to which their own temperament impels them to devote themselves *con amore*.

I have now sketched — very briefly and inadequately it is true — both the extreme types and the more healthy types of the 'Intermediate' man and woman: types which can be verified from history and literature, though more certainly and satisfactorily perhaps from actual life around us. And unfamiliar though the subject is, it begins to appear that it is one which modern thought and science will have to face. Of the latter and more normal types it may be said that they exist, and have always existed, in considerable abundance, and from that circumstance alone there is a strong probability that they have their place and purpose. As pointed out there is no particular indication of morbidity about them, unless the special nature of their love-sentiment be itself accounted morbid; and in the alienation of the sexes from each other, of which complaint is so often made to-day, it must be admitted that they do much to fill the gap.

The instinctive artistic nature of the male of this class, his sensitive spirit, his wavelike emotional temperament, combined with hardihood of intellect and body; and the frank, free nature of the female, her masculine independence and strength wedded to thoroughly feminine grace of form and manner; may be said to give them both, through their double nature, command of life in all its phases, and a certain freemasonry of the secrets of the two sexes which may well favour their function as reconcilers and interpreters. Certainly it is remarkable that some of the world's greatest leaders and artists have been dowered either wholly or in part with the Uranian temperament — as in the cases of Michel Angelo, Shakespeare, Marlowe, Alexander the Great, Julius Caesar, or among women, Christine of Sweden, Sappho the poetess, and others.

3. The Homogenic Attachment

In its various forms, so far as we know them, Love seems always to have a deep significance and a most practical importance to us little mortals. In one form, as the mere semi-conscious Sex-love, which runs through creation and is common to the lowest animals and plants, it appears as a kind of organic basis for the unity of all creatures; in another, as the love of the mother for her offspring — which may also be termed a passion — it seems to pledge itself to the care and guardianship of the future race; in another, as the marriage of man and woman, it becomes the very foundation of human society. And so we can hardly believe that in its homogenic form, with which we are here concerned, it has not also a deep significance, and social uses and functions which will become clearer to us, the more we study it.

To some perhaps it may appear a little strained to place this last-mentioned form of attachment on a level of import-ance with the others, and such persons may be inclined to deny to the homogenic[1] or homosexual love that intense, that penetrating, and at times overmastering character which would entitle it to rank as a great human passion. But in truth, this view, when entertained, arises from a want of acquaintance with the actual facts; and it may not be amiss here, in the briefest possible way, to indicate what the world's History, Literature, and Art has to say to us on this aspect of the subject, before going on to further consider-ations. Certainly, if the confronting of danger and the endurance of pain and distress for the sake of the loved one, if sacrifice, unswerving devotion and life-long union, constitute proofs of the reality and intensity (and let us say healthiness) of an affection, then these proofs have been given in numberless cases of such attachment, not only as existing between men, but as between women, since the world began. The records of chivalric love, the feats of enamoured knights for their ladies' sakes, the stories of Hero and Leander, etc., are easily paralleled, if not surpassed, by the stories of the Greek comrades-in-arms and tyrannicides — of Cratinus and Aristodemus, who offered themselves together as a voluntary sacrifice for the purifi-cation of Athens; of Chariton and Melanippus,[2] who attempted to assassinate Phalaris, the tyrant of Agrigentum; or of Cleomachus who in like manner, in a battle between the Chalkidians and Eretrians, being entreated to charge the latter, 'asked the youth he loved, who was standing by, whether he would be a spectator of the fight; and when he said he would, and affectionately kissed Cleomachus and put his helmet on his head, Cleomachus with a proud joy placed himself in the front of the bravest of the Thessalians and charged the enemy's cavalry with such impetuosity that he threw them into disorder and routed them; and the Eretrian cavalry fleeing in consequence, the Chalkidians won a splendid victory.'[3]

The annals of all nations contain similar records — though probably among none has the ideal of this love been quite so enthusiastic and heroic as among the post-Homeric Greeks. It is well known that among the Polynesian

Islanders — for the most part a very gentle and affectionate people, probably inheriting the traditions of a higher culture than they now possess — the most romantic male friendships are (or were) in vogue. Says Herman Melville in *Omoo* (chap. 39), 'The really curious way in which all Polynesians are in the habit of making bosom friends is deserving of remark . . . In the annals of the island (Tahiti) are examples of extravagant friendships, unsurpassed by the story of Damon and Pythias — in truth much more wonderful; for notwithstanding the devotion — even of life in some cases — to which they led, they were frequently entertained at first sight for some stranger from another island.' So thoroughly recognised indeed were these unions that Melville explains (in *Typee*, chap. 18) that if two men of hostile tribes or islands became thus pledged to each other, then each could pass through the enemy's territory without fear of molestation or injury; and the passionate nature of these attachments is indicated by the following passage from *Omoo* (another book of Melville's): 'Though little inclined to jealousy in ordinary love-matters, the Tahitian will hear of no rivals in his *friendship*.'

Even among savage races lower down than these in the scale of evolution, and who are generally accused of being governed in their love-relations only by the most animal desires, we find a genuine sentiment of comradeship beginning to assert itself — as among the Balonda[4] and other African tribes, where regular ceremonies of the betrothal of comrades take place, by the transfusion of a few drops of blood into each other's drinking-bowls, by the exchange of names,[5] and the mutual gift of their most precious possessions; but unfortunately, owing to the obtuseness of current European opinion on this subject, these and other such customs have been but little investigated and have by no means received the attention that they ought.

When we turn to the poetic and literary utterances of the more civilised nations on this subject we cannot but be struck by the range and intensity of the emotions expressed — from the beautiful threnody of David over his friend whose love was passing the love of women, through the vast panorama of the Homeric *Iliad*, of which the heroic friendship of Achilles and his dear Patroclus forms really the basic theme, down to the works of the great Greek age — the splendid odes of Pindar burning with clear fire of passion, the lofty elegies of Theognis, full of wise precepts to his beloved Kurnus, the sweet pastorals of Theocritus, the passionate lyrics of Sappho, or the more sensual raptures of Anacreon. Some of the dramas of Aeschylus and Sophocles — as the *Myrmidones* of the former and the *Lovers of Achilles*[6] of the latter — appear to have had this subject for their motive; and many of the prose-poem dialogues of Plato were certainly inspired by it.

Then coming to the literature of the Roman age, whose materialistic spirit could only with difficulty seize the finer inspiration of the homogenic love, and which in such writers as Catullus and Martial could only for the most part give expression to its grosser side, we still find in Vergil, a noble and notable instance. His second *Eclogue* bears the marks of a genuine passion; and, according to some,[7] he there under the name of Alexis immortalises his own love for the youthful Alexander. Nor is it possible to pass over in this connection the great mass of Persian literature, and the poets Sadi, Hafiz, Jami, and many others, whose names and works are for all time, and whose marvellous love-songs ('Bitter and sweet is the parting kiss on the lips of a friend') are to a large extent, if not mostly, addressed to those of their own sex.[8]

Of the mediaeval period in Europe we have of course but few literary monuments. Towards its close we come upon the interesting story of Amis and Amile (thirteenth century), unearthed by Mr W. Pater from the Bibliotheca Elzeviriana.[9] Though there is historic evidence of the prevalence of the passion we may say of this period that its *ideal* was undoubtedly rather the chivalric love than the love of comrades. But with the Renaissance in Italy and the Elizabethan period in England the latter once more comes to evidence in a burst of poetic utterance,[10] which culminates perhaps in the magnificent sonnets of Michel Angelo and of Shakespeare; of Michel Angelo whose pure beauty of expression lifts the enthusiasm into the highest region as the direct perception of the divine in mortal form;[11] and of Shakespeare — whose passionate words and amorous spirituality of friendship have for long enough been a perplexity to hide-bound commentators. Thence through minor writers (not overlooking Winckelmann[12] in Germany) we pass to quite modern times — in which, notwithstanding the fact that the passion has been much misunderstood and misinterpreted, two names stand conspicuously forth — those of Tennyson, whose 'In Memoriam' is perhaps his finest work, and of Walt Whitman, the enthusiasm of whose poems on Comradeship is only paralleled by the devotedness of his labours for his wounded brothers in the American Civil War.

It will be noticed that here we have some of the very greatest names in all literature concerned; and that their utterances on this subject equal if they do not surpass, in beauty, intensity and humanity of sentiment, whatever has been written in praise of the other more ordinarily recognised love.

And when again we turn to the records of Art, and compare the way in which man's sense of Love and Beauty has expressed itself in the portrayal of the male form and the female form respectively we find exactly the same thing. The whole vista of Greek statuary shows the male passion of beauty in high degree. Yet though the statues of men and youths (by men sculptors) preponderate probably considerably, both in actual number and in devotedness of execution, over the statues of female figures, it is, as J. A. Symonds says in his *Life of Michel Angelo*, remarkable that in all the range of the former there are hardly two or three that show a base or licentious expression, such as is not so very uncommon in the female statues. Knowing as we do the strength of the male physical passion in the life of the Greeks, this one fact speaks strongly for the sense of proportion which must have characterised this passion — at any rate in the most productive age of their Art.

In the case of Michel Angelo we have an artist who with brush and chisel portrayed literally thousands of human forms; but with this peculiarity, that while scores and scores of his male figures are obviously suffused and inspired by a romantic sentiment, there is hardly one of his female figures that is so, — the latter being mostly representative of woman in her part as mother, or sufferer, or prophetess or poetess, or in old age, or in any aspect of strength or tenderness, except that which associates itself especially with romantic love. Yet the cleanliness and dignity of Michel Angelo's male figures are incontestable, and bear striking witness to that nobility of the sentiment in him, which we have already seen illustrated in his sonnets.[13]

This brief sketch may suffice to give the reader some idea of the place and position in the world of the particular sentiment which we are discussing; nor can it fail to impress him — if any reference is made to the authorities quoted — with a sense of the dignity and solidity of the sentiment, at any rate as handled by some of the world's greatest men. At the same time it would be affectation to ignore the fact that side by side with this view of the subject there has been another current of opinion leading people — especially in quite modern times in Europe — to look upon attachments of the kind in question with much suspicion and disfavour.[14] And it may be necessary here to say a few words on this latter view.

The origin of it is not far to seek. Those who have no great gift themselves for this kind of friendship — who are not in the inner circle of it, so to speak, and do not understand or appreciate its deep emotional and romantic character, have nevertheless heard of certain corruptions and excesses; for these latter leap to publicity. They have heard of the debaucheries of a Nero or a Tiberius; they have noted the scandals of the Police Courts; they have had some experience perhaps of abuses which may be found in Public Schools or Barracks; and they (not unnaturally) infer that these things, these excesses and sensualities, are the motive of comrade-attachments, and the object for which they exist; nor do they easily recognise any more profound and intimate bond. To such people physical intimacies of *any* kind (at any rate between males) seem inexcusable. There is no distinction in their minds between the simplest or most naive expression of feeling and the gravest abuse of human rights and decency; there is no distinction between a genuine heart-attachment and a mere carnal curiosity. They see certain evils that occur or have occurred, and they think, perfectly candidly, that any measures are justifiable to prevent such things recurring. But they do not see the interior love-feeling which when it exists does legitimately demand *some* expression. Such folk, in fact, not having the key in themselves to the real situation hastily assume that the homogenic attachment has no other motive than, or is simply a veil and a cover for, sensuality — and suspect or condemn it accordingly.

Thus arises the curious discrepancy of people's views on this important subject — a discrepancy depending on the side from which they approach it.

On the one hand we have anathemas and execrations, on the other we have the lofty enthusiasm of a man like Plato — one of the leaders of the world's thought for all time — who puts, for example, into the mouth of Phaedrus (in the *Symposium*) such a passage as this:[15] 'I know not any greater blessing to a young man beginning life than a virtuous lover, or to the lover than a beloved youth. For the principle which ought to be the guide of men who would nobly live — that principle, I say, neither kindred, nor honour, nor wealth, nor any other motive is able to implant so well as love. Of what am I speaking? Of the sense of honour and dishonour, without which neither states nor individuals ever do any good or great work... For what lover would not choose rather to be seen of all mankind than by his beloved, either when abandoning his post or throwing away his arms? He would be ready to die a thousand deaths rather than endure this. Or who would desert his beloved or fail him in the hour of danger? The veriest coward would become an inspired hero, equal to the bravest, at such a time; love would inspire him. That courage which, as Homer says, the god breathes into the soul of heroes, love of his own nature inspires into the lover'. Or again in the *Phaedrus* Plato makes Socrates say:[16] 'In like manner the followers of Apollo and of every other god, walking in the ways of their god, seek a love who is to be like their god, and when they have found him, they themselves imitate their god, and persuade their love to do the same, and bring him into harmony with the form and ways of the god as far as they can; for they have no feelings of envy or jealousy towards their beloved, but they do their utmost to create in him the greatest likeness of themselves and the god whom they honour. Thus fair and blissful to the beloved when he is taken, is the desire of the inspired lover, and the initiation of which I speak into the mysteries of true love, if their purposed is effected '.

With these few preliminary remarks we may pass on to consider some recent scientific investigations of the matter in hand. In late times — that is, during the last thirty years or so — a group of scientific and capable men chiefly in Germany, France, and Italy, have made a special and more or less impartial study of it. Among these may be mentioned Dr Albert Moll of Berlin; R. von Krafft-Ebing, one of the leading medical authorities of Vienna, whose book on 'Sexual Psychopathy' has passed into its 10th edition; Dr Paul Moreau (*Des Aberrations du sens génésique*); Cesare Lombroso, the author of various works on Anthropology; M. A. Raffalovich (*Uranisme et unisexualité*); Auguste Forel (*Die Sexuelle Frage*); Mantegazza; K. H. Ulrichs; and last but not least, Dr Havelock Ellis, of whose great work on the Psychology of Sex the second volume is dedicated to the subject of *Sexual Inversion*.[17] The result of these investigations has been that a very altered complexion has been given to the subject. For whereas at first it was easily assumed that the phenomena were of morbid character, and that the leaning of the love-sentiment towards one of the same sex was always associated with degeneracy or disease, it is very noticeable that step by step with the accumulation of reliable information this assumption has been abandoned. The point of view has changed; and the change has been most marked in the latest authors, such as A. Moll and Havelock Ellis.

It is not possible here to go into anything like a detailed account of the works of these various authors, their theories, and the immense number of interesting cases and observations which they have contributed; but some of the general conclusions which flow from their researches may be pointed out. In the first place their labours have established the fact, known hitherto only to individuals, that *sexual inversion* — that is the leaning of desire to one of the same sex — is in a vast number of cases quite instinctive and congenital, mentally and physically, and therefore twined in the very roots of individual life and practically ineradicable. To Men or Women thus affected with an innate homosexual bias, Ulrichs gave the name Urning,[18] since pretty widely accepted by scientists. Some details with regard to 'Urnings' ,I have given in the preceding paper, but it should be said here that too much emphasis cannot be laid on the distinction between these born lovers of their own kind, and that class of persons, with whom they are so often confused, who out of mere carnal curiosity or extravagance of desire, or from the dearth of opportunities for a more normal satisfaction (as in schools, barracks, etc.) adopt some homosexual practices. It is the latter class who become chiefly prominent in the public eye, and who excite, naturally enough, public reprobation. In their case, the attraction is felt, by themselves and all concerned, to be merely sensual and morbid. In the case of the others, however, the feeling is, as said, so deeply rooted and twined with the mental and emotional life that the person concerned has difficulty in imagining himself affected otherwise than he is; and to him at least his love appears healthy and natural, and indeed a necessary part of his individuality.

In the second place it has become clear that the number of individuals affected with 'sexual inversion' in some degree or other is very great — much greater than is generally supposed to be the case. It is however very difficult or perhaps impossible to arrive at satisfactory figures on the subject,[19] for the simple reasons that the proportions vary so greatly among different peoples and even in different sections of society and in different localities, and because of course there are all possible grades of sexual inversion to deal with, from that in which the instinct is *quite exclusively* directed towards the same sex, to the other extreme in which it is normally towards the opposite sex but capable, occasionally and under exceptional attractions, of inversion towards its own — this last condition being probably among some peoples very widespread, if not universal.

In the third place, by the tabulation and comparison of a great number of cases and 'confessions', it has become pretty well established that the individuals affected with inversion in marked degree do not after all differ from the rest of mankind, or womankind, in any other physical or mental particular which can be distinctly indicated.[20] No congenital association with any particular physical conformation or malformation has yet been discovered; nor with any distinct disease of body or mind. Nor does it appear that persons of this class are usually of a gross or specially low type, but if anything rather the opposite − being most of refined, sensitive nature and including, as Krafft-Ebing points out (*Psychopathia Sexualis*, 7th ed., p. 227) a great number 'highly gifted in the fine arts, especially music and poetry'; and, as Mantegazza says,[21] many persons of high literary and social distinction. It is true that Krafft-Ebing insists on the generally strong sexual equipment of this class of persons (among men), but he hastens to say that their emotional love is also 'enthusiastic and exalted',[22] and that, while bodily congress is desired, the special act with which they are vulgarly credited is in most cases repugnant to them.[23]

The only distinct characteristic which the scientific writers claim to have established is a marked tendency to nervous development in the subject, not infrequently associated with nervous maladies; but − as I shall presently have occasion to show − there is reason to think that the validity even of this characteristic has been exaggerated.

Taking the general case of men with a marked exclusive preference for persons of their own sex, Krafft-Ebing says (*op. cit.*, p. 256): 'The sexual life of these Homosexuals is *mutatis mutandis* just the same as in the case of normal sex-love... The Urning loves, deifies his male beloved one, exactly as the woman-wooing man does *his* beloved. For him, he is capable of the greatest sacrifice, experiences the torments of unhappy, often unrequited, love, of faithlessness on his beloved's part, of jealousy, and so forth. His attention is enchained only by the male form... The sight of feminine charms is indifferent to him, if not repugnant.' Then he goes on to say that many such men, notwithstanding their actual aversion to intercourse with the female, do ultimately marry − either from ethical, as sometimes happens, or from social considerations. But very remarkable — as illustrating the depth and tenacity of the homogenic instinct[24] — and pathetic too, are the records that he gives of these cases; for in many of them a real friendship and regard between the married pair was still of no avail to overcome the distaste on the part of one to sexual intercourse with the other, or to prevent the experience of actual physical distress after such intercourse, or to check the continual flow of affection to some third person of the same sex; and thus unwillingly, so to speak, this bias remained a cause of suffering to the end.

I have said that at the outset it was assumed that the Homogenic emotion was morbid in itself, and probably always associated with distinct disease, either physical or mental, but the progress of the inquiry has served more and more to dissipate this view; and that it is noticeable that the latest of the purely scientific authorities are the least disposed to insist upon the theory of morbidity. It is true that Krafft-Ebing clings to the opinion that there is generally some *neurosis*, or degeneration of a nerve-centre, or *inherited tendency in that direction*, associated with the instinct; see p. 190 (7th ed.), also p. 227, where he speaks, rather vaguely, of 'an hereditary neuropathic or psychopathic tendency' — *neuro(psycho)pathische Belastung*. But it is an obvious criticism on this that there are few people in modern life, perhaps none, who could be pronounced absolutely free from such a *Belastung*! And whether the Dorian Greeks or the Polynesian Islanders or the Albanian mountaineers, or any of the other notably hardy races among whom this affection has been developed, were particularly troubled by nervous degeneration we may well doubt!

As to Moll, though he speaks[25] of the instinct as morbid (feeling perhaps in duty bound to do so), it is very noticeable that he abandons the ground of its association with other morbid symptoms — as this association, he says, is by no means always to be observed; and is fain to rest his judgment on the *dictum* that the mere failure of the sexual instinct to propagate the species is itself pathological — a *dictum* which in its turn obviously springs from that pre-judgment of scientists that generation is the sole object of love,[26] and which if pressed would involve the good doctor in awkward dilemmas, as for instance that every worker-bee is a pathological specimen.

Finally we find that Havelock Ellis, one of the latest writers of weight on this subject, in chapter 6 of his *Sexual Inversion*, combats the idea that this temperament is necessarily morbid; and suggests that the tendency should rather be called an anomaly than a disease. He says (2nd edition, p. 186):[27] 'Thus in sexual inversion we have what may fairly be called a "sport" or variation, one of those organic aberrations which we see throughout living nature in plants and in animals'.[28]

With regard to the nerve-degeneration theory, while it may be allowed that sexual inversion is not uncommonly found in connection with the specially nervous temperament, it must be remembered that its occasional association with nervous troubles or disease is quite another matter; since such troubles ought perhaps to be looked upon as the results rather than the causes of the inversion. It is difficult of course for outsiders not personally experienced in the matter to realise the great strain and tension of nerves under which those persons grow up from boyhood to manhood — or from girl to womanhood — who find their deepest and strongest instincts under the ban of the society around them; who before they clearly understand the drift of their own natures discover that they are somehow cut off from the sympathy and understanding of those nearest to them; and who know that they can never give expression to their tenderest yearnings of affection without exposing themselves to the possible charge of actions stigmatised as odious crimes.[29] That such a strain, acting on one who is perhaps already of a nervous temperament, should tend to cause nervous prostration or even mental disturbance is of course obvious; and if such disturbances are really found to be commoner among homogenic lovers than among ordinary folk we have in these social causes probably a sufficient explanation of the fact.

Then again in this connection it must never be forgotten that the medico-scientific enquirer is bound on the whole to meet with those cases that *are* of a morbid character, rather than with those that are healthy in their manifestation, since indeed it is the former that he lays himself out for.

And since the field of his research is usually a great modern city, there is little wonder if disease colours his conclusions. In the case of Dr Moll, who carried out his researches largely under the guidance of the Berlin police (whose acquaintance with the subject would naturally be limited to its least satisfactory sides), the only marvel is that his verdict is so markedly favourable as it is. As Krafft-Ebing says in his own preface, 'It is the sad privilege of Medicine, and especially of Psychiatry, to look always on the reverse side of life, on the weakness and wretchedness of man.'

Having regard then to the direction in which science has been steadily moving in this matter, it is not difficult to see that the epithet 'morbid' will probably before long be abandoned as descriptive of the homogenic bias — that is, of the general sentiment of love towards a person of the same sex. That there are excesses of the passion — cases, as in ordinary sex-love, where mere physical desire becomes a mania — we may freely admit; but as it would be unfair to judge of the purity of marriage by the evidence of the Divorce courts, so it would be monstrous to measure the truth and beauty of the attachment in question by those instances which stand most prominently perhaps in the eye of the modern public; and after all deductions there remains, we contend, the vast body of cases in which the manifestation of the instinct has on the whole the character of normality and healthfulness — sufficiently so in fact to constitute this *a distinct variety of the sexual passion*. The question, of course, not being whether the instinct is *capable* of morbid and extravagant manifestation — for that can easily be proved of any instinct — but whether it is capable of a healthy and sane expression. And this, we think, it has abundantly shown itself to be.

Anyhow the work that Science has practically done has been to destroy the dogmatic attitude of the former current opinion from which itself started, and to leave the whole subject freed from a great deal of misunderstanding, and much more open than before. If on the one hand its results have been chiefly of a negative character, and it admits that it does not understand the exact place and foundation of this attachment; on the other hand since it recognises the deeply beneficial influences of an intimate love-relation of the usual kind on those concerned, it also allows that there are some persons for whom these necessary reactions can only come from one of the same sex as themselves.

'Successful love,' says Moll (p. 125) 'exercises a helpful influence on the Urning. His mental and bodily condition improves, and capacity of work increases — just as it happens in the case of a normal youth with *his* love.' And further on (p. 173) in a letter from a man of this kind occur these words: 'The passion is I suppose so powerful, just because one looks for everything in the loved man – Love, Friendship, Ideal, and Sense-satisfaction... As it is at present I suffer the agonies of a deep unresponded passion, which wake me like a nightmare from sleep. And I am conscious of physical pain in the region of the heart.' In such cases the love, in some degree physically expressed, of another person of the same sex, is allowed to be as much a necessity and a condition of healthy life and activity, as in more ordinary cases is the love of a person of the opposite sex.

If then the physical element which is sometimes present in the love of which we are speaking is a difficulty and a stumbling-block, it must be allowed that it is a difficulty that Nature confronts us with, and which cannot be disposed of by mere anathema and execration. The only theory — from K. H. Ulrichs to Havelock Ellis — which has at all held its ground in this matter, is that in congenital cases of sex-inversion there is a mixture of male and female elements in the same person; so that for instance in the same embryo the emotional and nervous regions may develop along feminine lines while the outer body and functions may determine themselves as distinctly masculine, or *vice versa*. Such cross-development may take place obviously in a great variety of ways, and thus possibly explain the remarkable varieties of the Uranian temperament; but in all such cases, strange as may be the problems thus arising, these problems are of Nature's own producing and can hardly be laid to the door of the individual who has literally to bear their cross. For such individuals expressions of feeling become natural, which to others seem out of place and uncalled for; and not only natural, but needful and inevitable. To deny to such people *all* expression of their emotion, is probably in the end to cause it to burst forth with the greater violence; and it may be suggested that our British code of manners, by forbidding the lighter marks of affection between youths and men, acts just contrary to its own purpose, and drives intimacies down into less open and unexceptional channels.

With regard to this physical element it must also be remembered that since the homogenic love — whether between man and man, or between woman and woman — can from the nature of the case never find expression on the physical side so freely and completely as is the case with the ordinary love, it must tend rather more than the latter to run along *emotional* channels, and to find its vent in sympathies of social life and companionship. If one studies carefully the expression of the Greek statues (see p.204) and the lesson of the Greek literature, one sees clearly that the *ideal* of Greek life was a very continent one: the trained male, the athlete, the man temperate and restrained, even chaste, for the sake of bettering his powers. It was round this conception that the Greeks kindled their finer emotions. And so of their love: a base and licentious indulgence was not in line with it. They may not have always kept to their ideal, but there it was. And I am inclined to think that the homogenic instinct (for the reasons given above) would in the long run tend to work itself out in this direction. And consonant with this is the fact that this passion in the past (as pointed out by J. Addington Symonds in his paper on 'Dantesque and Platonic Ideals of Love'[30]) has, as a matter of fact, inspired such a vast amount of heroism and romance — only paralleled indeed by the loves of Chivalry, which of course, owing to their special character, were subject to a similar Transmutation.

In all these matters the popular opinion has probably been largely influenced by the arbitrary notion that the function of love is limited to child-breeding; and that any love not concerned in the propagation of the race must necessarily be of dubious character. And in enforcing this view, no doubt the Hebraic and Christian tradition has exercised a powerful influence — dating, as it almost certainly does, from far-back times when the multiplication of the tribe was one of the first duties of its members, and one of the first necessities of corporate life.[31] But nowadays when the need has swung round all the other way it is not unreasonable to suppose that a similar revolution will take place in people's views of the place and purpose of the non-child-bearing love.[32]

I have now said enough I think to show that though much in relation to the homogenic attachment is obscure, and though it may have its special pitfalls and temptations — making it quite necessary to guard against a too great latitude on the physical side; yet on its ethical and social sides it is pregnant with meaning and has received at various times in history abundant justification. It certainly does not seem impossible to suppose that as the ordinary love has a special function in the propagation of the race, so the other has its special function in social and heroic work, and in the generation — not of bodily children — but of those children of the mind, the philosophical conceptions and ideals which transform our lives and those of society. J. Addington Symonds, in his privately printed pamphlet, *A Problem in Greek Ethics* (now published in a German trans-lation),[33] endeavours to reconstruct as it were the genesis of comrade-love among the Dorians in early Greek times. Thus: 'Without sufficiency of women, without the sanctities of established domestic life, inspired by the memories of Achilles and venerating their ancestor Herakles, the Dorian warriors had special opportunity for elevating comradeship to the rank of an enthusiasm. The incidents of emigration into a foreign country — perils of the sea, passages of rivers and mountains, assaults of fortresses and cities, landings on a hostile shore, night-vigils by the side of blazing beacons, foragings for food, picquet service in the front of watchful foes — involved adventures capable of shedding the lustre of romance on friendship. These circumstances, by bringing the virtues of sympathy with the weak, tenderness for the beautiful, protection for the young, together with corresponding qualities of gratitude, self-devotion, and admiring attachment into play, may have tended to cement unions between man and man no less firm than that of marriage. On such connections a wise captain would have relied for giving strength to his battalions, and for keeping alive the flames of enterprise and daring.' The author then goes on to suggest that though in such relations as those indicated the physical probably had some share, yet it did not at that time overbalance the emotional and spiritual elements, or lead to the corruption and effeminacy of a later age.

At Sparta the lover was called *eispnêlos*, the inspirer, and the younger beloved *aïtes*, the hearer. This alone would show the partly educational aspects in which comradeship was conceived; and a hundred passages from classic literature might be quoted to prove how deeply it had entered into the Greek mind that this love was the cradle of social chivalry and heroic life. Finally it seems to have been Plato's favourite doctrine that the relation if properly conducted led up to the disclosure of true philosophy in the mind, to the divine vision or mania, and to the remembrance or rekindling within the soul of all the forms of celestial beauty. He speaks of this kind of love as causing a 'generation in the beautiful'[34] within the souls of the lovers. The image of the beloved one passing into the mind of the lover and upward through its deepest recesses reaches and unites itself to the essential forms of divine beauty there long hidden — the originals as it were of all creation — and stirring them to life excites a kind of generative descent of noble thoughts and impulses, which henceforward modify the whole cast of thought and life of the one so affected.

If there is any truth — even only a grain or two — in these speculations, it is easy to see that the love with which we are specially dealing is a very important factor in society, and that its neglect, or its repression, or its vulgar misapprehension, may be matters of considerable danger or damage to the common-weal. It is easy to see that while on the one hand marriage is of indispensable importance to the State as providing the workshop as it were for the breeding and rearing of children, another form of union is almost equally indispensable to supply the basis for social activities of other kinds. Every one is conscious that without a close affectional tie of some kind his life is not complete, his powers are crippled, and his energies are inadequately spent. Yet it is not to be expected (though it may of course happen) that the man or woman who have dedicated themselves to each other and to family life should leave the care of their children and the work they have to do at home in order to perform social duties of a remote and less obvious, though may be more arduous, character. Nor is it to be expected that a man or woman single-handed, without the counsel of a helpmate in the hour of difficulty, or his or her love in the hour of need, should feel equal to these wider activities. If — to refer once more to classic story — the love of Harmodius had been for a wife and children at home, he would probably not have cared, and it would hardly have been his business, to slay the tyrant. And unless on the other hand each of the friends had had the love of his comrade to support him, the two could hardly have nerved themselves to this audacious and ever-memorable exploit. So it is difficult to believe that anything can supply the force and liberate the energies required for social and mental activities of the most necessary kind so well as a comrade-union which yet leaves the two lovers free from the responsibilities and impediments of family life.

For if the slaughter of tyrants is not the chief social duty nowadays, we have with us hydra-headed monsters at least as numerous as the tyrants of old, and more difficult to deal with, and requiring no little courage to encounter. And beyond the extirpation of evils we have solid work waiting to be done in the patient and life-long building up of new forms of society, new orders of thought, and new institutions of human solidarity — all of which in their genesis must meet with opposition, ridicule, hatred, and even violence. Such campaigns as these — though different in kind from those of the Dorian mountaineers described above — will call for equal hardihood and courage, and will stand in need of a comradeship as true and valiant. And it may indeed be doubted whether the higher heroic and spiritual life of a nation is ever quite possible without the sanction of this attachment in its institutions, adding a new range and scope to the possibilities of love.[35]

Walt Whitman, the inaugurator, it may almost be said, of a new world of democratic ideals and literature, and — as one of the best of our critics has remarked — the most Greek in spirit and in performance of modern writers, insists continually on this social function of 'intense and loving comradeship, the personal and passionate attachment of man to man.' 'I will make,' he says, 'the most splendid race the sun ever shone upon, I will make divine magnetic lands... I will make inseparable cities with their arms about each others' necks, by the love of comrades.' And again, in *Democratic Vistas*, 'It is to the development, identification, and general prevalence of that fervid comradeship (the adhesive love at least rivaling the amative love hitherto possessing imaginative literature, if not going beyond it), that I look for the counterbalance and offset of materialistic and vulgar American Democracy, and for the spiritualisation thereof... I say Democracy infers such loving comradeship, as its most inevitable twin or counterpart, without which it will be incomplete, in vain, and incapable of perpetuating itself.'

Yet Whitman could not have spoken, as he did, with a kind of authority on this subject, if he had not been fully aware that through the masses of the people this attachment was already alive and working — though doubtless in a somewhat suppressed and un-self-conscious form — and if he had not had ample knowledge of its effects and influence in himself and others around him. Like all great artists he could but give form and light to that which already existed dim and inchoate in the heart of the people. To those who have dived at all below the surface in this direction it will be familiar enough that the homogenic passion ramifies widely through all modern society, and that among the masses of the people as among the classes, even below the stolid surface and reserve of British manners, letters pass and enduring attachments are formed, differing in no very obvious respect from those correspondences which persons of the opposite sex knit with each other under similar cirumstances; but that hitherto while this relation has occasionally, in its grosser forms and abuses, come into public notice through the police reports, etc., its more sane and spiritual manifestations — though really a moving force in the body politic — have remained unrecognised.

It is hardly needful in these days when social questions loom so large upon us to emphasise the importance of a bond which by the most passionate and lasting compulsion may draw members of the different classes together, and (as it often seems to do) none the less strongly because they are members of different classes. A moment's consideration must convince us that such a comradeship may, as Whitman says, have 'deepest relations to general politics'. It is noticeable, too, in this deepest relation to politics that the movement among women towards their own liberation and emancipation, which is taking place all over the civilised world, has been accompanied by a marked development of the homogenic passion among the female sex. It may be said that a certain strain in the relations between the opposite sexes which has come about owing to a growing conscious-ness among women that they have been oppressed and unfairly treated by men, and a growing unwillingness to ally themselves unequally in marriage — that this strain has caused the womenkind to draw more closely together and to cement alliances of their own. But whatever the cause may be it is pretty certain that such comrade-alliances — and of quite devoted kind — are becoming increasingly common, and especially perhaps among the more cultured classes of women, who are working out the great cause of their sex's liberation; nor is it difficult to see the importance of such alliances in such a campaign. In the United States where the battle of women's independence is also being fought, the tendency mentioned is as strongly marked.

A few words may here be said about the legal aspect of this important question. It has to be remarked that the present state of the Law, both in Germany and Britain — arising as it does partly out of some of the misapprehensions above alluded to, and partly out of the sheer unwillingness of legislators to discuss the question — is really impracticable. While the Law rightly seeks to prevent acts of violence or public scandal, it may be argued that it is going beyond its province when it attempts to regulate the private and voluntary relations of adult persons to each other. The homogenic affection is a valuable social force, and in some cases a necessary element of noble human character — yet the Act of 1885 makes almost any familiarity in such cases the possible basis of a criminal charge. The Law has no doubt had substantial ground for previous statutes on this subject — dealing with a certain gross act; but in so severely condemning the least familiarity between male persons[36] we think it has gone too far. It has undertaken a censorship over private morals (entirely apart from social results) which is beyond its province, and which — even if it were its province — it could not possibly fulfil;[37] it has opened wider than ever before the door to a real, most serious social evil and crime — that of blackmailing; and it has thrown a shadow over even the simplest and most ordinary expressions of an attachment which may, as we have seen, be of great value in the national life.

That the homosexual feeling, like the heterosexual, may lead to public abuses of liberty and decency; that it needs a strict self-control; and that much teaching and instruction on the subject is needed; we of course do not deny. But as, in the case of persons of opposite sex, the law limits itself on the whole to a maintenance of public order, the protection of the weak from violence and insult,[38] and of the young from their inexperience; so we think it should be here. The much-needed teaching and the true morality on the subject must be given — as it can only be given — by the spread of proper education and ideas, and not by the clumsy bludgeon of the statute-book.[39]

Having thus shown the importance of the homogenic or comrade-attachment, in some form, in national life, it would seem high time now that the modern peoples should recognise this in their institutions, and endeavour at least in their public opinion and systems of education to understand this factor and give it its proper place. The undoubted evils which exist in relation to it, for instance in our public schools as well as in our public life, owe their experience largely to the fact that the whole subject is left in the gutter so to speak — in darkness and concealment. No one offers a clue of better things, nor to point a way out of the wilderness; and by this very non-recognition the passion is perverted into its least satisfactory channels. All love, one would say, must have its responsibilities, else it is liable to degenerate, and to dissipate itself in mere sentiment or sensuality. The normal marriage between man and woman leads up to the foundation of the household and the family; the love between parents and children implies duties and cares on both sides. The homogenic attachment left unrecognised, easily loses some of its best quality and becomes an ephemeral or corrupt thing. Yet, as we have seen, and as I am pointing out in the following chapter, it may, when occurring between an elder and younger, prove to be an immense educational force; while, as between equals, it may be turned to social and heroic uses, such as can hardly be demanded or expected from the ordinary marriage. It would seem high time, I say, that public opinion should recognise these facts; and so give to this attachment the sanction and dignity which arise from public recognition, as well as the definite form and outline which would flow from the existence of an accepted ideal or standard in the matter. It is often said how necessary for the morality of the ordinary marriage is some public recognition of the relation, and some accepted standard of conduct in it. May not, to a lesser degree, something of the same kind (as suggested in the next chapter) be true of the homogenic attachment? It has had its place as a recognised and guarded institution in the elder and more primitive societies; and it seems quite probable that a similar place will be accorded to it in the societies of the future.

4. Affection in Education

The place of Affection, and the need of it, as an educative force in school-life, is a subject which is beginning to attract a good deal of attention. Hitherto Education has been concentrated on intellectual (and physical) development; but the affections have been left to take care of themselves. Now it is beginning to be seen that the affections have an immense deal to say in the building up of the brain and the body. Their evolution and organisation in some degree is probably going to become an important part of school management.

School friendships of course exist; and almost every one remembers that they filled a large place in the outlook of his early years; but he remembers, too, that they were not recognised in any way, and that in consequence the main part of their force and value was wasted. Yet it is evident that the first unfolding of a strong attachment in boyhood or girlhood must have a profound influence; while if it occurs between and elder and a younger school-mate, or — as sometimes happens — between the young thing and its teacher, its importance in the educational sense can hardly be overrated.

That such feelings sometimes take quite intense and romantic forms few will deny. I have before me a letter, in which the author, speaking of an attachment he experienced when a boy of sixteen for a youth somewhat older than himself, says:

'I would have died for him ten times over. My devices and plannings to meet him (to come across him casually, as it were) were those of a lad for his sweetheart, and when I saw him my heart beat so violently that it caught my breath, and I could not speak. We met in — —, and for the weeks that he stayed there I thought of nothing else — thought of him night and day — and when he returned to London I used to write him weekly letters, veritable love-letters of many sheets in length. Yet I never felt one particle of jealousy, though our friendship lasted for some years. The passion, violent and extravagant as it was, I believe to have been perfectly free from sex-feeling and perfectly wholesome and good for me. It distinctly contributed to my growth. Looking back upon it and analysing it as well as I can, I seem to see as the chief element in it an escape from the extremely narrow Puritanism in which I was reared, into a large sunny ingenuous nature which knew nothing at all of the bondage of which I was beginning to be acutely conscious.'

Shelley in his fragmentary 'Essay on Friendship' speaks in the most glowing terms of an attachment he formed at school, and so does Leigh Hunt in his *Autobiography*. Says the latter:

'If I had reaped no other benefit from Christ Hospital, the school would be ever dear to me from the recollection of the friendships I formed in it, and of the first heavenly taste it gave me of that most spiritual of the affections... I shall

never forget the impression it made on me. I loved my friend
for his gentleness, his candour, his truth, his good repute,
his freedom even from my own livelier manner, his calm
and reasonable kindness. . . . I doubt whether he ever had a
conception of a tithe of the regard and respect I entertained
for him, and I smile to think of the perplexity (though he
never showed it) which he probably felt sometimes at my
enthusiastic expressions; for I thought him a kind of angel.'

It is not necessary, however, to quote authorities on such
a subject as this.[1] Any one who has had experience of
schoolboys knows well enough that they are capable of
forming these romantic and devoted attachments, and that
their alliances are often of the kind especially referred to as
having a bearing on education – i.e., between an elder and a
younger. They are genuine attractions, free as a rule, and at
their inception, from secondary motives. They are not
formed by the elder one for any personal ends. More often,
indeed, I think they are begun by the younger, who naively
allows his admiration of the elder one to become visible.
But they are absorbing and intense, and on either side their
influence is deeply felt and long remembered.

That such attachments *may* be of the very greatest value
is self-evident. The younger boy looks on the other as a
hero, loves to be with him, thrills with pleasure at his words
of praise or kindness, imitates, makes him his pattern and
standard, learns exercises and games, contracts habits, or
picks up information from him. The elder one, touched,
becomes protector and helper; the unselfish side of his
nature is drawn out, and he develops a real affection and
tenderness towards the younger. He takes all sorts of trouble
to initiate his *protégé* in field sports or studies; is proud of
the latter's success; and leads him on perhaps later to share
his own ideals of life and thought and work.

Sometimes the alliance will begin, in a corresponding
way, from the side of the elder boy. Sometimes, as said,
between a boy and a master such an attachment, or the
germ of it, is found; and indeed it is difficult to say what
gulf, or difference of age, or culture, or class in society, is so
great that affection of this kind will not on occasion over-
pass it. I have by me a letter which was written by a boy of
eleven or twelve to a young man of twenty-four or twenty-

five. The boy was rather a wild, 'naughty' boy, and had given his parents (working-class folk) a good deal of trouble. He attended, however, some sort of night-school or evening class and there conceived the strongest affection (evidenced by this letter) for his teacher, the young man in question, quite spontaneously, and without any attempt on the part of the latter to elicit it; and (which was equally important) without any attempt on his part to *deny* it. The result was most favourable; the one force which could really reach the boy had, as it were, been found; and he developed rapidly and well.

The following extract is from a letter written by an elderly man who has had large experience as a teacher. He says:

'It has always seemed to me that the *rapport* that exists between two human beings, whether of the same or of different sexes, is a force not sufficiently recognised, and capable of producing great results. Plato fully understood its importance, and aimed at giving what to his countrymen was more or less sensual, a noble and exalted direction... As one who has had much to do in instructing boys and starting them in life, I am convinced that the great secret of being a good teacher consists in the possibility of that *rapport*; not only of a merely intellectual nature, but involving a certain physical element, a personal affection, almost indescribable, that grows up between pupil and teacher, and through which thoughts are shared and an influence created that could exist in no other way.'

And it must be evident to every one that to the expanding mind of a small boy to have a relation of real affection with some sensible and helpful elder of his own sex must be a priceless boon. At that age love to the other sex has hardly declared itself, and indeed is not exactly what is wanted. The unformed mind requires an ideal of itself, as it were, to which it can cling or towards which it can grow. Yet it is equally evident that the relation and the success of it, will depend immensely on the character of the elder one, on the self-restraint and tenderness of which he is capable, and on the ideal of life which he has in his mind. That, possibly, is the reason why Greek custom, at least in the early days of Hellas, not only recognised friendships between elder and younger youths as a national institution of great importance, but laid down very distinct laws or rules concerning the conduct of them, so as to be a guide and a help to the elder in what was acknowledged to be a position of responsibility.

In Crete, for instance,[2] the friendship was entered into in quite a formal and public way, with the understanding and consent of relatives; the position of the elder was clearly defined, and it became his business to train and exercise the younger in skill of arms, the chase, etc.; while the latter could obtain redress at law if the elder subjected him to insult or injury of any kind. At the end of a certain period of probation, if the younger desired it he could leave his comrade; if not, he became his squire or henchman — the elder being bound to furnish his military equipments — and they fought thenceforward side by side in battle, 'inspired with double valour, according to the notions of the Cretans, by the gods of war and love.'[3] Similar customs prevailed in Sparta, and, in a less defined way, in other Greek states; as, indeed, they have prevailed among many semi-barbaric races on the threshold of civilisation.

When, however, we turn to modern life and the actual situation, as for instance in the public schools of today, it may well be objected that we find very little of the suggested ideal, but rather an appalling descent into the most uninspiring conditions. So far from friendship being an institution whose value is recognised and understood, it is at best scantily acknowledged and is often actually discountenanced and misunderstood. And though attachments such as we have portrayed exist, they exist underground, as it were, at their peril, and half-stifled in an atmosphere which can only be described as that of the gutter. Somehow the disease of premature sexuality seems to have got possession of our centres of education; wretched practices and habits abound, and (what is perhaps their worst feature) cloud and degrade the boys' conception of what true love or friendship may be.

To those who are familiar with large public schools the state of affairs does not need describing. A friend (who has placed some notes at my disposal) says that in his time a certain well-known public school was a mass of uncleanness, incontinence, and dirty conversation, while at the same time a great deal of genuine affection, even to heroism, was shown among the boys in their relations with one another. But 'all these things were treated by masters and boys alike as more or less unholy, with the result that they were either sought after or flung aside according to the sexual or emotional instinct of the boy. No attempt was made at discrimination. A kiss was by comparison as unclean as the act of *fellatio*, and no one had any gauge or principle whatever on which to guide the cravings of boyhood.' The writer then goes into details which it is not necessary to reproduce here. He (and others) were initiated in the mysteries of sex by the dormitory servant; and the boys thus corrupted mishandled each other.

Naturally in any such atmosphere as this the chances *against* the formation of a decent and healthy attachment are very large. If the elder youth happens to be given to sensuality he has here his opportunity; if on the other hand he is *not* given to it, the ideas current around probably have the effect of making him suspect his own affection, and he ends by smothering and disowning the best part of his nature. In both ways harm is done. The big boys in such places become either coarse and licentious or hard and self-righteous; the small boys, instead of being educated and strengthened by the elder ones, become effeminate little wretches, the favourites, the petted boys, and the 'spoons' of the school. As time goes on the public opinion of the school ceases to believe in the possibility of a healthy friendship; the masters begin to presume (and not without reason) that all affection means sensual practices, and end by doing their best to discourage it.

Now this state of affairs is really desperate. There is no need to be puritanical, or to look upon the lapses of boyhood as unpardonable sins; indeed, it may be allowed, as far as that goes, that a little frivolity is better than hardness and self-righteousness; yet every one feels, and must feel, who knows anything about the matter, that the state of our schools is bad.

And it is so because, after all, purity (in the sense of continence) *is* of the first importance to boyhood. To prolong the period of continence in a boy's life is to prolong the period of *growth*. This is a simple physiological law, and a very obvious one; and whatever other things may be said in favour of purity, it remains perhaps the most weighty. To introduce sensual and sexual habits — and one of the worst of these is self-abuse — at an early age, is to arrest growth, both physical and mental.

And what is even more, it means to arrest the capacity for affection. I believe affection, attachment — whether to the one sex or the other — springs up normally in the youthful mind in a quite diffused, ideal, emotional form — a kind of longing and amazement as at something divine — with no definite thought or distinct consciousness of sex in it. The sentiment expands and fills, as it were like a rising tide, every cranny of the emotional and moral nature; and the longer (of course within reasonable limits) its definite outlet towards sex is deferred, the longer does this period of emotional growth and development continue, and the greater is the refinement and breadth and strength of character resulting. All experience shows that a too early outlet towards sex cheapens and weakens affectional capacity.

Yet the early outlet it is which is the great trouble of our public schools. And it really does not seem unlikely that the peculiar character of the middle-class man of today, his undeveloped affectional nature and something of brutishness and woodenness, is largely due to the prevalent condition of the places of his education. The Greeks, with their wonderful instinct of fitness, seem to have perceived the right path in all this matter; and, while encouraging friendship, as we have seen, made a great point of modesty in early life — the guardians and teachers of every well-born boy being especially called upon to watch over the sobriety of his habits and manners.[4]

We have then in education generally, it seems to me (and whether of boys or of girls), two great currents to deal with, which cannot be ignored, and which certainly ought to be candidly recognised and given their right direction. One of these currents is that of friendship. The other is that of the young thing's natural curiosity about sex. The latter is of course, or should be, a perfectly legitimate interest. A boy at puberty naturally wants to know — and ought to know — what is taking place, and what the uses and functions of his body are. He does not go very deep into things; a small amount of information will probably satisfy him; but the curiosity is there, and it is pretty certain that the boy, if he is a boy of any sense or character, *will* in some shape or another get to satisfy it.

The process is really a *mental* one. Desire — except in some abnormal cases — has not manifested itself strongly; and there is often perhaps generally, an actual repugnance at first to anything like sexual practices; but the wish for information exists and is, I say, legitimate enough.[5] In almost all human societies except, curiously, the modern nations, there have been institutions for the initiation of the youth of either sex into these matters, and these initiations have generally been associated, in the opening blossom of the young mind, with inculcation of the ideals of manhood and womanhood, courage, hardihood, and the duties of the citizen or the soldier.[6]

But what does the modern school do? It shuts a trap-door down on the whole matter. There is a hush; a grim silence. Legitimate curiosity soon becomes illegitimate of its kind; and a furtive desire creeps in, where there was no desire before. The method of the gutter prevails. In the absence of any recognition of schoolboy needs, contraband information is smuggled from one to another; chaff and 'smut' take the place of sensible and decent explanations; unhealthy practices follow; the sacredness of sex goes its way, never to return, and the school is filled with premature and morbid talk and thought about a subject which should, by rights, only just be rising over the mental horizon.

The meeting of these two currents, of ideal attachment and sexual desire, constitutes a rather critical period, even when it takes place in the normal way — i.e., later on, and at the matrimonial age. Under the most favourable conditions a certain conflict occurs in the mind at their first encounter. But in the modern school this conflict, precipitated far too soon, and accompanied by an artificial suppression of the nobler current and a premature hastening of the baser one, ends in simple disaster to the former. Masters wage war against incontinence, and are right to do so. But how do they wage it? As said, by grim silence and fury, by driving the abscess deeper, by covering the drain over, *and* by confusing when it comes before them — both in their own minds and those of the boys — a real attachment with that which they condemn.

Not long ago the headmaster of a large public school coming suddenly out of his study chanced upon two boys embracing each other in the corridor. Possibly, and even probably, it was the simple and natural expression of an unsophisticated attachment. Certainly, it was nothing that in itself could be said to be either right or wrong. What did he do? He haled the two boys into his study, gave them a long lecture on the nefariousness of their conduct, with copious hints that he knew *what such things meant*, and *what they led to*, and ended by punishing both condignly. Could anything be more foolish? If their friendship was clean and natural, the master was only trying to make them feel that it was unclean and unnatural, and that a lovely and honourable thing was disgraceful; if the act was — which at least is improbable — a mere signal of lust — even then the best thing would have been to assume that it was honourable, and by talking to the boys, either together or separately, to try and inspire them with a better ideal; while if, between these positions, the master really thought the affection though honourable would lead to things undesirable, then, plainly, to punish the two was only to cement their love for each other, to give them a strong reason for concealing it, and to hasten its onward course. Yet every one knows that this is the *kind* of way in which the subject is treated in schools. It is the method of despair. And masters (perhaps not unnaturally) finding that they have not the time which would be needed for personal dealing with each boy, nor the forces at their command by which they might hope to introduce new ideals of life and conduct into their little community, and feeling thus utterly unable to cope with the situation, allow themselves to drift into a policy of mere silence with regard to it, tempered by outbreaks of ungoverned and unreasoning severity.

I venture to think that schoolmasters will never successfully solve the difficulty until they boldly recognise the two needs in question, and proceed candidly to give them their proper satisfaction.

The need of information — the legitimate curiosity — of boys (and girls) must be met, (1) partly by classes on physiology, (2) partly by private talks and confidences between elder and younger, based on friendship. With regard to (1) classes of this kind are already, happily, being carried on at a few advanced schools, and with good results. And though such classes can only go rather generally into the facts of motherhood and generation they cannot fail, if well managed, to impress the young minds, and give them a far grander and more reverent conception of the matter than they usually gain.

But (2) although some rudimentary teaching on sex lessons in physiology may be given in classes, it is obvious that further instruction and indeed any real help in the conduct of life and morals can only come through very close and tender confidences between the elder and the younger, such as exist where there is a strong friendship to begin with. It is obvious that effective help *can* only come in this way, and that this is the only way in which it is desirable that it should come. The elder friend in this case would, one might say, naturally be, and in many instances may be, the parent, mother or father — who ought certainly to be able to impress on the clinging child the sacredness of the relation. And it is much to be hoped that parents will see their way to take this part more freely in the future. But for some unexplained reason there is certainly often a gulf of reserve between the (British) parent and child; and the boy who is much at school comes more under the influence of his elder companions than his parents. If, therefore, boys and youths cannot be trusted and encouraged to form decent and loving friendships with each other, and with their elders or juniors — in which many delicate questions could be discussed and the tradition of sensible and manly conduct with regard to sex handed down — we are indeed in a bad plight and involved in a vicious circle from which escape seems difficult.

And so (we think) the need of attachment must also be met by full recognition of it, and the granting of it expression within all reasonable limits; by the dissemination of a good ideal of friendship and the enlistment of it on the side of manliness and temperance. Is it too much to hope that schools will in time recognise comradeship as a regular institution — considerably more important, say, than 'fagging' — an institution having its definite place in the school life, in the games and in the studies, with its own duties, responsibilities, privileges, etc., and serving to ramify through the little community, hold it together, and inspire its members with the two qualities of heroism and tenderness, which together form the basis of all great character?

But here it must be said that if we are hoping for any great change in the conduct of our large boys' schools, the so-called public schools are not the places in which to look for it — or at any rate for its inception. In the first place these institutions are hampered by powerful traditions which naturally make them conservative; and in the second place their mere size and the number of boys make them difficult to deal with or to modify. The masters are overwhelmed with work; and the (necessary) division of so many boys into separate 'houses' has this effect that a master who introduces a better tradition into his own house has always the prospect before him that his work will be effaced by the continual and perhaps contaminating contact with the boys from the other houses. No, it will be in smaller schools, say of from 50 to 100 boys, where the personal influence of the headmaster will be a real force reaching each boy, and where he will be really able to mould the tradition of the school, that we shall alone be able to look for an improved state of affairs.[7]

No doubt the first steps in any reform of this kind are difficult; but masters are greatly hampered by the confusion in the public mind, to which we have already alluded — which so often persists in setting down any attachment between two boys, or between a boy and his teacher, to nothing but sensuality. Many masters quite understand the situation, but feel themselves helpless in the face of public opinion. Who so fit (they sometimes feel) to enlighten a young boy and guide his growing mind as one of themselves, when the bond of attachment exists between the two? Like the writer of a letter quoted in the early part of this paper they believe that 'a personal affection, almost indescribable, grows up between pupil and teacher, through which thoughts are shared and an influence created that could exist in no other way.' Yet when the pupil comes along of whom all this

might be true, who shows by his pleading looks the sentiment which animates him, and the profound impression
which he is longing, as it were, to receive from his teacher,
the latter belies himself, denies his own instinct and the
boy's great need, and treats him distantly and with coldness.
And why? Simply because he dreads, even while he desires
it, the boy's confidence. He fears the ingenuous and
perfectly natural expression of the boy's affection in caress or
embrace, because he knows how a bastard public opinion will
interpret, or misinterpret it; and rather than run such a risk
as this he seals the fountains of the heart, withholds the
help which love alone can give, and deliberately nips the
tender bud which is turning to him for light and warmth.[8]

The panic terror which prevails in England with regard to
the expression of affection of this kind has its comic aspect.
The affection exists, and is known to exist, on all sides; but
we must bury our heads in the sand and pretend not to see
it. And if by any chance we are compelled to recognise it, we
must show our vast discernment by *suspecting* it. And thus
we fling on the dust-heap one of the noblest and most
precious elements in human nature. Certainly, if the denial
and suspicion of all natural affection were beneficial, we
should find this out in our schools; but seeing how complete
is its failure there to clarify their tone it is sufficiently
evident that the method itself is wrong.

The remarks in this paper have chiefly had reference to
boys' schools; but they apply in the main to girls' schools,
where much the same troubles prevail — with this difference, that in girls' schools friendships instead of being
repressed are rather encouraged by public opinion; only
unfortunately they are for the most part friendships of a
weak and sentimental turn, and not very healthy either in
themselves or in the habits they lead to. Here too, in girls'
schools, the whole subject wants facing out; friendship
wants setting on a more solid and less sentimental basis; and
on the subject of sex, so infinitely important to women,
there needs to be sensible and consistent teaching, both
public and private. Possibly the co-education of boys and girls
may be of use in making boys less ashamed of their feelings,
and girls more healthy in the expression of them.

At any rate the more the matter is thought of, the clearer I believe will it appear that a healthy affection must in the end be the basis of education and that the recognition of this will form the only way out of the modern school-difficulty. It is true that such a change would revolutionise our school-life; but it will have to come, all the same, and no doubt will come *pari passu* with other changes that are taking place in society at large.

5. The Place of the Uranian in Society

Whatever differing views there may be on the many problems which the Intermediate sexes present — and however difficult of solution some of the questions involved — there is one thing which appears to me incontestable: namely that a vast number of intermediates do actually perform most valuable social work, and that they do so partly on account and by reason of their special temperament.

This fact is not generally recognised as it ought to be, for the simple reason that the Uranian himself is not recognised, and indeed (as we have already said) tends to conceal his temperament from the public. There is no doubt that if it became widely known *who are* the Uranians, the world would be astonished to find so many of its great or leading men among them.

I have thought it might be useful to indicate some of the lines along which valuable work is being performed, or has been performed, by people of this disposition; and in doing this I do not of course mean to disguise or conceal the fact that there are numbers of merely frivolous, or feeble or even vicious homosexuals, who practically do no useful work for society at all — *just as there are of normal people*. The existence of those who do no valuable work does not alter the fact of the existence of others whose work is of great importance. And I wish also to make it clearly understood that I use the word Uranians to indicate simply those whose lives and activities are inspired by a genuine friendship or love for their own sex, without venturing to specify their individual and particular habits or relations towards those whom they love (which relations in most cases we have no means of knowing). Some Intermediates of light and leading — doubtless not a few — are physically very reserved and continent; others are sensual in some degree or other. The point is that they are all men, or women, whose most powerful motive comes from the dedication to their own kind, and is bound up with it in some way. And if it seems strange and anomalous that in such cases work of considerable importance to society is being done by people whose affections and dispositions society itself would blame, this is after all no more than has happened a thousand times before in the history of the world.

As I have already hinted, the Uranian temperament (probably from the very fact of its dual nature and swift and constant interaction between its masculine and feminine elements) is exceedingly sensitive and emotional; and there is no doubt that, going with this, a large number of the artist class, musical, literary or pictorial, belong to this description. That delicate and subtle sympathy with every wave and phase of feeling which makes the artist possible is also very characteristic of the Uranian (the male type), and makes it easy or natural for the Uranian man to become an artist. In the 'confessions' and 'cases' collected by Krafft-Ebing, Havelock Ellis and others, it is remarkable what a large percentage of men of this temperament belong to the artist class. In his volume on *Sexual Inversion*, speaking of the cases collected by himself, Ellis says: 'An examination of my cases reveals the interesting fact that thirty-two of them, or sixty-eight per cent, possess artistic aptitude in varying degree. Galton found, from the investigation of nearly one thousand persons, that the general average showing artistic taste in England is only about thirty per cent. It must also be said that my figures are probably below the truth, as no special point was made of investigating the matter, and also that in many of my cases the artistic aptitudes are of high order. With regard to the special avocations of my cases, it must of course be said that no occupation furnishes a safeguard against inversion. There are, however, certain occupations to which inverts are specially attracted. Acting is certainly one of the chief of these. Three of my cases belong to the dramatic profession, and others have marked dramatic ability. Art, again, in its various forms, and music, exercise much attraction. In my experience, however, literature is the avocation to which inverts seem to feel chiefly called, and that moreover in which they may find the highest degree of success and reputation. At least half-a-dozen of my cases are successful men of letters.'

Of Literature in this connection, and of the great writers of the world whose work has been partly inspired by the Uranian love, I have myself already spoken. ² It may further be said that those of the modern artist-writers and poets who have done the greatest service in the way of interpreting and reconstructing *Greek* life and ideals — men like Winckel-mann, Goethe, Addington Symonds, Walter Pater — have had a marked strain of this temperament in them. And this has been a service of great value, and one which the world could ill have afforded to lose.

The painters and sculptors, especially of the renaissance period in Italy, yield not a few examples of men whose work has been similarly inspired — as in the cases of Michel Angelo, Leonardo, Bazzi, Cellini, and others. As to music, this is certainly the art which in its subtlety and tenderness — and perhaps in a certain inclination to *indulge* in emotion — lies nearest to the Urning nature. There are few in fact of this nature who have not some gift in the direction of music — though, unless we cite Tschaikowsky, it does not appear that any thorough-going Uranian has attained to the highest eminence in this art.

Another direction along which the temperament very naturally finds an outlet is the important social work of Education. The capacity that a man has, in cases, of devoting himself to the welfare of boys or youths, is clearly a thing which ought not to go wasted — and which may be most precious and valuable. It is incontestable that a great number of men (and women) are drawn into the teaching profession by this sentiment — and the work they do is, in many cases, beyond estimation. Fortunate the boy who meets with such a helper in early life! I know a man — a rising and vigorous thinker and writer — who tells me that he owes almost everything mentally to such a friend of his boyhood, who took the greatest interest in him, saw him almost every day for many years, and indeed cleared up for him not only things mental but things moral, giving him the affection and guidance his young heart needed. And I have myself known and watched not a few such teachers, in public schools and in private schools, and seen something of the work and of the real inspiration they have been to boys under them. Hampered as they have been by the readiness of the world to misinterpret, they still have been able to do most precious service. Of course here and there a case occurs in which privilege is abused; but even then the judgment of the world is often unreasonably severe. A poor boy once told me with tears in his eyes of the work a man had done for him. This man had saved the boy from drunken parents, taken him from the slums, and by means of a club helped him out into the world. Many other boys he had rescued, it appeared, in the same way — scores and scores of them. But on some occasion or other he got into trouble, and was accused of improper familiarities. No excuse, or record of a useful life, was of the least avail. Every trumpery slander was believed, every mean motive imputed, and he had to throw up his position and settle elsewhere, his life-work shattered, never to be resumed.

The capacity for sincere affection which causes an elder man to care so deeply for the welfare of a youth or boy, is met and responded to by a similar capacity in the young thing of devotion to an elder man. This fact is not always recognised; but I have known cases of boys and even young men who would feel the most romantic attachments to quite mature men, sometimes as much as forty or fifty years of age, and only for them — passing by their own contemporaries of either sex, and caring only to win a return affection from these others. This may seem strange, but it is true. And the fact not only makes one understand what riddles there are slumbering in the breasts of our children, but how greatly important it is that we should try to read them — since here, in such cases as these, the finding of an answering heart in an elder man would probably be the younger one's salvation.

How much of the enormous amount of philanthropic

work done in the present day — by women among needy or
destitute girls of all sorts, or by men among like classes of
boys — is inspired by the same feeling, it would be hard to
say; but it must be a very considerable proportion. I think
myself that the best philanthropic work — just because it is
the most personal, the most loving, and the least merely
formal and self-righteous — has a strong fibre of the Uranian
heart running through it; and if it should be said that work
of this very personal kind is more liable to dangers and
difficulties on that account, it is only what is true of the best
in almost all departments.

Eros is a great leveller. Perhaps the true Democracy rests,
more firmly than anywhere else, on a sentiment which
easily passes the bounds of class and caste, and unites in the
closest affection the most estranged ranks of society. It is
noticeable how often Uranians of good position and breeding are drawn to rougher types, as of manual workers, and
frequently very permanent alliances grow up in this way,
which although not publicly acknowledged have a decided
influence on social institutions, customs and political
tendencies — and which would have a good deal more
influence could they be given a little more scope and
recognition. There are cases that I have known (although
the ordinary commercial world might hardly believe it) of
employers who have managed to attach their workmen, or
many of them, very personally to themselves, and whose
object in running their businesses was at least as much to
provide their employees with a living as themselves; while
the latter, feeling this, have responded with their best
output. It is possible that something like the guilds and
fraternities of the middle ages might thus be reconstructed,
but on a more intimate and personal basis than in those
days; and indeed there are not wanting signs that such a
reconstruction is actually taking place.

The *Letters of Love and Labour* written by Samuel M.
Jones of Toledo, Ohio, to his workmen in the engineering
firm of which he was master, are very interesting in this
connection. They breathe a spirit of extraordinary personal
affection towards, and confidence in, the employees, which
was heartily responded to by the latter; and the whole
business was carried on, with considerable success, on the

principle of a close and friendly co-operation all around.

These things indeed suggest to one that it is possible that the Uranian spirit may lead to something like a general enthusiasm of Humanity, and that the Uranian people may be destined to form the advance guard of that great movement which will one day transform the common life by substituting the bond of personal affection and compassion for the monetary, legal and other external ties which now control and confine society. Such a part of course we cannot expect the Uranians to play unless the capacity for their kind of attachment also exists — though in a germinal and undeveloped state — in the breast of mankind at large. And modern thought and investigation are clearly tending that way — to confirm that it does so exist.

Dr E. Bertz in his late study of Whitman as a person of strongly homogenic temperament[4] brings forward the objection that Whitman's gospel of Comradeship as a means of social regeneration is founded on a false basis — because (so Dr Bertz says) the gospel derives from an abnormality in himself, and therefore cannot possibly have a universal application or create a general enthusiasm. But this is rather a case of assuming the point which has to be proved. Whitman constantly maintains that his own disposition at any rate is normal, and that he represents the average man. And it *may* be true, even as far as his Uranian temperament is concerned, that while this was specially developed in him the germs of it *are* almost, if not quite, universal. If so, then the Comradeship on which Whitman founds a large portion of his message may in course of time become a general enthusiasm, and the nobler Uranians of today may be destined, as suggested, to be its pioneers and advance guard. As one of them himself has sung:

> These things shall be! A loftier race,
>   Than e'er the world hath known, shall rise
> With flame of freedom in their souls,
>   And light of science in their eyes.
> Nation with nation, land with land,
>   In-armed shall live as comrades free;
> In every heart and brain shall throb
>   The pulse of one fraternity.[5]

To proceed. The Uranian, though generally high-strung and sensitive, is by no means always dreamy. He is sometimes extraordinarily and unexpectedly practical; and such a man may, and often does, command a positive enthusiasm among his subordinates in a business organisation. The same is true of military organisation. As a rule the Uranian temperament (in the male) is not militant. War with its horrors and savagery is somewhat alien to the type. But here again there are exceptions; and in all times there have been great generals (like Alexander, Caesar, Charles XII of Sweden, or Frederick II of Prussia — not to speak of more modern examples) with a powerful strain in them of the homogenic nature, and a wonderful capacity for organisation and command, which combined with their personal interest in, or attachment to, their troops, and the answering enthusiasm so elicited, have made their armies well-nigh invincible.

The existence of this great practical ability in some Uranians cannot be denied; and it points to the important work they may some day have to do in social reconstruction. At the same time I think it is noticeable that *politics* (at any rate in the modern sense of the word, as concerned mainly with party questions and party government) is not as a rule congenial to them. The personal and affectional element is perhaps too remote or absent. Mere 'views' and 'questions' and party strife are alien to the Uranian man, as they are on the whole to the ordinary woman.

If politics, however, are not particularly congenial, it is yet remarkable how many royal personages have been decidedly homogenic in temperament. Taking the Kings of England from the Norman Conquest to the present day, we may count about thirty. And three of these, namely, William Rufus, Edward II, and James I were homosexual in a marked degree — might fairly be classed as Urnings — while some others, like William III had a strong admixture of the same temperament. Three out of thirty reveals a high ratio — ten per cent — and considering that sovereigns do not generally choose themselves, but come into their position by accident of birth, the ratio is certainly remarkable. Does it suggest that the general percentage in the world at large is equally high, but that it remains unnoticed, except in the fierce light that beats upon thrones? Or is there some other explanation with regard to the special liability of royalty to inversion? Hereditary degeneracy has sometimes been suggested. But it is difficult to explain the matter even on this theory; for though the epithet 'degenerate' might possibly apply to James I, it would certainly not be applicable to William Rufus and William III, who, in their different ways, were both men of great courage and personal force — while Edward II was by no means wanting in ability.

But while the Uranian temperament has, in cases, specially fitted its possessors to become distinguished in art or education or war or administration, and enabled them to do valuable work in these fields, it remains perhaps true that above all it has fitted them, and fits them, for distinction and service in affairs of the heart.

It is hard to imagine human beings more skilled in these matters than are the Intermediates. For indeed no one else can possibly respond to and understand, as they do, all the fluctuations and interactions of the masculine and feminine in human life. The pretensive coyness and passivity of women, the rude invasiveness of men; lust, brutality, secret tears, the bleeding heart; renunciation, motherhood, finesse, romance, angelic devotion — all these things lie slumbering in the Uranian soul, ready on occasion for expression; and if they are not always expressed are always there for purposes of divination or interpretation. There are few situations, in fact, in courtship or marriage which the Uranian does not instinctively understand; and it is strange to see how even an unlettered person of this type will often read Love's manuscript easily in cases where the normal man or woman is groping over it like a child in the dark. (Not of course that this means to imply any superiority of *character* in the former; but merely that with his double outlook he necessarily discerns things which the other misses.)

That the Uranians do stand out as helpers and guides, not only in matters of Education, but in affairs of love and marriage, is tolerably patent to all who know them. It is a common experience for them to be consulted now by the man, now by the woman, whose matrimonial conditions are uncongenial or disastrous — not generally because the consultants in the least perceive the Uranian nature, but because they instinctively feel that here is a strong sympathy with and understanding of their side of the question. In this way it is often the fate of the Uranian, himself unrecognised, to bring about happier times and a better comprehension of each other among those with whom he may have to deal. Also he often becomes the confidant of young things of either sex, who are caught in the tangles of love or passion, and know not where to turn for assistance.

I say that I think perhaps of all the services the Uranian may render to society it will be found some day that in this direction of solving the problems of affection and of the heart he will do the greatest service. If the day is coming as we have suggested — when Love is at last to take its rightful place as the binding and directing force of society (instead of the Cash-nexus), and society is to be transmuted in consequence to a higher form, then undoubtedly the superior types of Uranians — prepared for this service by long experience and devotion, as well as by much suffering — will have an important part to play in the transformation. For that the Urnings in their own lives put Love before everything else — postponing to it the other motives like money-making, business success, fame, which occupy so much space in most people's careers — is a fact which is patent to everyone who knows them. This may be saying little or nothing in favour of those of a poor and frivolous sort; but in the case of those others who see the god in his true light, the fact that they serve him in singleness of heart and so unremittingly raises them at once into the position of the natural leaders of mankind.

From this fact — i.e. that these folk think so much of affairs of the heart — and from the fact that their alliances and friendships are formed and carried on beneath the surface of society, as it were, and therefore to some extent beyond the inquisitions and supervisions of Mrs. Grundy, some interesting conclusions flow.

For one thing, the question is constantly arising as to how Society would shape itself if *free*: what form, in matters of Love and Marriage, it would take, if the present restrictions and sanctions were removed or greatly altered. At present in these matters, the Law, the Church, and a strong pressure of public opinion interfere, compelling the observance of certain forms; and it becomes difficult to say how much of the existing order is due to the spontaneous instinct and common sense of human nature, and how much to mere outside compulsion and interference: how far, for instance, Monogamy is natural or artificial; to what degree marriages would be permanent if the Law did not make them so; what is the rational view of Divorce; whether jealousy is a necessary accompaniment of Love; and so forth. These are questions which are being constantly discussed, without finality; or not infrequently with quite pessimistic conclusions.

Now in the Urning societies a certain freedom (though not complete, of course) exists. Underneath the surface of general Society, and consequently unaffected to any great degree by its laws and customs, alliances are formed and maintained, or modified or broken, more in accord with inner need than with outer pressure. Thus it happens that in these societies there are such opportunities to note and observe human grouping under conditions of freedom, as do not occur in the ordinary world. And the results are both interesting and encouraging. As a rule I think it may be said that the alliances are remarkably permanent. Instead of the wild 'general post' which so many good people seem to expect in the event of law being relaxed, one finds (except of course in a few individual cases) that common sense and fidelity and a strong tendency to permanence prevail. In the ordinary world so far has doubt gone that many to-day disbelieve in life-long free marriage. Yet among the Uranians such a thing is, one may almost say, common and well known; and there are certainly few among them who do not believe in its possibility.

Great have been the debates, in all times and places, concerning Jealousy; and as to how far jealousy is natural and instinctive and universal, and how far it is the product of social opinion and the property sense, and so on. In ordinary marriage what may be called social and proprietary jealousy is undoubtedly a very great factor. But this kind of jealousy hardly appears or operates in the Urning societies. Thus we have an opportunity in these latter of observing conditions where only the natural and instinctive jealousy exists. This of course is present among the Urnings — sometimes rampant and violent, sometimes quiescent and vanishing almost to *nil*. It seems to depend almost entirely upon the individual; and we certainly learn that jealousy though frequent and widespread, is not an absolutely necessary accompaniment of love. There are cases of Uranians (whether men or women) who, though permanently allied, do not object to lesser friendships on either side — and there are cases of very decided objection. And we may conclude that something the same would be true (is true) of the ordinary Marriage, the property considerations and the property jealousy being once removed. The tendency anyhow to establish a dual relation more or less fixed, is seen to be very strong among the Intermediates, and may be concluded to be equally strong among the more normal folk.

Again with regard to Prostitution. That there are a few natural-born prostitutes is seen in the Urning-societies; but prostitution in that world does not take the important place which it does in the normal world, partly because the law-bound compulsory marriage does not exist there, and partly because prostitution naturally has little chance and cannot compete in a world where alliances are free and there is an open field for friendship. Hence we may see that freedom of alliance and of marriage in the ordinary world will probably lead to the great diminution or even disappearance of Prostitution.

In these and other ways the experience of the Uranian world forming itself freely and not subject to outside laws and institutions comes as a guide — and really a hopeful guide — towards the future. I would say however that in making these remarks about certain conclusions which we are able to gather from some spontaneous and comparatively unrestricted associations, I do not at all mean to argue *against* institutions and forms. I think that the Uranian love undoubtedly suffers from want of a recognition and a standard. And though it may at present be better off than if subject to a foolish and meddlesome regulation; yet in the future it will have its more or less fixed standards and ideals, like the normal love. If one considers for a moment how the ordinary relations of the sexes would suffer were there no generally acknowledged codes of honour and conduct with regard to them, one then indeed sees that reasonable forms and institutions are a help, and one may almost wonder that the Urning circles are so well-conducted on the whole as they are.

I have said that the Urning men in their own lives put love before money-making, business success, fame, and other motives which rule the normal man. I am sure that it is also true of them as a whole that they put love before lust. I do not feel *sure* that this can be said of the normal man, at any rate in the present stage of evolution. It is doubtful whether on the whole the merely physical attraction is not the stronger motive with the latter type. Unwilling as the world at large is to credit what I am about to say, and great as are the current misunderstandings on the subject, I believe it is true that the Uranian men are superior to the normal men in this respect − in respect for their love-feeling − which is gentler, more sympathetic, more considerate, more a matter of the heart and less one of mere physical satisfaction than that of ordinary men.[6] All this flows naturally from the presence of the feminine element in them, and its blending with the rest of their nature. It should be expected *a priori*, and it can be noticed at once by those who have any acquaintance with the Urning world. Much of the current misunderstanding with regard to the character and habits of the Urning arises from his confusion with the ordinary *roué* who, though of normal temperament, contracts homosexual habits out of curiosity and so forth − but this is a point which I have touched on before, and which ought now to be sufficiently clear. If it be once allowed that the love-nature of the Uranian is of a sincere and essentially humane and kindly type then the importance of the Uranian's place in Society, and of the social work he may be able to do, must certainly also be acknowledged.

Intermediate Types among Primitive Folk

Introduction

That between the normal man and the normal woman there
exist a great number of intermediate types – types, for
instance, in which the body may be perfectly feminine,
while the mind and feelings are decidedly masculine, or *vice
versa* – is a thing which only a few years ago was very little
understood. But today – thanks to the labours of a number of
scientific men – the existence of these types is generally
recognised and admitted; it is known that the variations in
question, whether affecting the body or the mind, are
practically always congenital; and that similar variations
have existed in considerable abundance in all ages and
among all races of the world. Since the Christian era these
intermediate types have been much persecuted in some
periods and places, while in others they have been mildly
tolerated; but that they might possibly fulfil a positive and
useful function of any kind in society is an idea which
seems hardly if ever to have been seriously considered.

Such an idea, however, must have been familiar in
pre-Christian times and among the early civilisations, and if
not consciously analysed or generalised in philosophical
form, it none the less underran the working customs and life
of many, if not most primitive tribes – in such a way that
the intermediate people and their corresponding sex-
relationships played a distinct part in the life of the tribe or
nation, and were openly acknowledged and recognised as
part of the general polity.

It is probably too early at present to formulate any
elaborate theory as to the various workings of this element
in the growth of society. It might be easy to enter into a

tirade against sex-inversion in general and to point out and insist on all the evils which may actually or possibly flow from it. But this would not be the method either of common-sense or of science; and if one is to understand any widespread human tendency it is obvious that the procedure has to be different from this. One has to enquire first what advantages (if any) may have flowed, or been reported to flow, from the tendency, what place it may possibly have occupied in social life, and what (if any) were its healthy, rather than its unhealthy, manifestations. Investigating thus in this case, we are surprised to find how often – according to the views of these early peoples themselves – inversion in some form was regarded as a necessary part of social life, and the Uranian man accorded a certain meed of honour.

It would seem – as a first generalisation on this unexplored subject – that there have been two main directions in which the intermediate types have penetrated into the framework of normal society, and made themselves useful if not indispensable. And the two directions have been in some sense opposite, the one being towards service in Warfare and the other towards the service of Religion. It would seem that where the homosexual tendency was of the robuster and more manly sort, leading men to form comrade alliances with each other in the direction of active and practical life, this tendency was soon reinforced and taken advantage of by the military spirit. Military comradeship grew into an institution, and the peoples who adopted it became extraordinarily successful in warfare, and overcoming other tribes spread their customs among them. Such was the case with the Dorian Greeks, whose comradeship institutions form the subjects of chapters 5, 6, and 7 of this book; and such also appears to have been the case in a somewhat different way with the Samurai of Japan (chapter 8) in the twelfth and succeeding centuries; and in lesser degree with many Mohammedan peoples in Arabia, Persia, Afghanistan, and elsewhere.

On the other hand, it would seem that where the homosexual tendency was of a more effeminate and passive sort, it led to a distaste, on the part of those individuals or groups who were affected by it, for the ordinary masculine occupations and business of the world, and to an inclination to retire into the precincts of the Temples and the services (often sexual) of Religion – which, of course in primitive days, meant not only the religious life in our sense, but the dedication to such things as Magic, learning, poetry, music, prophecy, and other occupations not generally favoured by the normal man, the hunter and the warrior. There are also some considerations which go to show that this class of Intermediate did actually tend to develop faculties like divination, clairvoyance, ecstasy, and so forth, which are generally and quite naturally associated with religion.

This connection of homosexuality with divination and religion I have made the special subject of the first portion of this book; and it certainly is remarkable to find – even from this slight study – how widespread the connection has been among the primitive peoples and civilisations.

(I: The Intermediate in the Service of Religion)

1. As Prophet or Priest

A curious and interesting subject is the connection of the Uranian temperament with prophetic gifts and divination. It is a subject which, as far as I know, has not been very seriously considered – though it has been touched upon by Elie Reclus, Westermarck, Bastian, Iwan Bloch, and others. The fact is well known, of course, that in the temples and cults of antiquity and of primitive races it has been a widespread practice to educate and cultivate certain youths in an effeminate manner, and that these youths in general become the priests or medicine-men of the tribe; but this fact has hardly been taken seriously, as indicating any necessary connection between the two functions, or any relation in general between homosexuality and psychic powers. Some such relation or connection, however, I think we must admit as being obviously indicated by the following facts; and the admission leads us on to the further enquiry of what the relation may exactly be, and what its *rationale* and explanation.

Among the tribes, for instance, in the neighbourhood of Behring's Straits — the Kamchadales, the Chukchi, the Aleuts, Inoits, Kadiak islanders, and so forth, homosexuality is common, and its relation to shamanship or priesthood most marked and curious. Westermarck, in his well-known book, *The Origin and Development of the Moral Ideas,*[1] quoting from Dr Bogoraz, says: 'It frequently happens that, under the supernatural influence of one of their shamans, or priests, a Chukchi lad at sixteen years of age will suddenly relinquish his sex and imagine himself to be a woman. He adopts a woman's attire, lets his hair grow, and devotes himself altogether to female occupation. Furthermore, this disclaimer of his sex takes a husband into the *yurt* (hut) and does all the work which is usually incumbent on the wife, in most unnatural and voluntary subjection ... These abnormal changes of sex imply the most abject immorality in the community, and appear to be strongly encouraged by the shamans, who interpret such cases as an injunction of their individual deity.' Further, Westermarck says 'the change of sex was usually accompanied by future shamanship; indeed nearly all the shamans were former delinquents of their sex.' Again he says: 'In describing the Koriaks, Krasheninnikoff makes mention of the *ke'yev,* that is men occupying the position of concubines, and he compares them with the Kamchadale *koe'kcuc,* as he calls them, that is men transformed into women. Every *koe'kcuc,* he says, "is regarded as a *magician* and interpreter of dreams ... The *koe'kcuc* wore women's clothes, did women's work, and were in a position of wives or concubines." ' And (on p. 472) 'There is no indication that the North American aborigines attached any opprobrium to men who had intercourse with those members of their own sex who had assumed the dress and habits of women. In Kadiak such a companion was on the contrary regarded as a great acquisition; and the effeminate men, far from being despised, were held in repute by the people, most of them being wizards.'

This connection with wizardry and religious divination is particularly insisted upon by Elie Reclus, in his *Primitive Folk* (Contemporary Science Series). Speaking of the Inoits (p. 68) he says: 'Has a boy with a pretty face also a graceful demeanour? The mother no longer permits him to associate with companions of his own age, but clothes him and brings him up as a girl. Any stranger would be deceived as to his sex, and when he is about fifteen he is sold for a good round sum to a wealthy personage.[2] "*Choupans*", or youths of this kind are highly prized by the Konyagas. On the other hand, there are to be met with here and there among the Esquimaux or kindred populations, especially in Youkon, *girls* who decline marriage and maternity. Changing their sex, so to speak, they live as boys, adopting masculine manners and customs, they hunt the stag, and in the chase shrink from no danger, in fishing from no fatigue.'

Reclus then says that the *choupans* commonly dedicate themselves to the priesthood; but all are not qualified for this. 'To become an *angakok* it is needful to have a very marked vocation, and furthermore a character and temperament which every one has not. The priests in office do not leave the recruiting of their pupils to chance; they make choice at an early age of boys or girls, not limiting themselves to one sex – a mark of greater intelligence than is exhibited by most other priesthoods' (p. 71). The pupil has to go through considerable ordeals: 'Disciplined by abstinence and prolonged vigils, by hardship and contraint, he must learn to endure pain stoically and to subdue his bodily desires, to make the body obey unmurmuringly the commands of the spirit. Others may be chatterers; he will be silent, as becomes the prophet and the soothsayer. At an early age the novice courts solitude. He wanders throughout the long nights across silent plains filled with the chilly whiteness of the moon; he listens to the wind moaning over the desolate floes; – and then the aurora borealis, that ardently sought occasion for "drinking in the light", the *angakok* must absorb all its brilliancies and splendours . . . And now the future sorcerer is no longer a child. Many a time he has felt himself in the presence of Sidné, the Esquimaux Demeter, he has divined it by the shiver which ran through his veins, by the tingling of his flesh and the bristling of his hair ... He sees stars unknown to the profane; he asks the secrets of destiny from Sirius, Algol, and Altair; he passes through a series of initiations, knowing well that his spirit will not be loosed from the burden of dense matter and crass ignorance, until the moon has looked him in the face, and darted a certain ray into his eyes. At last his own Genius, evoked from the bottomless depths of existence, appears to him, having scaled the immensity of the heavens, and climbed across the abysses of the ocean. White, wan, and solemn, the phantom will say to him: "Behold me, what dost thou desire?" Uniting himself with the Double from beyond the grave, the soul of the *angakok* flies upon the wings of the wind, and quitting the body at will, sails swift and light through the universe. It is permitted to probe all hidden things, to seek the knowledge of all mysteries, in order that they may be revealed to those who have remained mortal with spirit unrefined' (p. 73).

Allowing something for poetic and imaginative expression, the above statement of the ordeals and initiations of the *angakok*, and their connection with the previous career of the *choupan* are well based on the observations of many authorities, as well as on their general agreement with similar facts all over the world. There is also another passage of Reclus (p. 70) on the duties of the *angakok*, which seems to throw considerable light on certain passages in the Bible referring to the *kedeshim* and *kedeshoth* of the Syrian cults, also on the *kosio* of the Slave Coast and the early functions of the priesthood in general: 'As soon as the *choupan* has moulted into the *angakok*, the tribe confide to him the girls most suitable in bodily grace and disposition; he has to complete their education – he will perfect them in dancing and other accomplishments, and finally will initiate them into the pleasures of love. If they display intelligence, they will become seers and medicine-women, priestesses and prophetesses. The summer *kachims* (assemblies), which are closed to the women of the community, will open wide before these. It is believed that these girls would be unwholesome company if they had not been purified by commerce with a man of God.'

Catlin, in his *North American Indians* (vol. 1, pp. 112–114), describes how on one occasion he was in a large tent occupied in painting portraits of some of the chiefs of the tribe (the Mandans) among whom he was staying, when he noticed at the door of the tent, but not venturing to come in, three or four young men of handsome presence and rather elegantly dressed, but not wearing the eagle's feathers of warriors. He mentally decided to paint the portrait of one of these also; and on a later day when he had nearly done with the chiefs, he invited one of these others to come in and stand for him. The youth was overjoyed at the compliment, and smiled all over his face. He was clad from head to foot in the skin of the mountain goat, which for softness and whiteness is almost like Chinese crape, embroidered with ermine and porcupine quills; and with his pipe and his whip in his hand, and his long hair falling over neck and shoulders, make a striking and handsome figure, which showed, too, a certain grace and gentleness as of good breeding. 'There was nought about him of the terrible,' says Catlin, 'and nought to shock the finest, chastest intellect.' But to Catlin's surprise, no sooner had he begun to sketch his new subject, than the chiefs rose up, flung their buffalo robes around them, and stalked out of the tent.

Catlin's interpreter afterwards explained to him the position of these men and the part they played in the tribal life; and how the chiefs were offended at the idea of their being placed on an equality with themselves. But the offence, it seemed, was not on any ground of immorality; but – and this is corroborated by the customs of scores of other tribes – arose simply from the fact that the young men were associated with the *women*, and shared their modes of life, and were not worthy therefore to rank among the *warriors*. In their own special way they held a position of some honour.

'Among the Illinois Indians,' says Westermarck (vol. 2, p. 473), the effeminate men assist in [i.e. are present at] all the juggleries and the solemn dance in honour of the calumet, or sacred tobacco-pipe, for which the Indians have such a deference. . . . but they are not permitted either to dance or to sing. They are called into the councils of the Indians, and nothing can be decided without their advice; for because of their extraordinary manner of living they are looked upon as *manitous*, or supernatural beings, and persons of consequ-

ence.' 'The Sioux, Sacs, and Fox Indians,' he continues, 'give
once a year, or oftener, a feast to the *berdashe*, or
i-coo-cco-a, who is a man dressed in women's clothes, as he
has been all his life.' And Catlin (*N. A. Indians*, vol. 2, p.
214) says of this *berdashe*: 'For extraordinary privileges
which he is known to possess, he is driven to the most
servile and degrading duties, which he is not allowed to
escape; and he being the only one of the tribe submitting to
this disgraceful degradation is looked upon as *medicine* and
sacred, and a feast is given to him annually; and initiatory to
it a dance by those few young men of the tribe who can – as
in the illustration – dance forward and publicly make their
boast (without the denial of the *berdashe*) that' [then follow
three or four unintelligible lines of some native dialect; and
then] 'such and such only are allowed to enter the dance and
partake of the feast.'

In this connection it may not be out of place to quote
Joaquin Miller (who spent his early life as a member of an
Indian tribe) on the prophetic powers of these people. He
says (*Life Among the Modocs*, p. 360) 'If there is a race of
men that has the gift of prophecy or prescience I think it is
the Indian. It may be a keen instinct sharpened by
meditation that makes them foretell many things with such
precision, but I have seen some things that looked much
like the fulfilment of prophecies. They believe in the gift of
prophecy thoroughly, and are never without their seers.'

In this connection we may quote the curious remark of
Herodotus, who after mentioning (1, 105) that some of the
Scythians suffered from a disease of effeminacy (θήλεια
νόσυς), and were called Enarees, says (4, 67) that 'these
Enarees, or Androgyni, were endowed by Venus with the
power of *divination*,' and were consulted by the king of the
Scythians when the latter was ill.*

The Jesuit father Lafitau, who published in 1724, at Paris,
an extremely interesting book on the manners and customs
of the North American tribes among whom he had been a
missionary,[3] after speaking of warlike women and Amazons, says (vol. 1, p. 53): 'If some women are found
possessing virile courage, and glorying in the profession of
war, which seems only suitable to men; there exist also men
so cowardly as to live like women. Among the Illinois,

among the Sioux, in Louisiana, in Florida, and in Yucatan, there are found youths who adopt the garb of women and preserve it all their lives, and who think themselves honoured by stooping to all their occupations; they never marry; they take part in all ceremonies in which religion seems to be concerned; and this profession of an extraordinary life causes them to pass for beings of a superior order, and above the common run of mankind. Would not these be the same kind of folk as the Asiatic worshippers of Cybele, or those Easterns of whom Julius Firmicus speaks (*Lib. de Errore prof. Relig.*), who consecrated to the Goddess of Phrygia, or to Venus Urania, certain priests, who dressed as women, who affected an effeminate countenance, who painted their faces, and disguised their true sex under garments borrowed from the sex which they wished to counterfeit.'

The instance, just quoted, of the Enarees among the Scythians, who by excessive riding were often rendered impotent and effeminate, is very curiously paralleled in quite another part of the world by the so-called *mujerados* (or feminised men) among the Pueblo Indians of Mexico. Dr W. A. Hammond, who was stationed, in 1850, as military doctor, in New Mexico, reported[4] that in each village one of the strongest men, being chosen, was compelled by unintermitted riding to pass through this kind of metamorphosis. 'He then became indispensable for the religious orgies which were celebrated among the Pueblo Indians in the same way as they once were among the old Greeks, Egyptians, and other people . . . These Saturnalia take place among the Pueblos in the Spring of every year, and are kept with the greatest secrecy from the observation of non-Indians.'[5] And again, 'To be a *mujerado* is no disgrace to a Pueblo Indian. On the contrary, he enjoys the protection of his tribes-people, and is accorded a certain amount of honour.'

Similar customs to those of the American Indians were found among the Pacific islanders. Captain James Wilson,[6] in visiting the South Sea Islands in 1796–8, found there men who were dressed like women and enjoyed a certain honour; and expresses his surprise at finding that 'even their women do not despise these fellows, but form friendships with

them.' While William Ellis, also a missionary, in his
Polynesian Researches[7] (vol. 1, p. 340), says that they not
only enjoyed the sanction of the priests, but even the direct
example of one of their divinities. He goes on to say that
when he asked the natives why they made away with so
many more female than male children, 'they generally
answered that the *fisheries*, the *service of the temple* and
especially *war* were the only purposes for which they
thought it desirable to rear children!'

But one of the most interesting examples of the connection we are studying is that of Apollo with the temple of
Delphi. Delphi, of course, was one of the chief seats of
prophecy and divination in the old world, and Apollo, who
presided at this shrine, was a strange blend of masculine and
feminine attributes. It will be remembered that he was
frequently represented as being very feminine in form –
especially in the more archaic statues.* He was the patron of
song and music. He was also, in some ways, the representative divinity of the Uranian love, for he was the special god
of the Dorian Greeks, among whom comradeship became an
institution.[8] It was said of him that to expiate his pollution
by the blood of the Python (whom he slew), he became the
slave and devoted favorite of Admetus; and Müller[9] describes a Dorian religious festival, in which a boy, taking the
part of Apollo, 'probably imitated the manner in which the
god, as herdsman and slave of Alcestis, submitted to the
most degrading service.' Alcestis, in fact, the wife of
Admetus, said of Apollo (in a verse of Sophocles cited by
Plutarch): οὑμὸς δ'ἀλέκτωρ αὐτον η'γε πρὸς 'μύλην'.* When
we consider that Apollo, as Sun god, corresponds in some
points to the Syrian Baal (masculine), and that in his epithet
Karneios, used among the Dorians,[10] he corresponds to the
Syrian Ashtaroth *karnaim* (feminine), we seem to see a
possible clue connecting certain passages in the Bible –
which refer to the rites of the Syrian tribes and their
occasional adoption in the Jewish Temple – with some
phases of the Dorian religious ritual.

'The Hebrews entering Syria,' says Richard Burton,[11]
'found it religionised by Assyria and Babylonia, when the
Accadian Ishtar had passed West, and had become
Ashtoreth, Ashtaroth, or Ashirah, the Anaitis of Armenia,

the Phœnician Astarte, and the Greek Aphrodite, the great Moon-goddess who is queen of Heaven and Love . . . She was worshipped by men habited as women, and *vice versa*; for which reason, in the Torah (Deut. 22, 5), the sexes are forbidden to change dress.'

In the account of the reforming zeal of King Josiah (2 Kings 23) we are told (v. 4) that 'the King commanded Hilkiah, the high priest, and the priests of the second order, and the keepers of the door, to bring forth out of the temple of the Lord all the vessels that were made for Baal, and for the grove, and for all the host of heaven; and he burned them without Jerusalem in the fields of Kidron . . . And he brake down the houses of the sodomites, that were by the house of the Lord, where the women wove hangings for the grove.'

The word here translated 'sodomites' is the Hebrew word *kedeshim*, meaning the 'consecrated ones' (males), and it occurs again in 1 Kings 14, 24; 15, 12; and 22, 46. And the word translated 'grove' is *asherah*. There is some doubt, I believe, as to the exact function of these *kedeshim* in the temple ritual, and some doubt as to whether the translation of the word given in our Authorised Version is justified.[12] It is clear, however, that these men corresponded in some way to the *kedeshoth* or sacred women, who were – like the *devadasis* of the Hindu temples – a kind of courtesan or prostitute dedicated to the god, and strange as it may seem to the modern mind, it is probable that they united some kind of sexual service with prophetic functions. Dr Frazer, speaking[13] of the sacred slaves or *kedeshim* in various parts of Syria, concludes that 'originally no sharp line of distinction existed between the prophets and the *kedeshim*; both were "men of God," as the prophets were constantly called; in other words they were inspired mediums, men in whom the god manifested himself from time to time by word and deed, in short, temporary incarnations of the deity. But while the prophets roved freely about the country, the *kedeshim* appears to have been regularly attached to a sanctuary, and among the duties which they performed at the shrines there were clearly some which revolted the conscience of men imbued with a purer morality.'

As to the *asherah*, or sometimes plural *asherim*, translated 'grove' – for which the women wove hangings – the most generally accepted opinion is that it was a wooden post or tree stripped of its branches and planted in the ground beside an altar, whether of Jehovah or other gods.[14] Several biblical passages, like Jeremiah 2, 27, suggest that it was an emblem of Baal or of the male organ, and others (e.g. Judges 2, 13, and 3, 7) connect it with Ashtoreth, the female partner of Baal; while the weaving of hangings or garments for the 'grove' suggests the combination of female with male in one effigy.[15] At any rate we may conclude pretty safely that the thing or things had a strongly sexual signification.

Thus it would seem that in the religious worship of the Canaanites there were male courtesans attached to the temples and inhabiting their precincts, as well as consecrated females, and that the ceremonies connected with these cults were of a markedly sexual character. These ceremonies had probably originated in an ancient worship of sexual acts as being symbolical of, and therefore favourable to, the fertility of Nature and the crops. But though they had penetrated into the Jewish temple they were detested by the more zealous adherents of Jehovah, because – for one reason at any rate – they belonged to the rival cult of the Syrian Baal and Ashtoreth, the *kedeshim* in fact being 'consecrated to the Mother of the Gods, the famous Dea Syria.'[16] And they were detestable, too, because they went hand in hand with the cultivation of 'familiar spirits' and 'wizards' – who of course knew nothing of Jehovah! Thus we see (2 Kings 22) that Manasseh followed the abominations of the heathen, building up the high places and the 'groves' and the altars for Baal. 'And he made his son pass through the fire, and observed times, and used enchantments,[17] and dealt with familiar spirits and wizards, and wrought much wickedness . . . and he set a graven image of the "grove" in the house of the Lord.' But Josiah, his grandson, reversed all this, and drove the familiar spirits and the wizards out of the land, together with the *kedeshim*.

So far with regard to Syria and the Bible. But Dr Frazer points out the curious likeness here to customs existing today among the Negroes of the Slave Coast of West Africa. In that region, women called *kosio*, are attached to the temples as wives, priestesses and temple prostitutes of the python-god. But besides these 'there are male *kosio* as well as femal *kosio*, that is there are dedicated men as well as dedicated women, priests as well as priestesses, and the idea and customs in regard to them seem to be similar.'[18] 'Indeed', he says, 'the points of resemblance between the prophets of Israel and of West Africa are close and curious.'[19] It must be said, however, that Dr Frazer does not in either case insist on the inference of homosexuality. On the contrary, he rather endeavours to avoid it, and of course it would be unreasonable to suppose any *invariable* connection of these 'sacred men' with this peculiarity. At the same time the general inference in that direction is strong and difficult to evade.

Throughout China and Japan and much of Malaysia, the so-called Bonzes, or Buddhist priests, have youths or boys attached to the service of the temples. Each priest educates a novice to follow him in the ritual, and it is said that the relations between the two are often physically intimate. Francis Xavier, in his letters from Japan (in 1549), mentions this. He says that the Bonzes themselves allowed that this was so, but maintained that it was no sin. They said that intercourse with woman was for them a deadly sin, or even punishable with death; but that the other relation was, in their eyes, by no means execrable, but harmless and even commendable.[20] And, as it was then, so on the whole it appears to be now, or to have been till very lately. In all the Buddhist sects in Japan (except Shinto) celibacy is imposed on the priests, but homosexual relations are not forbidden.

And to return to the New World, we find Cieza de Leon – who is generally considered a trustworthy authority – describing practices and ceremonials in the temples of New Granada in his time (1550) strangely similar to those referred to in the Hebrew Bible: 'Every temple or chief house of worship keeps one or two men, or more, according to the idol – who go about attired like women, even from their childhood, and talk like women, and imitate them in their manner, carriage, and all else.'[21] These served in the temples, and were made use of 'almost as if by way of sanctity and religion' (*casi come por via de santidad y religion*); and he concludes that 'the Devil had gained such mastery in that land that, not content with causing the people to fall into mortal sin, he had actually persuaded them that the same was a species of holiness and religion, in order that by so doing he might render them all the more subject to him. And this,' he says, 'Fray Domingo told me in his own writing – a man of whom everyone knows what a lover of truth he is.'

Thus, as Richard Burton remarks,[22] these same usages in connection with religion have spread nearly all over the world and 'been adopted by the priestly castes from Mesopotamia to Peru.'

It is all very strange and difficult to understand. Indeed, if the facts were not so well-established and so overwhelmingly numerous, it would appear incredible to most of us nowadays that the conception of 'sacredness' or 'consecration' could be honestly connected, in the mind of any people, with the above things and persons. And yet is is obvious, when one sums up the whole matter, that though in cases Cieza de Leon may have been right in suggesting that religion was only brought in as a cloak and excuse for licentiousness, yet in the main this explanation does not suffice. There must have been considerably more at the back of it all than that: a strange conviction apparently, or superstition, if one likes to call it so, that unusual powers of divination and prophecy were to be found in homosexual folk, and those who adopted the said hybrid kind of life – a conviction moreover (or superstition) so rooted and persistent that it spread over the greater part of the world.

Is any explanation, we may ask, of this strange and anomalous belief possible? Probably a *complete* explanation, in the present state of our knowledge, is not possible. Yet some suggestions in that direction we may perhaps venture to give. Before doing so, however, it may be as well to dwell for a moment on the further and widely prevalent belief in the connection between homosexuality and sorcery.

2. As Wizard or Witch

Perhaps – as it is now generally considered that the belief in Magic preceded what we call religion, and that the wizard came in order of development before the priest – I ought to have placed the present chapter first; but for some reasons the order adopted seems the better. Anyhow it is certain that among primitive folk the prophet, the priest, the wizard, and the witch-doctor largely unite their functions, and are not easily distinguishable from one another; and therefore, from what has already been said, we may naturally expect to find an association between homosexuality and sorcery.

Westermarck (vol. 1, p. 477) mentions the ancient Scandinavians as regarding passive homosexuals in the light of sorcerers; and refers (p. 484, note) to Thomas Falkner, who, in his *Description of Patagonia* (1775), p. 117, says that among the Patagonians 'the wizards are of both sexes. The male wizards are obliged (as it were) to leave their sex, and to dress themselves in female apparel, and are not permitted to marry, though the female ones or witches may. They are generally chosen for this office when they are children, and a preference is always shown to those who at that early time of life discover an effeminate disposition. They are clothed very early in female attire, and presented with the drum and rattles belonging to the professsion they are to follow.'

The following is an account given by Dawydow, the Russian traveller,[1] of the quite similar custom prevalent in his time (about 1800) among the Konyagas in the Alaska region: 'There are here (in the island of Kadiak) men with tatooed chins, who work only as women; who always live with the women-kind, and like the latter, have husbands – not infrequently even two. Such men are called *achnutschik*. They are not by any means despised, but, on the contrary, are respected in the settlements, and are for the most part *wizards*. The Konyaga, who possesses an *achnutschik* instead of a wife, is even thought fortunate. When father or mother regard their son as feminine in his bearing they will often dedicate him in earliest childhood to the vocation of *achnutschik*. Sometimes it will happen that the parents have in mind beforehand to have a daughter, and when they find themselves disappointed they make their new-born son an *achnutschik*.'

Here we have the association between homosexuality and sorcery clearly indicated for the very extremes, South and North, of the American continent; and, as a matter of fact, and as appears from various other passages in the present work, the same association may be traced among countless tribes of the middle regions of the same continent, and all over the world. There was a legend current among the North American Indians at one time[2] about a *berdache*, or man of this kind, who was shot at by an enraged warrior of his own tribe; but when the onlookers ran to the place where the transfixed man fell they found only an arrow sticking in a heap of stones. The man had disappeared!

With regard to the attribution of homosexuality also to female wizards, or witches, I believe that, rightly or wrongly, this was very common in Europe a few centuries ago. Leo Africanus (1492) in his description of Morocco[3] says: 'The third kind of diviners are women-witches, which are affirmed to have familiarity with divels. Changing their voices they fain the divell to speak within them: then they which come to enquire ought with greate feare and trembling (to) aske these vile and abominable witches such questions as they mean to propound, and lastly, offering some fee unto the divell, they depart. But the wiser and honester sort of people call these women *sahacat*, which in Latin signifieth *fricatrices*, because they have a damnable custom to commit unlawful venerie among themselves, which I cannot express in any modester terms.' He then goes on to say that these witches, carnally desiring some of the young women who come to 'enquire,' entrap them and corrupt them so far as actually to cause them in some cases to 'desire the companie of those witches' (and to that end, he explains, deceive their husbands). Whether this is all true or not – it shows the kind of thing that was believed at that time about witches.

In some cases the adoption of the life of priest or sorcerer is accompanied by a change of dress (as we have seen), but this is by no means always so. Speaking of the Pelew Islanders, Dr Frazer[4] attributes the adoption by the priests of female attire to the fact that 'it often happens that a goddess chooses a man, not a woman, for her minister and inspired mouthpiece. When that is so, the favoured man is thenceforth regarded and treated as a woman.' And he continues: 'This pretended change of sex under the inspiration of a female spirit perhaps explains a custom widely spread among savages, in accordance with which some men dress as women and act as women through life.'

This explanation is certainly not very convincing – though it is just possible that in certain cases of men of this kind in early times, the feminine part of their natures may have personified itself, and presented itself to them as a vision of a female spirit or goddess; and thus the explanation might be justified. But anyhow it should not be overlooked that the same impulse (for men to dress as women, and women to dress as men) perseveres today in quite a large percentage of our modern civilised populations; and whatever its explanations, the impulse is often enormously powerful, and its satisfaction a source of great delight. It must also not be overlooked, in dealing with this complex and difficult subject, that the mere fact of a person delighting to adopt the garb of the opposite sex does not in itself prove that his or her love-tendency is abnormal – i.e. cross-dressing does not *prove* homosexuality. There are not a few cases of men in the present day (and presumably the same in past times) who love to dress as women, and yet are perfectly normal in their sex-relations; and therefore too sweeping generalisations on this subject must be avoided.[5]

On the whole, however, cross-dressing must be taken as a general indication of, and a cognate phenomenon to, homosexuality; and its wide prevalence in early times, especially in connection with the priesthood, must give us much matter for thought. Dr Frazer, in his *Adonis, Attis, and Osiris*, continuing the passage I have just quoted, says: 'These unsexed creatures often, perhaps generally, profess the arts of sorcery and healing, they communicate with spirits and are regarded sometimes with awe and sometimes with contempt, as beings of a higher or lower order than common folk. Often they are dedicated or trained to their vocation from childhood. Effeminate sorcerers or priests of this sort are found among the Sea Dyaks of Borneo, the Bugis of South Celebes, the Patagonians of South America ... In Madagascar we hear of effeminate men who wore female attire and acted as women, thinking thereby to do God service. In the kingdom of Congo there was a sacrificial priest who commonly dressed as a woman and gloried in the title of the grandmother.' And Dr Karsch, in his *Uranismus bei den Naturvölkern*, after enumerating the above and many other instances, says that among many or most of these tribes the main object of the cross-dressing seems to be something of a religious or mystical character, since the persons concerned are accounted as beings of a higher order, priests or sorcerers; but that fact does not stand in the way of the homosexual relationship, which certainly prevails in many cases.

An important point in all this matter, and one which on the one hand gives an air of sincerity to the phenomenon, and on the other may easily have connected it with magic or sorcery in the primitive mind, is the rapidity and decisiveness with which the sexual transformation sometimes seems to take place. This is indicated in Dr Frazer's just-quoted passage on the Pelew Islanders; and in such cases we seem to be witnessing a veritable metamorphosis, and cannot help wondering whether a real psychological or physiological transmutation may not be in progress. For though sometimes, as we have seen, children are brought up from an early age to play this exchanged or inverted part in life, yet often they take it up themselves, and cannot be persuaded to abandon it; and often they quite suddenly adopt it as young men (or women) or in mature age – as the result of some supposed dream or inspiration. Wied, lately quoted, says concerning the *berdaches*: 'These generally assert that a dream or some high impulse has commanded them to adopt this state as their "medicine" or salvation, and nothing then can turn them away from their purpose. Many a father has sought even by force to divert his child from this object, has reasoned with him at first, offered him fine weapons and masculine articles of dress in order to inspire him with a taste for manly occupations; and when this proved useless, has handled him sternly, punished and beaten him; yet all in vain.'[6]

John T. Irving, in his *Indian Sketches* (1835) — a description of the Pawnee and other American Indians — has a whole chapter (ch. 13) entitled 'The Metamorphosis' and dealing with this subject. He there describes how among a group of female Indians occupied in drying shelled corn in the sun, he one day noticed what seemed a particularly tall and powerful woman — who, on enquiry, turned out to be a man. This man's story was as follows. Once an Otoe brave of the highest renown, he on one occasion, after a desperate fight with the Osages, returned home, and refusing to speak to anyone, threw himself on his bed for the night. In the morning he rose up an altered man. 'He collected his family round him, and informed them that the Great Spirit had visited him in a dream, and had told him he had now reached the zenith of his reputation; that no voice had more weight in the Council; no arm was heavier in battle. But that he must thenceforth relinquish all claim to the rank of a warrior and assume the dress and avocations of a female.' His friends heard him in sorrow, but did not attempt to dissuade him, 'for they listened to the communications of the deity with a veneration equal to his own.' So he snapped his bow in twain, buried his tomahawk and rifle, washed off his war paint, discarded the eagle plume from his scalplock, and ceased to be numbered among the warriors, relinquishing all 'for the lowly and servile duties of a female.'

Years had elapsed, says the author, since that act of renunciation, but the man had kept to his resolve.

These strange changes, induced in childhood, or spontaneously adopted in youth, maturity, and even old age, have been observed amongst almost all the North American Indian tribes. Wied mentions the Sauks, Foxes, Mandans, Crows, Blackfeet, Dakotas, Assiniboins, and others. And their connection with the Moon seems to be frequently believed in. W. H. Keating, in his *Expedition to Lake Winnipeck* (2 vols, 1824), says that the Sun among the Winnebagos is held to be propitious to man; but 'the Moon, on the contrary, they held to be inhabited by an adverse female deity, whose delight is to cross man in all his pursuits. If, during their sleep, this deity should present herself to them in their dreams, the Indians consider it enjoined on them by duty to become *cinœdi*; and they ever after assume the female garb. It is not impossible,' continues Keating, 'that this may have been the source of the numerous stories of hermaphrodites related by all the old writers on America.'

Whatever may be the truth about the connection between these strange changes of sexual habit and visionary appearances of the deities (a subject on which I shall touch again later on), we cannot help seeing, as I say, that the fervent belief in such connection is a testimony to the sincerity and actuality of the transformations, as well as a partial explanation of why sorcerous and miraculous powers were credited to the transformed persons. At any rate, the total mass of facts connecting homosexualism in general with religion and divination, or with unusual psychic powers, and on the same lines as those already presented in this and the preceding chapter, is enormously large; and we need delay no longer on their further accumulation. We may, however, venture to say a few words in possible explanation of the connection.

Dr Iwan Bloch, in his monumental work *Die Prostitution*,[7] leans to the general explanation that homosexuality, just on account of its strange and inexplicable character, was by primitive people accounted as something divine and miraculous, and the homosexual man or woman therefore credited with supernatural powers. He says (vol. 1, p. 101): 'This riddle, which despite all our efforts, present-day science has not yet satisfactorily solved, must to the primitive intelligence have appeared even more inexplicable than to us; and a man born with the inclination towards his own sex must have been regarded as something extraordinary, as one of those strange freaks of Nature which among Primitives are so easily accounted divine marvels and honored as such. The by no means scanty supply of ethnological facts on this subject which we possess confirms the above view, and shows in what odour of sanctity homosexual individuals have often stood among Nature-folk – for which reason they frequently played an important part in religious rituals and festivals.'

Bloch also quotes a theory of Adolf Bastian, who, in his great work *Der Mensch in der Geschichte* supposes that the priests among early peoples, as representatives of the *bisexual* principle in Nature, encouraged homosexual rites in the temples on the same footing as heterosexual rites. 'The men,' says Bastian, 'prayed to the active powers of Nature, and the women, in privacy and retirement, to the feminine powers; while the priests, who had to satisfy the demands of both parties, learned the idea of sex-changes from the Moon, and served the masculine gods in masculine attire, and the goddesses in feminine garments, or set up images of a bearded Venus and of a Herkules spinning at the wheel.*

Neither of these explanations seems to me to be quite adequate. That of Bloch is hardly sufficient; for though it is true that freaks of Nature are often regarded with superstitious awe by savages, that fact does not quite suffice to explain the world-wide attribution of magic powers to homosexuals, nor the systematic adoption of the services of such folk in the temples. The theory of Bastian, on the other hand, is quite opposed to that of Bloch, for it presupposes a very wide original prevalence of homosexuality in the human race, which was only preserved (and not instituted) by the priests in the tradition of the religious rituals; and therefore it cuts away the speculation that the homosexual man was divinised on account of his rarity. Moreover, the theory of Bastian suffers from the fact that the supposed wide prevalence of bisexuality in aboriginal times is by no means proved, or indeed easily provable – although, of course, it may have existed. However, on the subject of bisexuality I shall touch in a later chapter.

For myself, I think that there are two quite possible and not unreasonable theories on the whole matter. The first and most important is that there really *is* a connection between the homosexual temperament and divinatory or unusual psychic powers; the second is (that there is no such particular connection, but) that the idea of sorcery or witchcraft naturally and commonly springs up round the ceremonials of an old religion or morality when that religion is being superseded by a new one. This is, of course, a well-recognised fact. The gods of one religion become the devils of its successor; the poetic rites of one age become the black magic of the next. But in the case of the primitive religions of the earth their ceremonials were, without doubt, very largely sexual, and even homosexual. Consequently, when new religious developments set in, the homosexual rites, which were most foreign to the later religionists and most disturbing to their ideas, associated themselves *most* strongly with the notion of sorcery and occult powers.

For myself I am inclined to accept both explanations, and – leaving out, of course, the clause in brackets in the second – to combine them. I think there *is* an organic connection between the homosexual temperament and unusual psychic or divinatory powers; but I think also that the causes mentioned in the second explanation have in many cases led to an exaggerated belief in such connection, and have given it a sorcerous or demonic aspect.

To take the second point first. Just as, according to Darwin, the sharpest rivalry occurs between a species and the closely allied species from which it has sprung, so in any religion there is the fiercest theological hatred against the form which has immediately preceded it. Early Christianity could never say enough against the Pagan cults of the old world (partly for the very reason that it embodied so much of their ceremonial and was in many respects their lineal descendant). They were the work and inspiration of the devil. Their Eucharists and baptismal rites and initiations – so strangely and diabolically similar to the Christian rites – were sheer black magic; their belief in the sacredness of sex mere filthiness. Similarly the early Protestants could never say malignant things enough against the Roman Catholics; or the Secularists in their turn against the Protestants. In all these cases there is an element of fear – fear because the thing supposed to have been left behind lies after all so close, and is always waiting to reassert itself – and this fear invests the hated symbol or person with a halo of devilish potency. Think, for instance, what sinister and magical powers and influence have been commonly ascribed to the Roman Catholic priests in the ordinary Protestant parlours and circles!

It is easy, therefore, to understand that when the Jews established their worship of Jehovah as a great reaction against the primitive nature-cults of Syria – and in that way to become in time the germ of Christianity – the first thing they did was to denounce the priests and satellites of Baal-Peor and Ashtoreth as wizards and sorcerers, and wielders of devilish faculties. These cults were frankly sexual – probably the most intimate meaning of them, as religions, being the glory and sacredness of sex; but the Jews (like the later Christians) blinding themselves to this aspect, were constrained to see in sex only filthiness, and in its religious devotees persons in league with Beelzebub and the powers of darkness. And, of course, the homosexual elements in these cults, being the most foreign to the new religion, stood out as the *most* sorcerous and the most magical part of them. Westermarck points out (*Moral Ideas*, vol. 2, 489) that the Mediæval Christianity constantly associated homosexuality with heresy – to such a degree in fact that the French word *hérite* or *hérétique* was sometimes used in both connections; and that *bougre* or *Bulgarian* was commonly used in both, though to begin with it only denoted a sect of religious heretics who came from Bulgaria. And he thinks that the violent reprobation and punishment of homosexuality arose more from its connection in the general mind with heresy than from direct aversion in the matter – more in fact from religious motives than from secular ones.

But connecting with all this, we must not neglect the theory so ably worked out by Prof. Karl Pearson among others – namely that the primitive religions were not only sexual in character but that they were largely founded on an early matriarchal order of society, in which women had the predominant sway – descent being traced through them, and tribal affairs largely managed by them, and in which the chief deities were goddesses, and the priests and prophets mainly females. Exactly how far such an order of society really extended in the past is apparently a doubtful question; but that there are distinct traces of such matriarchal institutions in certain localities and among some peoples seems to be quite established. Karl Pearson, assuming the real prevalence of these institutions in early times points out, reasonably enough, that when Christianity became fairly established matriarchal rites and festivals, lingering on in out-of-the-way places among the peasantry, would at once be interpreted as being devilish and sorcerous in character, and the women (formerly priestesses) who conducted them and perhaps recited snatches of ancient half-forgotten rituals, would be accounted witches. 'We have, therefore,' he says,[8] 'to look upon the witch as essentially the degraded form of the old priestess, cunning in the knowledge of herbs and medicine, jealous of the rites of the goddess she serves, and preserving in spells and incantations such wisdom as early civilisation possessed.' This civilisation, he explains, included the 'observing of times and seasons,' the knowledge of weather-lore, the invention of the broom, the distaff, the cauldron, the pitchfork, the domestication of the goat, the pig, the cock and the hen, and so forth – all which things became symbols of the witch in later times, simply because originally they were the inventions of woman and the insignia of her office, and so the religious symbols of the Mother-goddess and her cult.

The connection of all this will homosexual customs is not at once clear; but it has been suggested – though I am not sure that Karl Pearson himself supports this – that the primitive religions of the Matriarchate may have ultimately led to men-priests dressing in female attire. For when the matriarchal days were passing away, and men were beginning to assert their predominance, it still may have happened that the old religious customs lingering on may have induced men to simulate the part of women and to dress as priestesses, or at least have afforded them an excuse for so doing.[9] In this way it seems just possible that the pendulum-swing of society from the matriarchate to the partriarchate may have been accompanied by some degree of crasis and confusion between the functions of the sexes, homosexual customs and tendencies may have come to the fore, and the connection of homosexuality with the priesthood may seem to be accounted for.

This explanation, however, though it certainly has a claim to be mentioned, seems to me too risky and insecure for very much stress to be laid upon it. In the first place the extent and prevalence of the matriarchal order of society is a matter still very much disputed, and to assume that at any early period of human history the same was pratically universal would be unjustified. In the second place, granting the existence of the matriarchal order and its transmutation into the patriarchal, the connection of this change with the development of homosexual customs is still only a speculation and a theory, supported by little direct evidence. On the other hand, the facts to be explained – namely, the connection of homosexuality with priesthood and divination – seem to be world-wide and universal. Therefore, though we admit that the causes mentioned – namely the attribution of magical qualities to old religious rites, and the introduction of feminine inversions and disguises through the old matriarchal custom – may account in part for the facts, and in particular may in certain localities have given them a devilish or sorcerous complexion, yet I think we must look deeper for the root-explanations of the whole matter, and consider whether there may not be some fundamental causes in human nature itself.

3. As Inventors of the Arts and Crafts

I have already said that I think there is an original connection of some kind between homosexuality and divination; but in saying this, of course, I do not mean that everywhere and always the one is associated with the other, or that the relationship between the two is extremely well marked; but I contend that a connection can be traced and that on *a priori* grounds its existence is quite probable.

And first, with regard to actual observation of such a connection, the fact of the widespread belief in it, which I have already noted as existing among the primitive tribes of the earth, and their founding of all sorts of customs on that belief, must count for something. Certainly the mere existence of a widespread belief among early and superstitious peoples – as for instance that an eclipse is caused by a dragon swallowing the sun – does not prove its truth; but in the case we are considering the matter is well within the range of ordinary observation, and the constant connection between the *choupan* and the *angakok*, the *ke'yev* and the *shamon*, the *berdache* and the witch-doctor, the ganymede and the temple-priest, and their correspondences all over the world, the *basir* among the Dyaks, the boy-priests in the temples of Peru, the same in the Buddhist temples of Ceylon, Burma and China – all these cases seem to point to some underlying fact, of the fitness or adaptation of the invert for priestly or divinatory functions. And though the tendency already alluded to, of a later religion to ascribe devilish potency to earlier cults, must certainly in many instances shed a sinister or sorcerous glamour over the invert, yet this exaggeration need not blind us to the existence of a residual fact behind it; and anyhow to a great many of the cases just mentioned it does not apply at all, since in them the question of one religion superseding another does not enter.

To come to more recent times, the frequency with which accusations of homosexuality have been launched against the religious orders and monks of the Catholic Church, the Knights Templars, and even the ordinary priests and clerics, must give us pause. Nor need we overlook the fact that in Protestant Britain the curate and the parson quite often appear to belong to some 'third sex' which is neither wholly masculine nor wholly feminine!

Granting, then, that the connection in question is to a certain degree indicated by the anthropological facts which we already possess – is there, we may ask, any rational ground for expecting this connection *a priori* and from psychological considerations? I think there is.

In the first place all science now compels us to admit the existence of the homosexual temperament as a fact of human nature, and an important fact; and not only so, but to perceive that it is widely spread among the various races of the earth, and extends back to the earliest times of which we have anything like historical knowledge. We can no longer treat it as a mere local and negligible freak, or put it in the category of a sinful and criminal disposition to be stamped out at all costs. We feel that it must have some real significance. The question is what that may be. The following is a suggestion that may cover part of the ground, though not, I think, the whole.

In the primitive societies the men (the quite normal men) are the warriors and hunters. These are their exlusive occupations. The women (the normal women) attend to domestic work and agriculture, and their days are consumed in those labours. But in the evolution of society there are many more functions to be represented than those simple ones just mentioned. And we may almost think that if it had not been for the emergence of intermediate types – the more or less feminine man and similarly the more or less masculine woman – social life might never have advanced beyond the primitive phases. But when the man came along who did not *want* to fight – who perhaps was more inclined to run away – and who did not particularly care about hunting, he necessarily discovered some other interest and occupation – composing songs or observing the qualities of herbs or the processions of the stars. Similarly with the woman who did not care about housework and child-rearing. The non-warlike men and the non-domestic women, in short, sought new outlets for their energies. They sought different occupations from those of the quite ordinary man and woman – as in fact they do today; and so they became the initiators of new activities. They became students of life and nature, inventors and teachers of arts and crafts, or wizards (as they would be considered) and sorcerers; they became diviners and seers, or revealers of the gods and religion; they became medicine-men and healers, prophets and prophetesses; and so ultimately laid the foundation of the priesthood, and of science, literature and art. Thus – on this view, and as might not unreasonably be expected – it was primarily a variation in the intimate sex-nature of the human being which led to these important differentiations in his social life and external activities.

In various ways we can see the likelihood of this thesis, and the probability of the intermediate man or woman becoming a forward force in human evolution. In the first place, as just mentioned, not wholly belonging to either of the two great progenitive branches of the human race, his nature would not find complete satisfaction in the activities of either branch, and he would necessarily create a new sphere of some kind for himself. Secondly, finding himself *different* from the great majority, sought after by some and despised by others, now an object of contumely and now an object of love and admiration, he would be forced to *think*. His mind turned inwards on himself would be forced to tackle the problem of his own nature, and afterwards the problem of the world and of outer nature. He would become one of the first thinkers, dreamers, discoverers. Thirdly, some of the Intermediates (though certainly not all) combining the emotionality of the feminine with the practicality of the masculine, and many other qualities and powers of both sexes, as well as much of their experience, would undoubtedly be greatly superior in ability to the rest of their tribe, and making forward progress in the world of thought and imagination would become inventors, teachers, musicians, medicine-men and priests; while their early science and art (for such it would be) – prediction of rain, determination of seasons, observation of stars, study of herbs, creation of chants and songs, rude drawings, and so forth – would be accounted quite magical and divinatory.

With regard to the early beginnings of poetry and music, we know that dancing had an important place; and there is an interesting passage in Leguével de Lacombe's *Voyage à Madagascar*[1] (vol. 1, pp. 97, 98), which indicates the connection of these arts, among the Tsecats of Madagascar, with sexual variation. 'Dancers form a distinct class in Madagascar, though they are not very numerous. They have their own manners and customs, and live apart; they do not marry, and even affect dislike for women – although they wear the dress of the latter and imitate their voices, gestures, and general habits. They wear large earrings of gold or silver, necklaces of coral or coloured beads, and bracelets of silver; they carefully extract the hair of their beards, and in short play the part of women so well that one is often deceived. For the rest these dancers have simple manners, and are very sober in their habits; they are continually on the move, and are well accepted wherever they go; sometimes, indeed, they receive considerable presents. I have seen chiefs who have been amused by them for some days make them a present, on their departure, of two or three slaves. They are the poets or the bards of the island, and they improvise rhapsodies in praise of those who are generous to them.'

Very similar customs connecting the wandering life of dancers, actors, and singers with a certain amount of inversion of temperament, are known to have existed among that strange and remarkable people, the Areoi of Polynesia: of whom Wm. Ellis, the missionary already quoted, says that they were honoured as gods, and were supposed to be inspired by the gods to become members of the Areoi society; also that their initiations began by submission to service and to various ordeals, and ended by a ceremonial in which the candidate snatched and appropriated the cloth worn by the chief *woman* present!

In all this – whether relating to primitive science or primitive art – there would, of course, really be nothing miraculous. It is easy to see that certain individuals, whose interests or abilities were turned in special or unusual directions, would seem to the general herd as having supernatural intuitions or powers. The 'rain-maker's' predictions in South Africa today may date from no more weatherlore than those of a British farmer; but to his tribe he appears a magician. Magic and early science have almost everywhere been interchangeable terms. The intermediate or Uranian man, from this point of view, would be simply an ordinary member of the tribe who from his double temperament would be rather more observant and acute and originative than the rest. There is, however, another point of view from which he might be credited with something distinctly additional in the way of faculty.

For, in the fourth place, I believe that at this stage an element of what might *really* be called divination would come in. I believe that the blending of the masculine and feminine temperaments would in some of these cases produce persons whose perceptions would be so subtle and complex and rapid as to come under the head of genius, persons of intuitive mind who would perceive things without knowing how, and follow far concatenations of causes and events without concerning themselves about the *why* – diviners and prophets in a very real sense. And these persons – whether they prophesied downfall or disaster, or whether they urged their people onward to conquest and victory, or whether by acute combinations of observation and experience they caught at the healing properties of herbs or determined the starry influences on the seasons and the crops – in almost all cases would acquire and did acquire a strange reputation for sanctity and divinity – arising partly perhaps out of the homosexual taboo, but also out of their real possession and command of a double-engine psychic power.

The double life and nature certainly, in many cases of inverts observed today, seems to give to them an extraordinary humanity and sympathy, together with a remarkable power of dealing with human beings. It may possibly also point to a further degree of evolution than usually attained, and a higher order of consciousness, very imperfectly realised, of course, but indicated. This interaction in fact, between the masculine and the feminine, this mutual illumination of logic and intuition, this combination of action and meditation, may not only raise and increase the power of each of these faculties, but it may give the mind a new quality, and a new power of perception corresponding to the blending of subject and object in consciousness. It may possibly lead to the development of that third order of perception which has been called the cosmic consciousness, and which may also be termed divination. 'He who knows the masculine,' says Lao-tsze, 'and at the same time keeps to the feminine, will be the whole world's channel. Eternal virtue will not depart from him, and he will return again to the state of an infant.' To the state of an infant! – that is, he will become undifferentiated from Nature, who is his mother, and who will lend him all her faculties.

It is not, of course, to be supposed that the witch-doctors and diviners of barbarian tribes have in general reached to the high order of development just described, yet it is noticeable, in the slow evolution of society, how often the late and high developments have been indicated in the germ in primitive stages; and it may be so in this case. Very interesting in this connection is the passage already quoted [p. 252] from Elie Reclus about the initiations of the Esquimaux *angakok* and the appearance to him of his own

Genius or Double from the world beyond, for almost exactly the same thing is supposed to take place in the initiation of the religious *yogi* in India – except that the god in this latter case appears to the pupil in the form of his teacher or *guru*. And how often in the history of the Christian saints has the divinity in the form of Jesus or Mary appeared to the strenuous devotee, apparently as the culminating result of his intense effort and aspiration, and of the opening out of a new plane of perception in his mind! It may be that with every great onward push of the growing soul, and every great crisis in which as it were a sheath or a husk falls away from the expanding bud, something in the nature of a metamorphosis does really take place; and the new order, the new revelation, the new form of life, is seen for a moment as a Vision in glorious state of a divine being within.[2]

4. Hermaphrodism among Gods and Mortals

In chapter 2 above, reference is made by one of the writers quoted to 'the numerous stories of hermaphrodites related by all the old writers on America.[1] That there are such numerous stories is quite correct. Jacobus Le Moyne, who travelled as artist with a French Expedition to Florida in 1564, left some very interesting drawings[1] representing the Indians of that region and their customs; and among them one representing the 'Hermaphrodites' – tall and powerful men, beardless but with long and abundant hair, and naked except for a loin-cloth, engaged in carrying wounded or dying fellow-Indians on their backs or on litters to a place of safety. He says of them that in Florida such folk of double nature are frequent, and that being robust and powerful, they are made use of in the place of animals for the carrying of burdens. 'For when their chiefs go to war the hermaphrodites carry the food; and when any of the tribe die of wounds or disease they construct litters . . . of wood and rushes . . . and so carry the dead to the place of burial. And indeed those who are stricken with any infectious disease are borne by the hermaphrodites to certain appointed places, and nursed and cared for by them, until they may be restored to full health.'

Similar stories are told by Charlevoix,[2] de Pauw,[3] and others; and one seems to get a glimpse in them of an intermediate class of human beings who made themselves useful to the community not only by their muscular strength, but by their ability and willingness to act as nurses and attendants on the sick and dying.

It is needless, of course, to say that these were *not* hermaphrodites in the strict sense of the term – i.e. human beings uniting in one person the functions both of male and female – since such beings do practically not exist. But it is evident that they *were* intermediate types – in the sense of being men with much of the psychologic character of women, or in some cases women with the mentality of men; and the early travellers, who had less concrete and reliable information on such subjects than we have, and who were already prepossessed by the belief in the prevalence of hermaphroditism, leapt easily to the conclusion that these strange beings were indeed of that nature. De Pauw, indeed, just mentioned, positively refuses to believe in the explanation that they were men dressed as women, and insists that they *were* hermaphrodites!

In 1889, a certain Dr A. B. Holder, anxious to settle positively the existence or non-existence of hermaphrodites, made some investigations among the Crow Indians of Montana – among whom the *berdaches* were called '*boté*'.[4] And Dr Karsch, summarising his report, says:[5] 'This word, *bo-té*, means literally "not man, not woman." A corresponding Tulalip word which the Indians of the Washington region make use of is, according to Holder, '*burdash*', which means 'half man, half woman' – and that without necessarily implying any anomalous structure of the sex-organs . . . The Crow tribe, in 1889, included five such *boté*, and possessed about the same number before. They form a class in every tribe, are well-known to each other, and knit friendly relations with their likes in other tribes, so that they become well acquainted with the Uranian relationships also in the neighbour tribes. They wear female attire, part their hair in the middle, and plait it in womanly style; they possess or cultivate feminine voices and gestures, and live continually in association with the women, just as if they belonged to that sex. All the same their voices, features, and figure never lose their masculine quality so completely as to make it hard for a careful observer to distinguish a *boté* from a woman. Such a *boté* among the Crows, carried on women's work, like sweeping, scrubbing, dish-washing, with such neatness and willingness that he would often obtain employment among the white folk. Usually the feminine attire is adopted in childhood, and the corresponding ways of life at an early age, but his special calling is not exercised by the *boté* till the age of puberty. A young scholar of an educational establishment – a boys' school in an Indian Agency – was often caught dressing himself in secret in women's clothes; and although punished on each occasion, he nevertheless, after leaving school, transformed himself into a *boté* – to which calling he has ever since remained true. A certain *boté*, well accredited among the Crow tribe, who belonged to the scouting-party of Dr Holder, was a Dakota Indian; he is described as a splendidly built young man of pleasing features, perfect health, brisk alertness, and the happiest disposition. Holder attached him to his own service, and finally persuaded him – though only after much unwillingness on his part – to allow himself to be personally examined.' The result of the examination was to prove him to be physically a complete man – and, moreover, an exceedingly modest one!

The Père Lafitau, whom I have quoted before, and who was a keen observer and a broad-minded man, says, in one passage of his *Sauvages Américains*: 'The spectacle of the men disguised as women surprised the Europeans who first landed in America. And, as they did not at all understand the motives of this sort of metamorphosis, they concluded that these were folk in whom the two sexes were conjoined: as a matter of fact our old records always term them hermaphrodites.' He goes on to say that though the spirit of religion which made these men embrace this mode of life caused them to be regarded as extraordinary beings, yet the suspicions which the Europeans entertained concerning them took such hold upon the latter 'that they invented every possible charge against them, and these imaginations inflamed the zeal of Vasco Nugnes de Vabra, the Spanish captain who first discovered the Southern Sea (*la mer du Sud*), to such an extent that he destroyed numbers of them by letting loose upon them those savage dogs, of whom his compatriots indeed made use for the purpose of exterminating a large proportion of the Indians.'

On the cruelties of the Spanish conquerors among the Indian tribes – only paralleled apparently by those of modern Commericalism among the same – we need not dwell. What interests us here is the evidence of the widespread belief in hermaphroditism current among the early European travellers. That a similar belief has ruled also among most primitive peoples is evident from a consideration of their gods. *Why* it should so have ruled is a question which I shall touch on towards the conclusion of this chapter. The whole matter, anyhow, belongs to the subjects we are discussing in this book. For clearly bisexuality links on to homosexuality, and the fact that this characteristic was ascribed to the gods suggests that in the popular mind it must have played a profound and important part in human life. I will, therefore, in concluding this portion of the book, give some instances of this divine bisexuality.

Brahm, in the Hindu mythology, is often represented as two-sexed. Originally he was the sole Being. But, 'delighting not to be alone he wished for the existence of another, and at once he became such, as male and female embraced (united). He caused his one self to fall in twain.'[6] Siva, also, the most popular of the Hindu divinities, is originally bisexual. In the interior of the great rockhewn Temple at Elephanta the career of Siva is carved in successive panels. And on the first he appears as a complete full-length human being conjoining the two sexes in one – the left side of the figure (which represents the female portion) projecting into a huge breast and hip, while the right side is man-like in outline, and in the centre (though now much defaced) the organs of both sexes. In the second panel, however, his evolution or differentiation is complete, and he is portrayed as complete male with his consort Sakti or Parvati standing as perfect female beside him.[7] There are many such illustrations in Hindu literature and art, representing the gods in their double or bisexual role – e.g. as Brahma Ardhanarisa, Siva Ardhanarisa (half male and half female).[8] And these again are interesting in connection with the account of Elohim in the first chapter of Genesis, and the supposition that he was such an androgynous deity. For we find (v. 27) that 'Elohim created man in his own image, in the image of Elohim created he him, *male and female* created he them.' And many commentators have maintained that this not only meant that the first man was hermaphrodite, but that the Creator also was of that nature. In the Midrasch we find that Rabbi Samuel-bar-Nachman said that 'Adam, when God had created him, was a man-woman (androgyne);' and the great and learned Maimonides supported this, saying that 'Adam and Eve were created together, conjoined by their backs, but God divided this double being, and taking one half (Eve), gave her to the other half (Adam) for a mate.' And the Rabbi Manasseh-ben-Israel, following this up, explained that when 'God took one of Adam's ribs to make Eve with,' it should rather be rendered 'one of his sides' – that is, that he divided the double Adam, and one half was Eve.[9]

In the Brihadaranyaka Upanishad (I Adhyaya, 4th-Brahmana) the evolution of Brahm is thus described:[10] 'In the beginning of this [world] was Self alone, in the shape of a person . . . But he felt no delight . . . He wished for a second. He was so large as man and wife together [i.e. he included male and female]. He then made this his Self to fall·in two; and thence arose husband and wife. Therefore, Yagnavalkya said: We two are thus (each of us) like half a shell [or as some translate, like a split pea].' The singular resemblance of this account to what has been said above about the creation of Adam certainly suggests the idea of Jehovah, like Brahm (and like Baal and other Syrian gods), was conceived of as double-sexed, and that primitive man was also conceived as of like nature. The author (Ralston Skinner) of *The Source of Measures* says (p. 159): 'The two words of which Jehovah is composed make up the original idea of male-female of the

birth-originator. For the Hebrew letter Jod (or J) was the
membrum virile, and Hovah was Eve, the mother of all
living, or the procreatrix Earth and Nature.'[11]

The tradition that mankind was anciently hermaphrodite
is world-old. It is referred to in Plato's *Banquet*, where
Aristophanes says: 'Anciently the nature of mankind was
not the same as now, but different. For at first there were
three sexes of human beings, not two only, namely male and
female, as at present, but a third besides, common to both
the others – of which the name remains, though the sex
itself has vanished. For the androgynous sex then existed,
both male and female; but now it only exists as a name of
reproach.' He then describes how all these three sorts of
human beings were originally double, and conjoined (as
above) back to back; until Jupiter, jealous of his supremacy,
divided them vertically 'as people cut apples before they
preserve them, or as they cut eggs with hairs' – after which,
of course, these divided and imperfect folk ran about over
the earth, ever seeking after their lost halves, to be joined to
them again.

I have mentioned the Syrian Baal as being sometimes
represented as double-sexed (apparently in combination
with Astarte). In the Septuagint (Hos. 2, 8, and Zeph. 1, 4) he
is called ἡ Baal (feminine) and Arnobius tells us that his
worshippers invoked him thus:[12] 'Here us, Baal! whether
thou be a god or goddess.' Similarly Bel and other Babylo-
nian gods were often represented as androgyne.[13] Mithras
among the Persians is spoken of by the Christian con-
troversialist Firmicus as two-sexed, and by Herodotus (1,
131) as identified with a goddess, while there are innumerable Mithraic monuments on which appear the symbols of
two deities, male and female combined.[14] Even Venus or
Aphrodite was sometimes worshipped in the double form.
'In Cyprus,' says Dr Frazer in his *Adonis, etc.* (p. 432, note),
'there was a bearded and masculine image of Venus
(probably Astarte) in female attire: according to Philochorus
the deity thus represented was the moon, and sacrifices
were offered to him or her by men clad as women, and by
women clad as men (see Macrobius, *Saturn* 3, 7, 2).' This
bearded female deity is sometimes also spoken of as
Aphroditus, or as Venus Mylitta. Richard Burton says:[15]

'The Phœnicians spread their androgynic worship over Greece. We find the consecrated servants and votaries of Corinthian Aphrodite called Hierodouloi* (Strabo, 8, 6), who aided the 10,000 courtesans in gracing the Venus-temple . . . One of the headquarters of the cult was Cyprus, where, as Sevius relates (Ad. Aen., 2, 632), stood the simulacre of a bearded Aphrodite with feminine body and costume, sceptred and mitred like a man. The sexes when worshiping it exchanged habits, and here the virginity was offered in sacrifice.'

The worship of this bearded goddess was mainly in Syria and Cyprus. But in Egypt also a representation of a bearded Isis has been found, with infant Horus in her lap;[16] while again there are a number of representations (from papyri) of the goddess Neith in androgyne form, with a male member (erected). And again, curiously enough, the Norse Freya, or Friga, corresponding to Venus, was similarly figured. Dr von Römer says:[17] 'Just as the Greeks had their Aphroditos as well as Aphrodite so the Scandinavians had their Friggo as well as their Friga. This divinity, too, was androgyne. Friga, to whom the sixth day of the week was dedicated, was sometimes thought of as hermaphrodite. She was represented as having the members of both sexes, standing by a column with a sword in her right hand, and in her left a bow.'

In the Orphic hymns we have:

Zeus was the first of all, Zeus the last, the lord of the lightning;
Zeus was the head, the middle, from him all things were created;
Zeus was Man, and again Zeus was the Virgin Eternal.

And in another passage, speaking of Adonis:

Hear me, who pray to thee, hear me O many-named and best of deities,
Thou, with thy gracious hair . . . both maiden and youth, Adonis.

Again, with regard to the latter, Ptolemaeus Hephaestius* (according to Photius) writes: 'They say that the androgyne Adonis fulfilled the part of a man for Aphrodite, but for

Apollo the part of a wife.'[18]

Dionysus, one of the most remarkable figures in the Greek Mythology, is frequently represented as androgyne. Euripides in his *Bacchae* calls him 'feminine-formed' (θηλύ-μορφος) or thelumorphos, and the Orphic hymns 'double-sexed' (διφύης) or diphues; and Aristides in his discourse on Dionysus says: 'Thus the God is both male and female. His form corresponds to his nature, since everywhere in himself he is like a double being; for among young men he is a maiden, and among maidens a young man, and among men a beardless youth overflowing with vitality.' In the museum at Naples there is a very fine sculptured head of Dionysus, which though bearded has a very feminine expression, and is remindful of the traditional head of Christ. 'In legend and art,' says Dr Frazer,[19] 'there are clear traces of an effeminate Dionysus, and in some of his rites and processions men wore female attire. Similar things are reported of Bacchus, who was, of course, another form of Dionysus. Even Hercules, that most masculine figure, was said to have dressed as a woman for three years, during which he was the slave of Omphale, queen of Lydia.' 'If we suppose,' says Dr Frazer,[20] 'that queen Omphale, like queen Semiramis, was nothing but the great Asiatic goddess, or one of her avatars, it becomes probable that the story of the womanish Hercules of Lydia preserves a reminiscence of a line or college of effeminate priests who, like the eunuch priests of the Syrian goddess, dressed as women in imitation of their goddess, and were supposed to be inspired by her. The probability is increased by the practice of the priests of Heracles at Antimachia in Cos, who, as we have just seen, actually wore female attire when they were engaged in their sacred duties. Similarly at the vernal mysteries of Hercules in Rome the men were draped in the garments of women.'

Such instances could be rather indefinitely multiplied. Apollo is generally represented with a feminine – sometimes with an extremely feminine – bust or figure. The great hero Achilles passed his youth among women, and in female disguise. Every one knows the recumbent marble Hermaphrodite in the Louvre.* There are also in the same collection two or three elegant bronzes of Aphrodite-like female figures in the standing position – but of masculine sex. What is the explanation of all this?

It is evident that the conception of a double sex, or of a sex combining the characters of male and female, haunted the minds of early people. Yet we have no reason for supposing that such a combination, in any complete and literal sense, ever existed. Modern physiological investigation has never produced a single case of a human being furnished with the complete organs of both sexes, and capable of fulfilling the functions of both. And the unfortunate malformations which do exist in this direction are too obviously abortive and exceptional to admit of their being generalised or exalted into any kind of norm or ideal. All we can say is that – though in the literal sense no double forms exist – certainly a vast number of intermediate forms of male and female are actually found, which are double in the sense that the complete organs of one sex are conjoined with some or nearly all of the (secondary) characters of the other sex; and that we have every reason to believe that these intermediate types have existed in considerable numbers from the remotest antiquity. That being so, it is possible that the observation or influence of these intermediate types led to a tentative and confused idealisation of a double type.

Anyhow the fact remains – that these idealisations of the double type are so numerous. And it is interesting to notice that while they begin in early times with being merely grotesque and symbolical, they end in the later periods by becoming artistic and gracious and approximated to the real and actual. The Indian Siva, with his right side masculine and his left side feminine, is in no way beautiful or attractive; any more than Brahma with twenty arms and twenty legs. And the same may be said of the bearded Egyptian Isis or the bearded Syrian Aphrodite. These were only rude and inartistic methods of conveying an idea. The later spirit, however, found a better way of expression. It took its cue from the variations of type to be seen every day in the actual world; and instead of representing the Persian Mithra as a two-sexed monster, it made him a young *man*, but of very feminine outline. The same with the Greek Apollo; while on the other hand, the female who is verging toward the male type is represented by Artemis or even by the Amazons.

It may be said: we can understand this representation of intermediate forms from actual life, but we do not see why such mingling of the sexes should be ascribed to the gods, unless it might be from a merely fanciful tendency to personify the two great powers of nature in one being – in which case it is strange that the tendency should have been so universal. To this we may reply that probably the reason or reasons for this tendency must be accounted quite deep-rooted and anything but fanciful. One reason, it seems to me, is the psychological fact that in the deeps of human nature (as represented by Brahm and Siva in the Hindu philosophy, by Zeus in the Orphic Hymns, by Mithra in the Zend-avesta, etc.) the sex-temperament *is* undifferentiated;[21] and it is only in its later and more external and partial manifestations that it branches decidedly into male and female; and that, therefore, in endeavouring through religion to represent the root facts of life, there was always a tendency to cultivate and honour hermaphroditism, and to ascribe some degree of this quality to heroes and divinities. The other possible reason is that as a matter of fact the great leaders and heroes *did* often exhibit this blending of masculine and feminine qualities and habits in their actual lives, and that therefore at some later period, when exalted to divinities, this blending of qualities was strongly ascribed to them and was celebrated in the rites and ceremonies of their religion and their temples. The feminine traits in genius (as in a Shelley or a Byron) are well marked in the present day. We have only to go back to the Persian Bâb of the last century[22] or to a St Francis or even to a Jesus of Nazareth, to find the same traits present in founders and leaders of religious movements in historical times. And it becomes easy to suppose the same again of those early figures – who once probably were men – those Apollos, Buddhas, Dionysus, Osiris, and so forth – to suppose that they too were somewhat bisexual in temperament, and that it was really largely owing to that fact that they were endowed with far-reaching powers and became leaders of mankind. In either case – whichever reason is adopted – it corroborates the general thesis and argument of this paper.

Self-Analysis for Havelock Ellis

My parentage is very sound and healthy. Both my parents (who belong to the professional middle class) have good general health; nor can I trace any marked abnormal or diseased tendency, of mind or body, in any records of the family.

Though of a strongly nervous temperament myself, and sensitive, my health is good. I am not aware of any tendency to physical disease. In early manhood, however, owing, I believe, to the great emotional tension under which I lived, my nervous system was a good deal shattered and exhausted. Mentally and morally my nature is pretty well balanced, and I have never had any serious perturbations in these departments.

At the age of eight or nine, and long before distinct sexual feelings declared themselves, I felt a friendly attraction toward my own sex, and this developed after the age of puberty into a passionate sense of love, which, however, never found any expression for itself till I was fully 20 years of age. I was a day-boarder at school and heard little of school-talk on sex subjects, was very reserved and modest besides; no elder person or parent ever spoke to me on such matters; and the passion for my own sex developed gradually, utterly uninfluenced from the outside. I never even, during all this period, and till a good deal later, learned the practice of masturbation. My own sexual nature was a mystery to me. I found myself cut off from the understanding of others, felt myself an outcast, and, with a highly loving and clinging temperament, was intensely miserable. I thought about my male friends – sometimes boys of my own age, sometimes elder boys, and once even a master – during the day and dreamed about them at night, but was too convinced that I was a hopeless monstrosity ever to make any effectual advances. Later on it was much the same, but gradually, though slowly, I came to find that there were others like myself. I made a few special friends, and at last it came to me occasionally to sleep with them and to satisfy my imperious need by mutual embraces and emissions. Before this happened, however, I was once or twice on the brink of despair and madness with repressed passion and torment.

Meanwhile, from the first, my feeling, physically, towards the female sex was one of indifference, and later on, with the more special development of sex desires, one of positive repulsion. Though having several female friends, whose society I like and to whom I am sincerely attached, the thought of marriage or cohabitation with any such has always been odious to me.

As a boy I was attracted in general by boys rather older than myself; after leaving school I still fell in love, in a romantic vein, with comrades of my own standing. Now – at the age of 37 – my ideal of love is a powerful, strongly built man, of my own age or rather younger – preferably of the working class. Though having solid sense and character, he need not be specially intellectual. If endowed in the latter way, he must not be too glib or refined. Anything effeminate in a man, or anything of the cheap intellectual style, repels me very decisively.

I have never had to do with actual pederasty, so called. My chief desire in love is bodily nearness or contact, as to sleep naked with a naked friend; the specially sexual, though urgent enough, seems a secondary matter. Pederasty, either active or passive, might seem in place to me with one I loved very devotedly and who also loved me to that degree; but I think not otherwise. I am an artist by temperament and choice, fond of all beautiful things, especially the male human form; of active, slight, muscular build; and sympathetic, but somewhat indecisive character, though possessing self-control.

I cannot regard my sexual feelings as unnatural or abnormal, since they have disclosed themselves so perfectly naturally and spontaneously within me. All that I have read in books or heard spoken about the ordinary sexual love, its intensity and passion, lifelong devotion, love at first sight, etc., seems to me to be easily matched by my own experiences in the homosexual form; and, with regard to the morality of this complex subject, my feeling is that it is the same as should prevail in love between man and woman, namely: that no bodily satisfaction should be sought at the cost of another person's distress or degradation. I am sure that this kind of love is, notwithstanding the physical difficulties that attend it, as deeply stirring and ennobling as the other kind, if not more so; and I think that for a perfect relationship the actual sex gratifications (whatever they may be) probably hold a less important place in this love than in the other.

Notes

Notes to Introduction

1. Gilbert Beith (ed.), *Edward Carpenter: In Appreciation* (London, 1931), p. 75.

2. 'Book Talk', BBC Home Service, 25 September 1944; Carpenter Collection (Sheffield), MSS. 387.5.

3. ibid.

4. *Edward Carpenter: In Appreciation*, p. 232; E.C. quoted by Charles Sixsmith. See also *My Days and Dreams* (London, 1916), p. 190.

5. *Edward Carpenter: In Appreciation*, p. 47.

6. ibid.

7. ibid., p. 86.

8. ibid., p. 25.

9. ibid., p. 21.

10. ibid., p. 90.

11. ibid., p. 104.

12. ibid., pp. 232–3.

13. ibid., p. 79.

14. ibid., p. 25.

15. Godfrey Elton, *England Arise!* (London, 1931), p. 10.

16. See note 2 above.

17. *Edward Carpenter: In Appreciation*, p. 61.

18. ibid., pp. 68–9.

19. *Towards Democracy* (London, 1949), pp. 14–15.

20. ibid., p. 18.

21. ibid., p. 25.

22. *Edward Carpenter: In Appreciation*, p. 79.

23. ibid., pp. 78.

24. *My Days and Dreams*, p. 14.

25. ibid., pp. 30–1.

26. *Towards Democracy*, p. 30.

27. ibid.

28. ibid.

29. *Edward Carpenter: In Appreciation*, p. 116.

30. *Towards Democracy*, p. 40.

31. *My Days and Dreams*, p. 94.
32. ibid., p. 97.
33. ibid., p. 98.
34. *Edward Carpenter: In Appreciation*, p. 110.
35. ibid., p. 182.
36. ibid., p. 110.
37. *My Days and Dreams*, p. 63.
38. ibid., pp. 64–5.
39. ibid., p. 68.
40. ibid., p. 79.
41. *Civilisation: Its Cause and Cure* (London, 1921), p. 183.
42. ibid., p. 189.
43. ibid., p. 186–7.
44. *Pagan and Christian Creeds* (London, 1920), p. 277.
45. *Towards Industrial Freedom* (London, 1918), p. 67.
46. *Civilisation: Its Cause and Cure*, p. 185.
47. *Towards Industrial Freedom*, p. 53.
48. ibid., pp. 53–4.
49. *Civilisation: Its Cause and Cure*, p. 199.
50. ibid., p. 204.
51. *Towards Industrial Freedom*, p. 54.
52. ibid., pp. 56–7.
53. *Love's Coming-of-Age*; above, p. 124.
54. *The Drama of Love and Death* (London, 1912), pp. 2–3.
55. *Towards Industrial Freedom*, p. 71.
56. *Civilisation: Its Cause and Cure*, p. 261.
57. *Towards Industrial Freedom*, p. 54.
58. *Civilisation: Its Cause and Cure*, p. 75.
59. *Towards Democracy*, p. 295.
60. *Sketches From Life* (London, 1908), p. 86.
61. *My Days and Dreams*, pp. 69–70.
62. ibid., p. 70.
63. *Edward Carpenter: In Appreciation*, p. 188.
64. *Towards Industrial Freedom*, pp. 64–5.
65. *Towards Democracy*, p. 15.
66. *My Days and Dreams*, p. 80.
67. Edward Carpenter to Charles Oates, 19 Dec. 1887; Carpenter Collection, MSS. 351.43.
68. George Merrill to Edward Carpenter, 8 Nov. 1896; C.C., MSS. 363.4.
69. George Merrill to Edward Carpenter, 26 Sept. 1896; C.C., MSS. 363.3.
70. George Hukin to Edward Carpenter, 26 Sept. 1886; C.C., MSS. 362.5.
71. George Hukin to Edward Carpenter, 21 May 1887; C.C., MSS. 362.10.
72. George Adams to Edward Carpenter, 17 Nov. 1887; C.C., MSS. 27.135.

73. ibid.

74. Edward Carpenter to Charles Oates, 19 Dec. 1887; C.C., MSS. 351.43.

75. George Hukin to Edward Carpenter, 24 May 1887; C.C., MSS. 362.11.

76. *Love's Coming-of-Age*; above, p. 179.

77. ibid., p. 178.

78. ibid.

79. ibid., p. 179.

80. *Towards Democracy*, p. 300.

81. ibid., pp. 26 and 27.

82. *Civilisation: Its Cause and Cure*, p. 52.

83. *My Days and Dreams*, p. 125.

84. *Towards Industrial Freedom*, p. 79–80.

85. ibid., p. 81.

86. ibid., p. 82.

87. ibid., pp. 82–3.

88. ibid., p. 85.

89. *My Days and Dreams*, p. 126.

90. ibid., p. 127.

91. ibid., p. 139.

92. ibid., pp. 114–5.

93. *Civilisation: Its Cause and Cure*, pp. 7–8.

94. ibid., p. 7.

95. *Sketches From Life*, p. 196.

96. ibid.

97. *My Days and Dreams*, p. 131.

98. ibid., pp. 247–8.

99. *Civilisation: Its Cause and Cure*, p. 16.

100. See note 2 above.

101. *My Days and Dreams*, p. 148.

102. ibid., p. 159.

103. *Towards Democracy*, p. 336.

104. *My Days and Dreams*, p. 161.

105. *My Days and Dreams*, p. 113.

106. ibid., pp. 143–4.

107. Edward Carpenter to George Hukin, 16 March 1891; C.C., MSS. 361.9.

108. George Hukin to Edward Carpenter, 22 Jan. 1891; C.C. 362.44.

109. *My Days and Dreams*, pp. 144–5.

110. ibid., p. 195.

111. ibid., pp. 195–6.

112. ibid., p. 196.

113. ibid., p. 197.

114. *Love's Coming-of-Age*; above, p. 108.

115. *My Days and Dreams*, p. 197.

116. See note 19 above.

117. *Towards Democracy*, p. 322.
118. ibid., p. 338.
119. ibid., p. 62.
120. See above, p. 92 and note.
121. *The Intermediate Sex*; above, p. 200.
122. ibid., p. 197.
123. In his prose essay *Democratic Vistas* (1871). Quoted in *The Intermediate Sex*; above, p. 218.
124. *The Intermediate Sex*; above, p. 217.
125. ibid., p. 219.
126. ibid., p. 200.
127. ibid., p. 240.
128. ibid., p. 241.
129. *My Days and Dreams*; below, p. 295.
130. *The Intermediate Sex*; above, pp. 207–8.
131. ibid., p. 191.
132. *Towards Democracy*, p. 331.
133. *The Intermediate Sex*; above, p. 238.
134. ibid.
135. *Love's Coming-of-Age*; above, pp. 97–8.
136. ibid.
137. ibid., p. 99.
138. ibid., p. 102.
139. ibid., p. 105.
140. ibid., pp. 119–20.
141. ibid., p. 125.
142. ibid., p. 127.
143. ibid., p. 147.
144. ibid., pp. 151–2.
145. ibid.
146. *Pagan and Christian Creeds*, p. 275.
147. *Love's Coming-of-Age*; above, pp. 158–9.
148. *Angels' Wings* (London, 1923), p. 131.
149. ibid., p. 242.
150. ibid., pp 118–19.
151. ibid., pp. 119 and 122.
152. ibid., pp. 128–9.
153. *The Drama of Love and Death*, p. 262.
154. ibid., p. 267.
155. ibid., pp. 251 and 268.
156. *Angels' Wings*, pp. 135–6.
157. *My Days and Dreams*, p. 303.
158. ibid., p. 314.
159. ibid., p. 302.
160. *Towards Democracy*, p. 230.
161. ibid., p. 13.

Notes to My Days and Dreams

Edward Carpenter's book *My Days and Dreams: being autobiographical notes* was begun in 1890, but only completed twenty-five years later, and published in 1916 by George Allen and Unwin. The excerpts reproduced here are taken from pages 13–15, 25–32, 46–47, 63–65, 66–67, 79 and 92–98. The final excerpt contains an open and explicit statement about Carpenter's homosexuality. Though he now had the relative protection of old age, this remains quite unique in English literature for the time, or indeed long after.

*

1. This is a subject which through the Freudian psychoanalysis has come now (1915) to be much better understood.
2. Many examples of this kind of temperament are given in Vol. 2 of Dr Havelock Ellis' classical work *Studies in the Psychology of Sex* – Philadelphia, 1901 and 1915. (See history vii, beginning 'My parentage is very sound', history xvii, etc.) And I will say that in my case the temperament has always been quite natural and associated with perfect healthiness of habit and general freedom from morbidity; and that it has been absolutely inborn, and not induced by any outside example or teaching. It is therefore a part of my nature, and a most intimate and organic part. And I have to thank Mr Edward Lewis that in his *Exposition and Appreciation of E. C.* (Methuen, 1915, pp. 200, 299, etc.) he has so clearly and firmly indicated this.

Notes to Love's Coming-of-Age

Love's Coming-of-Age was published in 1896, but the material contained in the first edition had largely appeared in three preceding pamphlets, *Sex-love: and its Place in a Free Society*, *Woman: and her Place in a Free Society*, and *Marriage in Free Society*. These were published by The Labour Press in Manchester in 1894. Carpenter combined, revised and expanded them for the London publisher Fisher Unwin, but Unwin reneged on the contract following the arrest of Oscar Wilde in April 1895. His reason was that Carpenter had also had printed at The Labour Press a fourth pamphlet on *Homogenic Love: and its Place in a Free Society*; though this was for private circulation only, and was not to be included in *Love's Coming-of-Age*, after Wilde's arrest 'a sheer panic prevailed over *all* questions of sex, and especially of course questions of the Intermediate Sex' (*My Days and Dreams*, London, 1916, p. 196). Unwin simultaneously withdrew from sale Carpenter's *Towards Democracy*. This rejection was echoed by other mainstream publishers, so 'there was nothing left for me but to return to my little Labour Press in Manchester' (*ibid.*). In 1902, however, *Love's Coming-of-Age* found a London publisher in Swan Sonnenschein (later absorbed, ironically enough, by George Allen and Unwin), and in 1906 Carpenter issued an enlarged edition. This included the essay on 'Homogenic Love', now re-worked and titled 'The Intermediate Sex'. Two further chapters were added in 1923, 'The Beginnings of Love' and 'Love's Ultimate Meaning', taken from Carpenter's 1912 book *The Drama of Love and Death*. 'The Beginnings of Love' is not included here, and also omitted are two of the Remarks and Notes ('On the Early Star and Sex Worships' and 'On the Primitive Group-Marriage') and an Appendix of further notes and supporting quotations. 'The Intermediate Sex' is reproduced on pp. 185–245 above.

*

The Sex-Passion

1. Though this is of course not true of *animal* food.
2. See Appendix.
3. See Appendix.
4. Taking union as the main point we may look upon the idealised Sex-love as a sense of contact pervading the whole mind and body — while the sex-organs are a specialisation of this faculty of union in the outermost sphere: union in the bodily sphere giving rise to bodily generation, the same as union in the mental and emotional spheres occasions generation of another kind.
5. These are (1) the curious, not yet explained, facts of 'Telegony' – i.e., the tendency (often noticed in animals) of the children of a dam by a second sire to resemble the first sire; (2) the probable survival, in a modified form, of the primitive close relation (as seen in the protozoa) between copulation and nutrition; (3) the great activity of the spermatozoa themselves.

Woman, the Serf

1. For other points of difference see Appendix.
2. *Man and Woman*, by Havelock Ellis. Contemporary Science Series, p. 371.
3. Physiologically speaking a certain excess of affectability and excitability in women over men seems to be distinctly traceable.

Woman in Freedom

1. The freedom of Woman must ultimately rest on the Communism of society — which alone can give her support during the

period of Motherhood, without forcing her into dependence on the arbitrary will of one man. While the present effort of women towards earning their own economic independence is a healthy sign and a necessary feature of the times, it is evident that it alone will not entirely solve the problem, since it is just during the difficult years of Motherhood, when support is most needed, that the woman is least capable of earning it for herself. (See Appendix.)

2. See Appendix.

3. See Appendix.

4. As to the maternal teaching of children, it must be confessed that it has, in late times, been most dismal. Whether among the masses or the classes the idea has been first and foremost to impress upon them the necessity of sliding through life as comfortably as possible, and the parting word to the boy leaving home to launch into the great world has seldom risen to a more heroic strain than 'Don't forget your flannels!'

Marriage: a Retrospect

1. It must be remembered too that to many women (though of course by no means a majority) the thought of Sex brings but little sense of pleasure, and the fulfilment of its duties constitutes a real, even though a willing, sacrifice. See Appendix.

2. Thus Bebel in his book on *Woman* speaks of 'the idle and luxurious life of so many women in the upper classes, the nervous stimulant afforded by exquisite perfumes, the overdosing with poetry, music, the stage — which is regarded as the chief means of education, and is the chief occupation, of a sex already suffering from hypertrophy of nerves and sensibility.'

3. See Appendix.

Marriage: a Forecast

1. It is curious that the early Church Service had 'Till death us depart,' but in 1661 this was altered to 'Till death us do part.'

2. See R. F. Burton's *Pilgrimage to El-Medinah and Meccah*, chap. 24. He says, however, 'As far as my limited observations go *polyandry* is the only state of society in which jealousy and quarrels about the sex are the exception and not the rule of life!'

3. See Appendix.

4. Perhaps one of the most sombre and inscrutable of these natural tragedies lies, for Woman, in the fact that the man to whom she first surrenders her body often acquires for her (whatever his character may be) so profound and inalienable a claim upon her heart. While, either for man or woman, it is almost impossible to thoroughly understand their own nature, or that of others, till they have had sex-experience, it happens so that in the case of the woman experience which should thus give the power of choice is

frequently the very one which seals her destiny. It reveals to her, as at a glance, the tragedy of a lifetime which lies before her, and yet which she cannot do other than accept.

Love's Ultimate Meaning

1. 'The disgrace which has overtaken the sexual act, and rendered it a deed of darkness, is doubtless largely responsible for the fact that the chief time for its consummation among modern civilised peoples is the darkness of the early night in stuffy bedrooms when the fatigue of the day's labours is struggling with the artificial stimulation produced by heavy meals and alcoholic drinks. This habit is partly responsible for the indifference or even disgust with which women sometimes view coitus.' (H. Ellis, *Studies in the Psychology of Sex*, vol. 6, p. 558.)

* (p. 160) 'I don't love unless I'm hurt.'

* (p. 161) This refers to the essay 'The Beginnings of Love', not included here. See above, p. 298.

2. See H. Ellis, vol 5, pp. 11 and 12.

3. See also Krafft-Ebing, *Psychopathia Sexualis*, 7th edition, p. 165.

4. *Modern Woman; Her Intentions*, p. 30.

* (p. 165) Lovers' quarrels are the renewal of love.

5. English edition, Heinemann, 1906.

6. Fischer, Berlin, p. 192.

7. Berlin, 1910, p. 290.

8. Berlin, 1905, p. 332. English translation, *Love and Marriage*, Putnam's, 1911.

The Free Society

* (p. 170) This is the essay 'The Intermediate Sex', printed here on pp. 189–200.

1. See Note on the Primitive Group-marriage.

2. Letourneau (*Evolution of Marriage*, p. 173) mentions also among the inferior races who have adopted Monogamy the Veddahs of Ceylon, the Bochimans of S. Africa, and the Kurnais of Australia.

3. See Remarks on the Early Star and Sex Worships.

4. Perhaps this accounts for the feeling, which so many have experienced, that a great love, even though not apparently returned, *justifies itself*, and *has* its fruition in its own time and its own way.

Notes to The Intermediate Sex

The panic that followed the conviction of Oscar Wilde did not prevent Carpenter from continuing to write openly about homosexuality. In July 1897 the *Reformer* magazine carried his article 'An Unknown People', also issued as a pamphlet, and in July 1899 the *International Journal of Ethics* published 'Affection in Education'. In 1902 the progressive London publisher Swan Sonnenschein, who now took over *Love's Coming-of-Age*, also published *Iölaus: an Anthology of Friendship*, in which Carpenter collected poems and essays on homogenic love, including Phaedrus' speech from Plato's *Symposium*, Michelangelo's sonnets, selections from Whitman, etc. In 1906, against the background of the militant women's movement and its increasing attacks on sexual taboos, Swan Sonnenschein felt able to include Carpenter's essay on 'The Intermediate Sex' in the enlarged edition of *Love's Coming-of-Age*, and two years later Carpenter was able to gather together his writings on homosexuality in book form, again for Sonnenschein. The title essay of *The Intermediate Sex* is taken virtually unchanged from the 1906 edition of *Love's Coming-of-Age*, while 'The Homogenic Attachment' and 'Affection in Education' are slightly revised versions of the magazine articles of 1897 and 1899. The book was rounded off with an 'Introductory' and the concluding essay on 'The Place of the Uranian in Society', as well as a substantial Appendix of notes and supporting quotations (forming about 30 per cent of the book) which is not reproduced here.

*

1. Introductory

1. For the derivation of these terms see p. [191].

2. The Intermediate Sex

1. See Appendix.
2. From *Uranos*, heaven; his idea being that the Uranian love was of a higher order than the ordinary attachment. For further about Ulrichs and his theories see Appendix.
3. Charles G. Leland ('Hans Breitmann') in his book *The Alternate Sex* (Welby, 1904), insists much on the frequent combination of the characteristics of both sexes in remarkable men and women, and has a chapter on ' The Female Mind in Man ', and another on ' The Male Intellect in Woman '.
4. Some late statistical inquiries (see *Statistische Untersuchungen* by Dr M. Hirschfeld (Leipzig, 1904) yield 1.5 to 2.0 per

cent as a probable ratio. See also Appendix.

5. For instances, see Appendix.

6. See De Joux, *Die Enterbten des Liebesglückes* (Leipzig, 1893), p. 21.

7. *Psychopathia Sexualis*, 7th ed., p. 276.

8. See Appendix.

9. A good deal in this description may remind readers of history of the habits and character of Henry III of France.

10. Perhaps, like Queen Christine of Sweden, who rode across Europe, on her visit to Italy, in jack-boots and sitting astride of her horse. It is said that she shook the Pope's hand, on seeing him, so heartily that the doctor had to attend to it afterwards!

3. The Homogenic Attachment

1. 'Homosexual', generally used in scientific works, is of course a bastard word. 'Homogenic' has been suggested, as being from two roots, both Greek, i.e., *'homos'*, same, and *'genos'*, sex.

2. *Athenaeus* 13, ch. 78.

3. See Plutarch's *Eroticus*, 17.

4. See *Natural History of Man*, by J. G. Wood, vol. *Africa*, p. 419.

5. See also Livingstone's *Expedition to the Zambesi* (Murray, 1865) p. 148.

6. Though these two plays, except for some quotations, are lost.

7. Mantegazza and Lombroso. See Albert Moll, *Conträre Sexualempfindung*, 2nd ed., p. 36.

8. Though in translation this fact is often by pious fraudulence disguised.

9. W. Pater's *Renaissance*, pp. 8-16.

10. Among *prose* writers of this period, Montaigne, whose treatment of the subject is enthusiastic and unequivocal, should not be overlooked. See Hazlitt's *Montaigne*, ch. 27.

11. I may be excused for quoting here the sonnet No. 54, from J. A. Symonds' translation of the sonnets of Michel Angelo:

'From thy fair face I learn, O my loved lord,
    That which no mortal tongue can rightly say:
    The soul, imprisoned in her house of clay,
    Holpen by thee to God hath often soared:
And though the vulgar, vain, malignant horde
    Attribute what their grosser wills obey,
    Yet shall this fervent homage that I pay,
    This love, this faith, pure joys for us afford,
Lo, all the lovely things we find on earth,
    Resemble for the soul that rightly sees,
    That source of bliss divine which gave us birth:
Nor have we first-fruits or remembrances
    Of heaven elsewhere. Thus, loving loyally,
    I rise to God, and make death sweet by thee.

The labours of von Scheffler, followed by J.A. Symonds, have now pretty conclusively established the pious frauds of the nephew, and the fact that the love-poems of the elder Michel Angelo were, for the most part, written to male friends.

12. See an interesting paper in W. Pater's *Renaissance*.

13. For a fuller collection of instances of this Friendship-love in the history of the world, see *Ioläus: an Anthology*, by E. Carpenter (George Allen, London, 3/- net). Also *Lieblingminne und Freundesliebe in der Weltliteratur*, by Elisar von Kuppfer (Adolf Brand, Berlin, 1900).

14. As in the case, for instance, of Tennyson's 'In Memoriam', for which the poet was soundly rated by the *Times* at the time of its publication.

15. Jowett's *Plato*, 2nd ed., vol. 2, p. 30.

16. Jowett, vol. 2. p. 130.

17. One ought also to mention some later writers, like Dr Magnus Hirschfeld and Dr von Römer, whose work though avowedly favourable to the Urning-movement, is in a high degree scientific and reliable in character.

18. From *Uranos* — see, for derivation, [p.191] — also Plato's *Symposium*, speech of Pausanias.

19. See, for estimates, Appendix.

20. Though there is no doubt a general *tendency* towards femininity of type in the male Urning, and towards masculinity in the female.

21. *Gli amori degli uomini.*

22. *Psychopathia Sexualis,* 7th ed., p. 227.

23. ibid., pp. 229 and 258. See Appendix.

24. 'How deep congenital sex-inversion roots may be gathered from the fact that the pleasure-dream of the male Urning has to do with male persons, and of the female with females.' — Krafft-Ebing, op. cit., 7th ed., p. 228.

25. *Conträre Sexualempfindung*, 2nd ed., p. 269.

26. See *Love's Coming of Age*, p. [107].

27. Pub. F. A. Davis, Philadelphia, 1901.

28. Otto Weininger even goes further, and regards the temperament as a natural intermediate form (*Sex and Character*, ch. 4). See also Appendix.

29. 'Though then before my own conscience I cannot reproach myself, and though I must certainly reject the judgment of the world about us, yet I suffer greatly. In very truth I have injured no one, and I hold my love in its nobler activity for just as holy as that of normally disposed men, but under the unhappy fate that allows us neither sufferance nor recognition I suffer often more than my life can bear.' — Extract from a letter given by Krafft-Ebing.

30. See *In the Key of Blue*, by J.A. Symonds (Elkin Mathews, 1893).

31. See Appendix.

32. See also *Love's Coming of Age*, p. [164].

33. See *Das Conträre Geschlechtsgefühl*, by Havelock Ellis and J.A. Symonds (Leipzig, 1896).

34. *Symposium*, speech of Socrates.

35. It is interesting in this connection to notice the extreme fervour, almost of romance, of the bond which often unites lovers of like sex over a long period of years, in an unfailing tenderness of treatment and consideration towards each other, equal to that shown in the most successful marriages. The love of many such men, says Moll (p. 119), 'developed in youth lasts at times the whole life through. I know of such men, who had not seen their first love for years, even decades, and who yet on meeting showed the old fire of their first passion. In other cases, a close love-intimacy will last unbroken for many years.'

36. Though, inconsistently enough, making no mention of females.

37. Dr. Moll maintains (2nd ed., pp. 314, 315) that if familiarities between those of the same sex are made illegal, as immoral, self-abuse ought much more to be so made.

38. Though it is doubtful whether the marriage-laws even do this.

39. In France, since the adoption of the Code Napoléon, sexual inversion is tolerated under the same restrictions as normal sexuality; and according to Carlier, formerly Chief of the French Police, Paris is not more depraved in this matter than London. Italy in 1889 also adopted the principles of the Code Napoléon on this point. For further considerations with regard to the Law, see Appendix.

4. Affection in Education

1. For further instances, see Appendix.

2. See Müller's *History and Antiquities of the Doric Race*.

3. Müller.

4. Cf. the incident at the end of Plato's *Lysis*, when the tutors of Lysis and Menexenus come in and send the youths home.

5. For a useful little manual on this subject, see *How We are Born*, by Mrs. N.J. (Daniel, London, price 2/-). For a general argument in favour of sex-teaching see *The Training of the Young in Laws of Sex*, by Canon Lyttelton, Headmaster of Eton College (Longmans, 2/6).

6. See, J.G. Wood's *Natural History of Man*, vol. *Africa*, p. 324 (the Bechuanas); also vol. *Australia*, p. 75

7. With the rapid rise which is taking place, in scope and social status, of the state day-schools, it is probable that some change of opinion will take place with regard to the wisdom of sending young boys of ten to fourteen to upper-class boarding-schools. For a boy of fifteen or sixteen and upwards the boarding-school system may

have its advantages. By that time a boy is old enough to understand some questions; he is old enough to have some rational idea of conduct, and to hold his own in the pursuit of it; and he may learn in the life away from home a lot in the way of discipline, organisation, self-reliance, etc. But to send a young thing, ignorant of life, and quite unformed of character, to take his chance by day and night in the public school as it at present exists, is — to say the least — a rash thing to do.

8. It should be also said, in fairness, that the fear of showing undue partiality, often comes in as a paralysing influence.

5. The Place of the Uranian in Society

1. *Studies in the Psychology of Sex*, vol. 2, p. 173.

2. See ch. 2, *supra*, also *Ioläus, an Anthology of Friendship*, by E. Carpenter.

3. Mr Jones became Mayor of Toledo; but died at the early age of 53. See also *Workshop Reconstruction*, by C. R. Ashbee, Appendix.

4. *Whitman: ein Charakterbild*, by Edward Bertz (Leipzig, Max Spohr).

5. John Addington Symonds.

6. See Appendix.

Notes to
Intermediate Types among Primitive Folk

The first part of this book, 'The Intermediate in the Service of Religion', which is reproduced here, forms four chapters out of eight, and first appeared in the *American Journal of Religious Psychology* for July 1911, under the title 'On the Connection between Homosexuality and Divination'. The second part, 'The Intermediate as Warrior', was added when *Intermediate Types* was published by George Allen in 1914.

Though the ethnographic material Carpenter draws on is somewhat dated, so little anthropological work has been done on the subject of homosexuality that his discussion is still a useful starting-point today. There is, however, a serious problem in Carpenter's theoretical approach, indicated by his own awareness that 'the word "Intermediate" hardly covers all the human types dealt with or spoken of' ('Conclusion', 1919 ed., p. 161).

Carpenter's view of homosexuality in contemporary Western society, as is clear from his previous writings, revolved around a rapprochement between the sexes, an attenuation of the gender division, and the liberation of women to equality with men. It is precisely in this that he prefigures so closely the radical sexual politics of today. And though reluctant to discard the defensive argument that gayness is congenital, Carpenter could at the same time proclaim that 'the capacity of their [the Uranians'] kind of attachment also exists – though in a germinal and undeveloped state – in the breast of mankind at large' (see above, p. 238).

This combination of a congenitally gay minority and a potentially gay majority was mediated for Carpenter by his Lamarckian concept of evolution, or exfoliation. The contradiction was only apparent, from focusing too narrowly on the immediate present. Indeed, it suggested an approach to less developed societies which looked for, and found, the ancestors of today's 'intermediates' in roles that had more recently emerged from the rigid gender system originally enforced by biology. But while this can account for one form of homosexuality, 'the intermediate in the service of religion' (and the life of the mind in general), where does it leave the other form, where 'the homosexual tendency was of the robuster and more manly sort . . . soon reinforced and taken advantage of by the military spirit' (above, p. 248)? Carpenter's solution, with which he himself shows signs of discomfort, is that while 'there are men who vary from the normal man-type in the feminine direction . . . there are also men who vary in the opposite direction'. These, he admits, 'can hardly be called "intermediate" ' (1919 ed., p. 161).

The second part of *Intermediate Types*, which deals with 'The Intermediate as Warrior', suffers from this unresolved theoretical problem. And though it is by no means devoid of interest, we have therefore prioritised other writings in the limited space available in this volume.

From the contemporary perspective, however, there seems no cause for Carpenter's confusion. Once the idea is abandoned that homosexuality and/or gender deviance are congenital, there is no need for institutionalised homosexuality to be necessarily associated with an underlying 'type' of individual. Even if this were the case with the 'religious' homosexuality of the berdache, etc., where a special social role is created for a minority, it is certainly not the case with the 'warrior' homosexuality of the Dorian Greeks and Japanese Samurai, this being universal practice at least within a certain caste. Homosexuality is indeed institutionalised in the two contrasting ways Carpenter outlines, but it is only the former that is in any sense 'intermediate'. The latter does not imply, as Carpenter supposes, that 'the Dorian Greeks or the Japanese Samurai must have counted among them men of . . . a "supervirile" quality' (*ibid.*, p. 163). These men were in every sense normal.

Yet far from undermining Carpenter's view of the role of 'intermediates' in contemporary Western society, the reality of warrior homosexuality actually strengthens it. For if this warrior homosexuality does not depend on the presence of 'supervirile' men, if in other words there have been societies where sexual love between ordinary, average men has been the norm, it should be even more possible for the homogenic attachment to revive, outside of any military connection, in the context of the attenuation of the gender system which Carpenter foresaw.

*

The editorial footnotes to *Intermediate Types among Primitive Folk* were compiled by Anton Everts.

*

1. As Prophet or Priest

1. 2 vols (Macmillan, 1908), vol. 2, p. 458.

2. See also Bancroft's *Native Races of the Pacific States*, vol. 1, p. 82.

* (p. 254) Like Aristotle in the *Nikomakhean Ethics* (7,7) Herodotos regards effeminacy as a hereditary defect. Both authors are likely to have been reflecting current opinion. Hippokrates also discusses the 'Anaries' and their condition (*On Airs, Waters, and Places*, 22), both regarding it as divinely inflicted and repeating the theory that excessive riding is a cause. He also introduces the reason that these rich Skythians (only the rich can afford to ride) wear trousers, so can't touch their genitals. However, neither Herodotos, Aristotle or Hippokrates specifically connect the Enarees with homosexual activity.

3. *Moeurs des Sauvages Amériquains, comparées aux moeurs des premiers temps*, by Père Lafitau (Paris, 1724).

4. W. A. Hammond in *American Journal of Neurology and Psychiatry* (August, 1882), p. 339.

5. See Dr Karsch *Jahrbuch für sexuelle Zwischenstufen*,vol. 3, p. 142.

6. *First Missionary Voyage to the South Sea Islands* (London, 1799), p. 200.

7. 2 vols (London, 1829).

* (p. 256) In these statues Apollo was portrayed not so much as feminine but rather as a youthful, beardless male.

8. See chapters 5, 6 and 7 in this volume. [Not included here; see introductory note to this text.]

9. *History and Antiquities of the Doric Race*, vol. 1, p. 338.

* (p. 256) Literally, 'my husband led him to the mill', probably meaning that Admetos made Apollo play a woman's role. Apollo is no longer thought of as a Sun god and indeed Müller himself rejected this idea. Karneios probably means Ram (*karnos*) god.

10. See *infra*, ch. 7. [See note 8 above.]

11. *The Thousand Nights and a Night* (1886), vol. 10, p. 229.

12. See Frazer's *Adonis, Attis and Osiris* (2nd ed., 1907), pp. 14, 64, note, etc.

13. ibid., p. 67.

14. See Frazer's *Adonis...*, p. 14, note, etc.

15. See a full consideration of this subject in *Ancient Pagan and Modern Christian Symbolism*, by Thomas Inman (2nd ed., 1874), pp. 120 *et seq.* Also a long article by A. E. Whatham in *The American Journal of Religious Psychology and Education*, for July, 1911, on 'The Sign of the Mother-goddess'.

16. See Westermarck's *Origin and Development of the Moral Ideas*, vol. 2, p. 488.

17. All this suggests the practice of some early and primitive science, and much resembles the accusations made in the thirteenth century against our own Roger Bacon, pioneer of modern science.

18. *Adonis...*, p.60.

19. ibid., p. 66.

20. See T. Karsch-Haack, *Forschungen über gleichgeschlecht-liche Liebe* (Munich), Die Japaner, p. 77. Also *The Letters of Fr. Xavier*, translated into German by Joseph Burg (3 vols, 1836–40).

21. See *La Chronica del Peru*, by Cieza de Leon (Antwerp, 1554), ch. 64.

22. op. cit., p. 243.

2. As Wizard or Witch

1. See 'Uranismus bei den naturvölkern', Dr F. Karsch, in *Jahrbuch für sexuelle Zwischenstufen*, vol. 3, pp. 161–2.

2. See Max. Prinz zu Wied, *Reise in das innere N. America* (2 vols, 1839 and 1841), vol. 2, p. 133.

3. Hakluyt Society (3 vols), vol. 2, p. 458.

4. *Adonis...*, p. 428.

5. See, in these connections, Dr Hirschfeld's remarkable book, *Die Transvestiten* (Berlin, 1910); also *Die Konträre Sexualemp-findung*, by Dr A. Moll (1893 ed.), pp. 82–90.

6. See Prinz zu Wied, *op. cit.* vol. 2, p. 133.

7. Berlin, 1912.

* (p 267) The bearded Venus (Aphroditos) was male, but wore a female robe. Here, as elsewhere, Carpenter often Latinises the Greek names.

8. *The Chances of Death and other studies*, by Karl Pearson (2 vols, 1897), vol. 2, p. 13.

9. See above, pp. 255 and 258, etc.

3. As Inventors of the Arts and Crafts

1. 2 vols (Paris, 1840).

2. It is probable also that the considerable degree of continence, to which many homosexuals are by nature or external necessity compelled, contributes to this visionary faculty.

4. Hermaphrodism among Gods and Mortals

1. *Indorum Floridam provinciam inhabitantium eicones*, etc. (Frankfurt, 1591). Also translation of the same with heliotypes of the engravings (Boston, J. R. Osgood & Co., 1875).

2. P. F. X. de Charlevoix, *La Nouvelle France*, 2 vols (Paris, 1744).

3. De Pauw, *Recherches sur les Américains*, 2 vols (Berlin, 1768).

4. See for his Report, *The New York Medical Journal*, vol. 50, no. 23 (7 December 1889).

5. 'Uranismus bei den Naturvölkern', *loc. cit.*, p. 138.

6. Quoted from the Yajur-Veda. See *Bible Folk-lore: a study in comparative mythology* (London, 1884), p. 104.

7. See *Adam's Peak to Elephanta* by E. Carpenter (1903), p. 308.

8. See drawings in *Ancient Pagan and Modern Christian Symbolism* by Thomas Inman (London, 1874).

9. These and some other references are taken from the learned and careful study 'Über die androgynische Idee des Lebens' by Dr von Römer of Amsterdam, which is to be found in vol. 5 of the *Jahrbuch für sexuelle Zwischenstufen* (Leipzig, 1903).

10. *Sacred Books of the East*, vol. 15, p. 85.

11. See H. P. Blavatsky, *Secret Doctrine*, vol. 2, p. 132; quoted in vol. 5, *Jahrbuch für sexuellen Zwischenstufen*, p. 76.

12. Inman's *Ancient Pagan and Modern Christian Symbolism* (Trubner, 1874), p. 119.

13. *Pagan Christs*, by John M. Robertson (1908), p. 308.

14. ibid., p. 307.

15. *The Thousand Nights and a Night*, vol. 10, p. 231.

* (p. 283) For a valuable discussion of the *hierodouloi*, see Geoffrey de Ste Croix, *Class Struggle in the Ancient Greek World* (London, 1981), p. 154.

16. See illustration in *Jahrbuch. . .*, vol. 5, p. 732.

17. See his study already quoted, *Jahrbuch. . .*, vol. 5, pp. 735–44.

* (p. 283) The author Photios cites here is in fact named simply as 'ho Hephaistionos', the son of Hephaistios.

18. See *Jahrbuch. . .*, as above, pp. 806, 807 and 809.

19. *Adonis. . .*, p. 432.

20. ibid., p. 431.

* (p. 284) In 4th century art Hermaphroditos – the offspring of Hermes and Aphroditos – is a beautiful boy with developed breasts, in later art an Aphroditos with male genitals. Though a unique dedication of the early 4th century attests the cult of Hermaphroditos in Attika (the region around and including Athens), Hermaphroditos only came into his/her own in the Hellenistic and Roman periods.

21. Compare the undifferentiated sex-tendencies of boys and girls at puberty and shortly after.

22. Ali Muhammed, who called himself the Bâb (or Gate), was born at Shiraz in 1820. In 1844 he commenced preaching his

gospel, which was very like that of Jesus, and which now has an
immense following. In 1850 he was shot, at Tabriz, as a malefector,
and his beloved disciple Mirza Muhammed Ali, refusing to leave
him, was shot with him.

Note to 'Self-Analysis for Havelock Ellis'

Havelock Ellis, active like Carpenter in the causes of socialism and
sexual freedom, wrote admiringly to Carpenter after coming upon a
copy of *Towards Democracy* in 1885. After the death in 1893 of
John Addington Symonds, who was collaborating with Ellis on his
book *Sexual Inversion*, Carpenter put a good deal of material at
Ellis's disposal, and wrote this case study of himself for Ellis's
book. This forms 'history vii' in the second (American) edition of
Studies in the Psychology of Sex, Vol. 2, part 1 (*Sexual Inversion*).

Index